A RUSKIN ALPHABET

Kevin Jackson

Z

A RUSKIN ALPHABET

Kevin Jackson

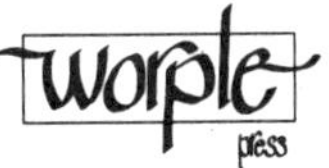

First published 2000 by
Worple Press
12 Havelock Road
Tonbridge
Kent TN9 1JE

ISBN 0 953947 2 3

The back cover photograph of Ruskin's gravestone was taken by the author (see *B is for Brantwood*).

Typeset and printed by Peepal Tree Press, Leeds

Acknowledgements

A much shorter version of this alphabet was published by *The Independent* on the centenary of Ruskin's death, 20 January 2000; it was commissioned by the Arts Editor, Ian Irvine. For this longer treatment of the theme, I have also incorporated some material from the documentary feature "People, Be Good" which I wrote and presented for broadcast by BBC Radio 3 on 17 January 2000; the producer was Abigail Appleton, who has my gratitude, as do our main contributors: Janet Barnes of the Crafts Council, David Barrie of The National Art Collections Fund, Dr Dinah Birch, Jonathan Glancey, Prof. Robert Hewison, Howard Hull, Tom Phillips, the Labour peer Tom Sawyer, Dr Nicholas Shrimpton, Dr Keith Thompson, and particularly my old friend Clive Wilmer - poet, scholar and editor of the Penguin edition of *Unto This Last* - to whom this slim work is dedicated. None of these eminent Ruskinians is to be held even slightly responsible for my errors of fact or tact.

For Clive Wilmer
il mare maggiore

"All letters are, therefore, to be considered as frightful things, and to be endured only upon occasion...."

- *The Seven Lamps of Architecture*,
Chapter IV, Sect. IX.

A is for ART

John Ruskin (1819-1900) was a writer of almost bewilderingly various talents. One of the most famous men of his age, he was, among other vocations, an artist and draughtsman, a geologist, an economist, a poet, a numismatist, a student of many aspects of the natural world, (from meteorology to what we would now call ecology), a social reformer, a botanist and gardener, a cultural historian, a teacher, an explorer and fabricator of mythology, a moralist and a visionary. He was awesomely prolific on all of these subjects: his *Works*, in the magnificent Library Edition of Cook and Wedderburn (published 1903-1912) run to 39 bulky volumes, and that vast printed edifice - a sort of literary Cabinet of Curiosities - does not include an almost equally formidable mass of unpublished letters, diaries and notes. But he was best known in his own time, and remains best known, as an impassioned critic and theorist of art and architecture - as the author, that is, of *Modern Painters, The Stones of Venice* and *The Seven Lamps of Architecture*.

For many Victorians, he was the man who had taught a once-blind nation to see. Charlotte Brontë famously observed to a friend that "Hitherto I have only had instinct to guide me in judging of art; I feel now as if I had been walking blindfold - this book seems to give me eyes." And although his work fell into disrepute during the twentieth century, languishing unread in library stacks and the back rooms of second-hand book shops, there has never been another British art critic remotely so influential as Ruskin. At the height of his career, he could make and ruin reputations with a single phrase - a state of affairs humorously recorded by *Punch*, which portrayed a once-successful Academician moaning that:

I paints and paints,
Hears no complaints,
And sells before I'm dry,
Till savage Ruskin
Sticks his tusk in,
And nobody will buy.

But he gradually grew dissatisfied with his role as "man-milliner" to the affluent; and the brilliant young art critic became a wrathful, despairing Old Testament prophet.

B is for BRANTWOOD

The home of Ruskin's last 28 years, overlooking Coniston Water in the Lake District, is now a centre devoted to his life and work, open to the public all year. The house itself, largely unremarkable in architectural terms save for the long seven-panelled window in the dining room (representing the *Seven Lamps of Architecture*, see below) and a small windowed turret on the upper storey which allowed the writer to gaze at the lake from his bedroom, contains a good deal of Ruskin memorabilia: paintings, geological specimens, and samples of the bright blue clothing of which he was always fond. (Ruskin was so attached to this bright colour that he even had his mother's coffin painted blue.)

The gardens, outside, continue Ruskin's interest in botany and agriculture: Brantwood's present director, Mr. Howard Hull, sometimes refers to these grounds as a sort of laboratory, and suggests that a walk through them is like a passage through the man's intricate mind. You can still go and sit in the rough stone chair Ruskin had made so that he could sit and contemplate the waterfall - running water always fascinated him - and then pass downwards to the most obviously symbolic part of the grounds. This takes the form of a zig-zag plantation rising up the hill, and was meant to represent the mountain of Purgatory from Dante's *Commedia*.

Anyone with so much as a passing interest in the man, or the subjects he wrote about, would be well advised to pay Brantwood a visit. (Tel: 015394 41396). It is the sort of place which can, and does, change lives: the architectural critic Jonathan Glancey recalls stumbling across Brantwood in the early seventies, when he was just fifteen. The house was so shabby in those days that he took it for an impoverished Old Folks' home, but he duly bought an old copy of *Unto This Last* (see below) for 40 pence, took it out to Ruskin's seat, read it into a single gulp, and stood up again with a new idea about what to do with his life.

After visiting Brantwood, a short walk into Coniston itself will take you to the Ruskin

Museum, recently restored with the aid of a Lottery Grant (churlish thought: would Ruskin have approved?) from its previous, somewhat ramshackle condition and kitted out with all sorts of inter-active delights, from computers to a set of "musical stones" - a sort of rough-hewn xylophone, of the type that Ruskin had made and enjoyed using in the 1880s. And then you can go on to the churchyard of St Andrew's, and follow the brown path worn in the grass by recent pilgrims, to Ruskin's fairly modest grave. (He might have been buried in Westminster Abbey, but made it known that the honour was unwelcome.) About a year after his death, on Ascension Day 1901, his friends put a stone monolith over his resting place, engraved by a local craftsman with symbols that recapitulate his life's work: on the eastern side, his artistic and architectural work, and on the west his social and ethical.

C is for CARLYLE

Thomas Carlyle (1795 - 1881), whose name is commonly linked with that of Ruskin in college courses on "Victorian Social Criticism" and the like, was a profound influence on his younger friend; Ruskin often called him "master". Carlyle, in his turn, was warmly encouraging when Ruskin began to turn his attention away from art (for which the older writer had little feeling) and towards social matters, and told him that Ruskin that he now felt less intellectually isolated - "in a minority of two, at any rate."

A recent biographer, Wolfgang Kemp, expresses one aspect of their relationship neatly: "Carlyle was largely responsible for identifying the work ethic as the dominant creed of the age; but Ruskin was the first to ask questions about the *quality* of work...":

The Desire of My Eyes, p190.

and for CHRISTIANITY

One of the several reasons for the decline in Ruskin's reputation in the years after his death is that Britain's increasingly secular intelligentsia, accurately noting the fervour of his Christian beliefs, were duly dismayed, repelled, embarrassed or bored.

But the history of Ruskin's faith is not as straightforward as his non-readers have sometimes assumed. His mother, Margaret (née Cock) was a fervent evangelical. "As soon as I was able to read with fluency, she began a course of Bible work with me, which never ceased till I went to Oxford." This study left him with an intimate knowledge of scripture and had, as one might expect, a lasting effect on his prose, even after he began to find her views not merely stifling but pernicious:

> "...it is neither Madonna-worship nor saint-worship, but the evangelical elf-worship and hell-worship - gloating, with an imagination as unfounded as it is foul, over the torments of the damned, instead of the glories of the blest, - which have in reality degraded the languid powers of christianity to their present state of shame and reproach."
>
> - *Fors Clavigera,* Letter XLI.

Though his father, John James Ruskin, was rather more worldly and easy-going in his faith, he none the less shared his wife's hope that Ruskin would become a notable preacher. When one of the family's friends, commiserating with Mr Ruskin, observed that John would have made a fine clergyman,

> "Yes," said my father with tears in his eyes - (true and tender tears, as ever father shed,) "He would have been a bishop."

In fact, Mr Ruskin had at one time entertained visions of the most brilliant of all clerical careers for his only son, a career made still more coruscating by literary and marital triumphs:

> "His ideal of my future, - now entirely formed in conviction of my genius, - was that I should enter at college into the best society, take all the prizes every year, and a double first to finish with; marry Lady Clara Vere de Vere; write poetry as good as Byron's, only

> pious; preach sermons as good as Bossuet's, only Protestant; be made, at forty, Bishop of Winchester, and at fifty, Primate of England."

Like other thoughtful men of his generation, Ruskin underwent a religious crisis; or, more accurately, a long and complex process of disaffiliation which came to a head at one dramatic moment. In July 1858 he was in Turin. One Sunday, since there were no other Protestant services to attend, he went into a Waldensian chapel, rapidly grew bored with the preacher's diatribe against worldly wickedness, and drifted off to the art gallery, where he was enraptured by Veronese's *Solomon and the Queen of Sheba*. "That day, my evangelical beliefs were put away, to be debated of no more". He later spoke of having experienced an "unconversion".

But the story does not end there. Ruskin seems gradually to have emerged from this unconverted state not exactly as a born-again Christian, but as an intensely spiritual man concerned with the truths expressed by or embodied in different world religions throughout history: hence his curious writings on Greek and Egyptian mythology. Late in life, he even developed an interest in spiritualism, and was persuaded that a medium had put him in touch with the spirit of his dead love, Rose La Touche (see below, *Y is for Young Girls*): he wrote in his diary that the events of this séance amounted to "the most overwhelming evidence of the other state of the world that has ever come over me".

D is for DAGUERROTYPES

Given Ruskin's views on the importance of drawing, it would be reasonable to assume that he was no friend to the new practice of making Daguerrotypes. This is not altogether wrong, but it stands in need of qualification. As he recalls in *Praeterita*, where he refers to photography by the charming phrase "the sun's drawing", he was something of a pioneer in the appreciation of this new form of representation:

"It must have been during my last days at Oxford that Mr. Liddell, the present Dean of Christ Church, told me of the original experiments of Daguerre. My Parisian friends obtained for me the best examples of his results; and the plates sent to me in Oxford were certainly the first examples of the sun's drawing that were ever seen in Oxford, and, I believe, the first sent to England."

Inspired by what he saw, Ruskin not only began to build up a collection of Daguerrotypes of French and Italian architecture ("Daguerrotypes taken by the vivid sunlight are glorious things"), but became a keen Daguerrotypist himself, and concluded that "Amongst all the mechanical poison that this terrible ninteenth century has poured upon men, it has given us at any rate one antidote - the Daguerrotype."

Then doubts began. By the time of his inaugural lectures on art at Oxford, he was utterly dimissive: "...they are not true, though they seem so. They are merely spoiled nature." For a more detailed discussion of this story, see Aaron Scharf, *Art and Photography* (Penguin, 1974), pp95-100.

and for DANTE

> "I admit two orders of poets, but no third; and by these two orders I mean the Creative (Shakspere [*sic*], Homer, Dante), and Reflective or Perceptive (Wordsworth, Keats, Tennyson)"
>
> \- *Modern Painters,* III.

Dante was one of the writers Ruskin read and re-read throughout his mature years, and who helped form his view not only of literature but of the universe. He said that the "best wisdom" of the ages has "been spoken in... strange enigmas - Dante's, Homer's, Hesiod's, Virgil's, Spenser's."

and for DARG

"You will never whistle at your dargs more, unless you are serving masters whom you can love."
- *Fors Clavigera,* Letter XXXII.

The meaning of "darg"? Ruskin himself glossed it as "doing". We would probably say "job", "task" or "work".

and for DEPRESSION

Ruskin was plagued by depression, as we would now call it, for much of his life. A tendency to gloom and worse was part of his physical inheritance: his grandfather, John Thomas Ruskin, was so tormented by melancholia that he eventually fell raving and, a couple of years later, committed suicide by cutting his throat. The long period of mental illness Ruskin suffered at the end of his life is often described as a form of profound depression.

and for DOMECQ

As cynics are quick to point out, Ruskin was a rich man, and - though astonishingly industrious - was never obliged to do a day's paid work in his life. His father, John James Ruskin, had made a fortune in the sherry trade as a partner of Ruskin, Telford and Domecq, a firm which which survives to this day as Allied Domecq. On his father's grave, Ruskin inscribed the verdict that John James had been "an entirely honest merchant":

> "He was an entirely honest merchant, and his memory is, to all who keep it, dear and helpful. His son, whom he loved to the uttermost and taught to speak truth, says this of him."

(Some of Ruskin's rage at merchants and the merchant class was prompted by what he saw as their failure to be as honest as his father.) John James Ruskin supported his son financially throughout his life, indulging - with a few exceptions that angered Ruskin terribly

- his every wish; and at his death in 1864, left him the then enormous sum of £120,000.

D is also for the Domecq daughters, who came to stay with the Ruskins in 1836. Their arrival hit the virginal 17-year old like a mortar shell. As he summed up the episode in *Praeterita*:

> "Virtually convent-bred more closely than the maids themselves, without a single sisterly or cousinly affection for refuge or lightning-rod, and having no athletic skill or pleasure to check my dreaming, I was thrown, bound hand and foot, in my unaccomplished simplicity, into the fiery furnace, or fiery cross, of these four girls, — who of course reduced me to a mere heap of white ashes in four days. Four days, at the most, it took to reduce me to ashes, but the Mercredi des cendres lasted four years.

> "Anything more comical in the externals of it, anything more tragic in the essence, could not have been invented by the skilfullest designer in either kind."

He was instantly smitten by the 15-year-old, oval-faced blonde Adèle Clotilde Domecq, and set about the doomed task of trying to woo her with all the grotesquely inappropriate means at his disposal: treating his "Spanish-born, Paris-bred and Catholic-hearted mistress" to his views on the Spanish Armada and the doctrine of Transubstantiation; writing and publishing a story about Neopolitan bandits ("Adèle laughed over it in rippling ecstasies of derision"); and bombarding her with letters in his doubtfully grammatical French once she had returned to Paris. He continued to pine for years:

> "I had neither the resolution to win Adèle, the courage to do without her, the sense to consider what was at last to come of it all, or the grace to think how disagreeable I was making my-

self at the time to everybody about me. There was really no more capacity nor intelligence in me than a just fledged owlet, or just open-eyed puppy, disconsolate at the existence of the moon."

He was, it is fair to say, never lucky in love: see *E is for Effie, Y is for Young Girls* for further sad details.

and for DRAWING

Drawing was a common accomplishment of the educated middle classes in Ruskin's day, but he took its practice far more seriously than most of his contemporaries; for Ruskin, drawing was virtually a mode of thought. He began to draw, often for many hours a day, in his childhood, and seldom abandoned the practice for very long even when knee-deep in writing and research. From 1854 onwards, he taught drawing (unpaid) at the new Working Men's College in London, and wrote three books on the subject: *The Elements of Perspective* (1859), *The Laws of Fesole* (1887-

8) and, most famously, *The Elements of Drawing* (1857). He wrote this last book by way of a response to the many requests he had recived for instruction in drawing after the publication of *Modern Painters*; it sold very well, and its teachings were eagerly received by amateurs and professionals alike. In the year of Ruskin's death, 1900, Monet told a journalist that "ninety per cent of the theory of Impressionist painting is in... Ruskin's *Elements of Drawing*."

For readers who despair of ever being able to draw, Ruskin has some pleasantly reassuring words: "...I can promise you that an hour's practice a day for six months, or an hour's practice every other day for twelve months... will give you sufficient power of drawing faithfully whatever you want to draw."

One biographer has pointed out that when Ruskin was in an emotional or mental crisis he would attempt to soothe and cure himself with drawing, and that an infallible sign of the onset of a crisis was a sudden loss of his ability to draw.

and for DÜRER

Ruskin, who thought all Germans arrogant, was none the less fond of quoting a proud phrase by "Albert Dürer" ("and he is the modestest German I know"), who said of his work, "Sir, it cannot be better done." In one of the few letters from Ruskin's last decade, Ruskin wrote to a young admirer that Dürer's engraving "The Knight, Death and the Devil" had been a friend and an encouragement to him throughout his life. He discusses the work, alongside *Melencolia,* in Volume V of *Modern Painters,* where he addresses the great German rhetorically as "Albert of Nuremberg".

E is for ECOLOGY

Ruskin is often spoken of - see above - as a prophet; a term which can be read in several ways. The most pertinent is his anguished concern for the rape of the environment by modern industry, and the literary record of his agony begins in the preface to *The Queen of the Air* (1869):

> "...I have seen strange evil brought upon every scene that I best loved, or tried to make beloved by others. The light which once flushed those pale summits with its rose at dawn, and purple at sunset, is now umbered and faint; the air which once inlaid the clefts of all their golden crags with azure is now defiled with languid coils of smoke, belched from worse than volcanic fires; their very glacier waves are ebbing, and their snows fading, as if Hell had breathed on them; the waters that once sank at their feet into crystalline rest are now dimmed and foul, from deep to deep, and shore to shore. These are no careless words - they are accurately - horribly - true...
>
> The light, the air, the waters, all defiled!"

This vein of Ruskin's writing reaches its climax, or apocalypse, in *The Storm-Cloud of the Nineteenth Century* (1884), where

Ruskin made his most desperate statement of the case that the sky itself had been damaged, perhaps beyond repair. His own time took this as a evidence of madness - understandably enough, for his reason did give way in his last years. But more recent research shows that he appears to have been quite right. The 1870s and 1880s were indeed a period of major climatic change: the skies grew more polluted (the sulphur dioxide content of the atmosphere reached its highest recorded level in 1880), temperatures in London were well below seasonal average for 18 of the 21 years between 1869 and 1889, respiratory illnesses grew worse and worse, thunderstorms were commonplace...

To be sure, Ruskin was far from being the only writer to have noticed these things, but the accuracy, the pain and the extremism of his response to environmental ruin make this aspect of his work peculiarly urgent for a generation which has grown wearily familiar with such phrases "global warming" and "ozone layer".

and for ECONOMICS

A subject on which Ruskin had unorthodox views. In reference to Adam Smith's classic observations on the division of labour, for example, Ruskin remarked that:

> "We have much studied and much perfected, of late, the great civilized invention of the division of labour; only we give it a false name. It is not, truly speaking, the labour that is divided; but the men: - divided into mere segments of men - broken into small fragments and crumbs of life."

He took similar exception to Mill's definition of economic man as one motivated entirely by the desire for the easiest path to the greatest possible gain; Mill admitted, of course, that such a pure-minded beast was not actually to be met with in the street, but was a necessary hypothesis of economic science. "For Ruskin", comments Clive Wilmer, "this was precisely the way science ought not to proceed. If such an individual did not exist, how could he be used as a model for understanding real human actions?" (Introduction to *Unto This Last*, Penguin, 1985.)

and for EFFIE

The sad story of Effie (Euphemia Chalmers) Gray, Ruskin's unfortunate young wife, is too well known to need retelling at any great length. Ruskin first met her when she was barely thirteen, and he was an undergraduate at Oxford; she asked him to write her a story, and he complied (See *K is for King of the Golden River*.) They met again in 1846, and Ruskin, probably still recovering from the final throes of his obsession with Adèle Domecq, was charmed by this pretty girl. The two hopelessly ill-suited young people became engaged in 1847, and were married on 10 April 1848: also the date of a major demonstration by the Chartists. The marriage was, notoriously, unconsummated, though probably not for the reason most commonly cited; see below, *P is for Pubic Hair*. In September 1849, after the reconquest of Venice by the Austrians, the couple set off for another of Ruskin's research trips to Venice: he hurled himself into work, she enjoyed a flirtation with an artillery officer. The pattern was set for the rest of their marriage: she liked to go out in society, he was engrossed in his studies. Ruskin's own summary is remarkably even-handed:

> "I married her, thinking her so young and affectionate that I might influence her as I chose, and make of her just such a wife as I wanted. It appeared that *she* married *me* thinking she could make of me just the *husband she* wanted. I was grieved and disappointed at finding I could not change her, and she was humiliated at finding she could not change me."

It was bound to end in tears, and soon did. In the summer of 1853, the Ruskins travelled to Glenfinlas in the Scottish Highlands, in the company of their new friend John Everett Millais, who was to paint their portraits. (He kept his part of the agreement: Millais's study of Ruskin standing on rocks by a stream is one of the most frequently reproduced images of the author.) The holiday fanned a passion which had already been sparked in London. On 26 April 1854, Effie left Ruskin. Their marriage was annulled on 15 July, 1854; Effie cited Ruskin's impotence as grounds. On July 3 1855 she married Millais.

At least five books, and one opera, have been written on the marriage.

and for EGYPT

In the summer of 1864, a few months after his father's death, Ruskin started to go to the British museum to immerse himself in Eyptian antiquities. By the autumn, this study had, he said, led him "into such an abyss of things I want to think over quietly." Some of the fruits of this thought can be found in *The Ethics of the Dust,* which contains strange digressions on Eyptian mythology.

On the other hand:

> "What Egyptian worship of garlic or crocodile [was] ever so damnable as modern English worship of money?"
> - *Fors,* Letter XLVI.

and for ETYMOLOGY

As his career progressed, Ruskin became increasingly fond of making arguments drawn from etymologies - often, though by no means always, fanciful. In the opening chapter of *The Bible of Amiens,* for instance, Ruskin refers to the English upper classes as "the scurviest louts that ever fouled God's earth with their carcasses". "The language appears to be violent", he later admitted, but insisted that "It is simply brief, and accurate", and he recommended his readers to take down their copies of Johnson's *Dictionary* to follow the history of the word "scurvy". As his critics pointed out, this habit of mind could lead him astray; but that straying ended in some interesting places.

and for EXECUTIONS

Ruskin approved of capital punishment, and purported to be unimpressed by the argument that innocent men sometimes go to the gallows:

> "It is only rogues who have a violent objection to being hanged, and only abettors of rogues who would desire anything else for them. Honest men don't in the least mind being hanged occasionally by mistake, so only that the general principle of the gallows be justly maintained; and they have the pleasure of knowing that the world they leave is positively minded to cleanse itself of the human vermin with which they have been classed by mistake.
>
> The contrary movement - so vigorously progressive in modern days - has its real root in a gradually increasing conviction on the part of the English nation that they are *all* vermin."
>
> - *Fors Clavigera,* Letter XXXV

F is for FLORENCE

Ruskin's initial response to Florence was unfavourable; he thought the Duomo "barbarous" and the Arno a "nasty muddy ditch". Even after he changed his mind about other aspects of the city, he continued to be enraged at the Florentines' attitude to their inheritance, which in his eyes was a compound of sheer neglect and ill-judged acts of restoration worse than any deliberate vandalism. His *Mornings in Florence* (1875-7), was conceived partly as a contradiction of more commercial guide-books, partly as an extension of his work as Slade Professor. Having made an experimental trial of its six recommended itineraries in 1995, I am in a position to confirm that the book can still be used with pleasure and profit by the English tourist.

and for FORS CLAVIGERA

Ruskin's cryptic, translation-defying title for the series of instructive letters (1871-84) he addressed in hope and fury to the working men of England; it eventually ran to some

1,900 pages, or 650,000 words. Hardly anyone would care to contradict the editors of his collected works when they say that "There is no other book in the world quite like it"; though a German critic has pointed out its affinities with Karl Kraus's *Die Fackel*, and the American poet Guy Davenport has pointed out its anticipations of Ezra Pound's *Cantos*: both works were composed in instalments, and have the air of being written on the hoof, in response to current events; both are concerned with economics (especially usury), Greek and other myths, the Middle Ages, Venice and Florence, coinage... See "The House that Jack Built" in *The Geography of the Imagination*.

Fors is a rambling, provocative, perplexing, exasperating, amazing work, and shows the workings of Ruskin's mind at its most forceful, idiosyncratic and creative pitch. (Or, for sceptics, its most cranky.) It has, like most of Ruskin's gigantic output, been long out of print, but the Ruskin scholar Dr Dinah Birch is about to publish an annotated selection.

So what exactly does the strange title mean? Several things, at different times. In Letter XLIII, Ruskin writes that

> "... the current and continual purpose of Fors Clavigera is to explain the powers of Chance, or Fortune (Fors), as she offers to men the conditions of prosperity; and as these conditions are accepted or refused, nails down and fastens their fate for ever, being thus 'Clavigera' - 'nail-bearing'. The image is one familiar in mythology: my own conception of it was first got from Horace, and developed by steady effort to read history with impartiality, and to observe the lives of men around me with charity. 'How you may make your fortune, or mar it,' is the expansion of the title."

and for FRONDES AGRESTES

Ruskin has long suffered from the reputation of being valuable chiefly as a writer of "purple passages" - a reputation which some of his followers unwittingly promoted by issuing small collections of just such lush flowerings. The best known of these, *Frondes Agrestes,* was compiled by his friend Miss Susan Beever from *Modern Painters,* and published in 1875.

and for FULLER

That is, Peter Fuller (1947-1990), the British art critic who began as a Marxist disciple of John Berger, passed through psychoanalytic theory and ended (in such works as *Theoria*) as a dedicated neo-Ruskinian - indeed, in the eyes of his more enthusiastic fans, as the heir to Ruskin's mission. In a lecture he gave shortly before his death, Fuller declared that "Ruskin was not just British literature's first major art critic, he was, I believe, the greatest critic the world has yet seen."

The critical journal Fuller founded, which is still a going concern, nailed his Ruskinian colours to the mast: he called it *Modern Painters.*

G is for GEOLOGY

Ruskin's earliest and most enduring intellectual passion was for rocks and stones and crystals; some of his most brilliant drawings are of rock formations. If his father lamented the loss of a potential archbishop when his son turned away from an ecclesiastical career, Ruskin himself mourned the untaken path that might have led him to become "probably the first geologist of my time in Europe." His knowledge of the subject was deepened, at Oxford, by his friendship with the magnificently eccentric Professor Buckland, and in 1840 he became a Fellow of the Geological Society. He wrote about Geology in many places, including *Modern Painters* and *Deucalion*; *The Ethics of the Dust* (1866), written in the form of a series of dialogues between an Old Lecturer and some very young schoolgirls, was his attempt at a primer in the subject. Geology, it should be added, was one of the studies which helped undermine (pun only slightly intended) his religious faith: in a much-quoted letter of 1851, he spoke of hearing the clink of the geologist's dreadful hammers "at the end of every cadence of the Bible verses."

and for GOTHIC

For Ruskin, an emotionally complex term denoting not only a style of architecture but a period of history, a Paradise Lost, an ethics of labour, a vision of order and beauty. His admiration for Gothic architecture (and contempt for neo-classicism) was inseparable from his Christian faith - he sometimes calls Gothic architecture, simply, "Christian architecture" - and from his care for nature, and his beliefs about the just society.

> "...go forth again to gaze upon the old cathedral front, where you have smiled so often at the fantastic ignorance of the old sculptors: examine once more those ugly goblins, and formless monsters, and stern statues, anatomiless and rigid; but do not mock them, for they are signs of the

> life and liberty of every workman who struck the stone; a freedom of thought, and rank in scale of being, such as no laws, no charters, no charities can secure; but which must be the first aim of all Europe at this day to regain for her children."

"The Nature of Gothic", the central chapter of the middle volume of *The Stones of Venice,* had far-reaching consequences. It was issued as a free pamphlet to students at the Working Men's College in London; and reissued, decades later, as a handsome Kelmscott Press volume by William Morris, who called it "one of the very few necessary and inevitable utterances of the century". He continued: "To some of us when we first read it, it seemed to point out a new road on which the world should travel."

Much more recently, Peter Fuller paraphrased the term "Gothic" by saying that it "might be described as the conditions under which the aesthetic dimension in human culture could flourish." (*Peter Fuller's Modern Painters,* 1993, p10).

and for THE GUILD OF ST GEORGE

Ruskin founded the Guild in 1878, as a sort of combined lobby group, revolutionary cell, mediaeval crafts guild and chivalric crusading army. It was the agency by which Ruskin hoped to bring about social change - indeed, to realise a version of Utopia (he frequently quoted from More's visionary work) - in Britain. He had in mind a combination of agrarian communism and strict hierarchy, and planned to begin by purchasing a plot of land:

> "We will try to take some small piece of English ground, beautiful, peaceful, and fruitful. We will have no steam-engines upon it, and no railroads; we will have no untended or unthought-of creatures on it; none wretched, but the sick; none idle but the dead. We will have no liberty upon it; but instant obedience to known law, and appointed persons: no equality upon it; but recognition of every betterness that we can find, and reprobation of every worseness.

> When we want to go anywhere, we will go there quietly and safely, not at forty miles an hour in the risk of our lives; when we want to carry anything anywhere, we will carry it either on the backs of beasts, or on our own, or in carts, or boats; we will have plenty of flowers and vegetables in our gardens, plenty of corn and grass in our fields, - and few bricks. We will have some music and poetry; the children shall learn to dance to it and sing it; - perhaps some of the old people, in time, may also."

As the reader will have noticed, the building of Ruskin's Utopia has had to be postponed indefinitely, though the Guild was not as ineffectual as might be assumed: among other substantial achievements, it could count the foundation of a worker's museum in Sheffield (still thriving; see below), a tea-shop in London, a reference library, the encouragement of various local crafts from linen production in Langdale to handweaving on the Isle of Man, and so on. And the Guild still exists, though not quite in the form Ruskin had envisaged. To-day, it is a charitable trust devoted to mainly to educational projects, particularly in the practice of crafts and the fields of agriculture, art history and the social sciences.

H is for HERNE HILL

The South London suburb where Ruskin grew up, and lived for the better part of his early life when he was not away on his European travels. The family came here in 1823, when his father took a lease at 28 Herne Hill, and remained for 19 years, when they made a short move to Denmark Hill. It might seem an unlikely breeding ground for the prophet of beauty, but Ruskin once remarked that it was the very aesthetic paucity of his early surroundings which helped sharpen his eye; more visually privileged children, he thought, often took beauty for granted. A "great part", he wrote,

> "of my acute perception and deep feeling of the beauty and architecture of scenery abroad, was owing to the well-formed habit of narrowing my-

self to happiness within the four brick walls of our fifty by one hundred yards of garden; and accepting with resignation the aesthetic external surroundings of a London suburb, and, yet more of a London chapel."

I is for "ILLTH"

Ruskin's coinage in *Unto This Last*: an antonym for "wealth".

and for INDUSTRY

By and large, Ruskin abhorred it, as a blight on craftsmanship, art, taste, the condition of the working man, and (see *E is for Ecology*) the natural world.

J is for DR JOHNSON

Different as they clearly are in many repects, John Ruskin and Samuel Johnson also have a striking number of qualities in common: both had astonishingly capacious minds, both were wonderfully prolific, both were deeply concerned with Christianity, both were tormented by melancholy and rage, both declared themselves Tories, both were noted conversationalists or monologuists, both made unsatisfactory and ill-judged marriages, both remained childless, both wrote remarkable travel books... and both are frequently assumed to be bores by those who have not troubled to read them much.

To what degree Ruskin acknowledged this affinity is uncertain, but he was happy to admit at least one major debt to Johnson:

> "No other author could have secured me, as he did, against all chance of being misled by my own sanguine and metaphysical temperament. He taught me carefully to measure life, and distrust fortune; and he secured me, by his adamantine common-sense, for ever, from being caught in the cobwebs of German metaphysics, or sloughed in the English drainage of them."

Finally, though Ruskin does not mention it, both men were also much possessed with the same Biblical phrase: when his family took the heraldic motto "Age quod agis", Ruskin recalls, he paraphrased it into a single word

> "...into "To-day", tacitly underlined to myself with the warning, "The night cometh, when no man can work"."

Boswell in *The Life of Johnson* recalls noting a short Greek inscription on the dial-plate of Johnson's watch

> "... being the first words of our SAVIOUR's admonition to the improvement of the time which is allowed us to prepare for eternity; "the night cometh when no man can work."...."

Strictly speaking, Ruskin's paraphrase was not one word, but three: TODAY TODAY TODAY.

and for JUVENILIA

A precocious child, Ruskin composed many stories and poems in his earliest years. At the age of seven, he wrote a short book about the adventures of "Harry and Lucy", a work largely inspired by Maria Edgeworth's children's books *Harry and Lucy* and *Frank*. This opuscule gives early note of his observation of natural processes ("Harry ran for an electrical apparatus which his father had given him and the cloud electrified his apparatus positively...."); it is curious to note that clouds drift over both the beginning and the end of his literary career; see above, *E is for Ecology*.

His other early works include short poems (his verses "On Skiddaw and Derwent Water" appeared in *The Spiritual Times* in 1830) and the 2,000 or so lines of a verse epic about a tour in the Lake District, the *Iteriad*. His first prose work, "Enquiries on the Causes of the Colour of the Water of the Rhine" was published in the *Magazine of Natural History* for September 1834.

Earlier, at the age of five, he composed and delivered a sermon, some eleven words long, which began: "People, be good". It would not be far from the truth to suggest that he went on saying the same thing, at rather greater length, for the rest of his life.

K is for KING OF THE GOLDEN RIVER

A fairy story written by Ruskin in 1841, at the request of young Effie, and said to be one of the first such tales - in England, at least - to have been completely made up by a modern writer rather than fabricated from earlier folk tales and legends. He was deprecating about its merits, but it proved immensely popular and has seldom been out of print. The American critic Northrop Frye contended that all of Ruskin's subsequent analyses of wealth might be read as commentaries on this fairy tale.

L is for D.H. LAWRENCE

Lawrence hated Ruskinians: "The deep damnation of self-righteousness... lies thick all over the Ruskinite, like painted feathers on a skinny peacock."

and for LECTURES

From about 1850 onwards, the Victorian middle classes (and not a few members of other classes) were gripped by a craze for attending lectures, and Ruskin was, with his friend Carlyle, the great star of the lecture circuit. Sometimes, though, his audiences got rather more than they had bargained for. In "Traffic" (published 1866), savage Ruskin stuck his tusk into the unwary businessmen of Yorkshire who had asked him to give them a little advice about the Exchange they planned to build. The result is a small masterpiece of angry irony, and one of the best introductions to Ruskin's work.

To judge by eye-witness accounts, he could be an electrifying performer. A. E. Housman wrote about one of the lectures he gave as Slade Professor: Ruskin brought in a framed and glassed picture by Turner, depicting the landscape near Leicester. To dramatise the horrors that industrialism had inflicted on earth, sky and water, Ruskin took up a paintbrush and slapped an indigo factory, a soap factory, an iron bridge and other eyesores onto the glass: "...A puff and a cloud of smoke all over Turner's sky; and then the brush thrown down, and Ruskin confronting modern civilization amid a tempest of applause..."

M is for MENIAL

"I suppose there is scarcely another word in the language which people more dislike having applied to them, or of which they less understand the application. It comes from a beautiful old Chaucerian word, 'meinie,', or many, signifying the attendant company of any one worth attending to; the disciples of a master, scholars of a teacher, soldiers of a leader, lords of a King. Chaucer says the God of Love came, in the garden of the Rose, with 'his many'; - in the court of the King of Persia spoke a Lord, one 'of his many'. Therefore there is nothing in itself dishonourable in being menial; the only question is - *whose* many you belong to, and

> whether he is a person worth belonging to, or even safe to be belonged to...." - *Fors Clavigera,* Letter XXVIII

Hence:

and for THE MIDDLE AGES

Ruskin loved almost everything about the Middle Ages (as he understood them) - the architecture, the art, the poetry - and saw in medieval society certain possibilities of order and beauty in both art and life that the modern world had sacrificed.

> "And at this day, though I have kind invitations enough to visit America, I could not, even for a couple of months, live in a country so miserable as to possess no castles."

Surprisingly, perhaps, many people were swayed by his love of such things, not least William Morris: see above, *G is for Gothic.*

and for MODERN PAINTERS

For many readers, Ruskin's greatest work, and certainly the one which brought him fame. It was not one book, but five separate volumes: a tale that grew in the telling, and became (among many other things) the history of how the teller grew in its making. It took the better part of eighteen years to complete - in a sense, he never completed it, only put it aside as a project that might never come to a true conclusion - and encompassed far more than he had originally intended. Volume One, which he set about writing on his graduation from Oxford and published in 1843, when he was only 24, was intended as a vindication of Turner (see below) against his conservative critics. Volume Two announced to the world his discovery of Italian religious art - Giotto, Fra Angelico, Bellini - but the writing of it sent him off on his investigation of European architecture. Volumes Three and Four, written rapidly and published in 1856, reflect his religious doubts and growing concern for social matters, as well as his deepening melancholia: all tendencies which reach their climax in Volume Five, published in 1860. One of the most florid tributes to the work comes from an unexpected source: Virginia Woolf: "The style in which page after page of *Modern Painters* is written takes our breath away. We find ourselves marvelling at the words, as if all the fountains of the English language had been set playing in the sunlight for our pleasure."

In more recent years, *Modern Painters* has also been the title of (a) an art magazine (see *F is for Fuller*) and (b) an opera by a young American composer based on Ruskin's life. This latter work, premiered at Santa Fé in 1995, was notable for an aria about trout sung by Ruskin's mother and for a final *coup* in which the singer playing Ruskin, his back to the audience, marched to the edge of the stage and fell off, while fireflies - the fireflies of Fonte Branda - twinkled all around.

N is for NATURE

Before he attended to art, Ruskin had worshipped the natural world; his passion for the one is inseparable from his love for the other. "You will never love art well", he wrote in his study of science *The Eagle's Nest* (1872) "till you love what she mirrors better".

and for NOVELS:

> "I wish I could write one; but I can't", Ruskin confessed in the 29th letter of *Fors*. On the other hand, he also said that "...George Eliot makes them end so wretchedly that they're worse than none - so she's no good, either."

O is for OBJECTIVE

When two or three are gathered together and the subject turns to art, there is a fair chance that someone will venture the proposition that all aesthetic judgements are "subjective". Ruskin would not, to put it mildly, have found this a sympathetic notion. In the third volume of *Modern Painters*, he notes that:

> "German dullness, and English affectation, have of late much multiplied among us the use of two of the most objectionable words that were ever coined by the troublesomeness of metaphysicians, - namely, "Objective" and "Subjective".
>
> "No words can be more exquisitely, and in all points, useless..."

and for OXFORD

Two significant periods of Ruskin's life were spent at Oxford. The first was the time he spent as an undergraduate - more exactly, as a gentleman-commoner - at Christ Church. His mother came along in case her precious child should fall ill and have no one to nurse him;

> "I count it is just a little to my credit that I was not ashamed, but pleased, that my mother came to Oxford with me to take such care of me as she could."

Her maternal anxiety was not altogether misplaced: Ruskin did fall ill at Oxford - in 1840, his body weakened by intensive cramming, he began to cough up blood - , and had to defer taking his degree until 1842, when he was awarded a Double Fourth.

He did not have a very high opinion of his aristocratic contemporaries:

> "men who had their drawers filled with pictures of naked bawds - who walked openly with their harlots in the sweet country lanes - men who swore, who diced, who drank, who knew *nothing* except the names of racehorses - who had no feelings but those of brutes - whose conversation at the very hall dinner table would have made prostitutes blush for them - and villains rebuke them - men who if they could, would have robbed me of my money at the gambling table - and laughed at me if I had fallen into their vices - & died of them."

But his undergraduate years were not without their pleasures and triumphs; he met Dr Buckland, who was busy eating his way through every type of animal in creation (and once debunked a supposedly miraculous manifestation of a saint's blood by tasting it and declaring it to be bat's urine); he wrote his most substantial work to date, the *Poetry of Architecture*, and had it published in the *Architectural Magazine* under the pseudonym "Kata Phusin" ("According to Nature"); and he managed to win the Newdigate Prize for poetry at his second attempt with a poem entitled "Salsette and Elephanta".

His return to the town and University came almost thirty years later, in 1869, when he was appointed as first Slade Professor of Fine Art. Despite this honour, relations between Ruskin and Oxford were often awkward. The most notorious of his exploits was the Hinksey Road project of "Useful Muscular Work", for which he recruited a crowd of ardent young disciples to go and act as manual labourers in a nearby village. One of the undergraduates who pitched in was, improbably enough (since no gentleman takes exercise), Oscar Wilde. He resigned the Professorship in March 1885; see *V is for Vivisection.*

P is for the PATHETIC FALLACY

Ruskin gave this phrase to the English language in *Modern Painters,* Vol. III:

> "The foam is not cruel, neither does it crawl. The state of mind which attributes to it these characters of a living creature is one in which the reason is unhinged by grief. All violent feelings have the same effect. They produce in us a falseness in all our impressions of external things, which I would generally characterize as the 'Pathetic fallacy'..."

and for PANTOMIMES

Ruskin not only loved going to see pantos, but thought they contained a powerful political burden. In pantomimes, he thought, one could discover

> "how the whole pleasure of life depends on the existence of Princes, Princesses and Fairies. One never hears of a Republican pantomime; one never thinks Cinderella would be a bit better off if there were no princes."

and for PRAETERITA

The final work of Ruskin's life was his unfinished autobiography, composed in the placid intervals between mental breakdown, and therefore inclined to dwell on the more agreeable aspects of his early life. (No mention, for example, of the Effie business.) Some readers consider it the most readable and delightful of Ruskin's works, though this view is disputable; compared, say, to the uncommon pleasures of *Fors*, it can be rather tepid fare.

Its concluding words, a memoir of a visit he made to Siena with his American friend Charles Eliot Norton, are often extracted and became famous as a prose poem, generally known as "The Fire-flies of Fonte Branda":

"*How* they shone! moving like fine-broken starlight through the purple leaves. How they shone! through the sunset that faded into thunderous night as I entered Siena three days before, the white edges of the mountainous clouds still lighted from the west, and the openly golden sky calm behind the Gate of Siena's heart, with its still golden words, "Cor magis tibi Sena pandit," and the fireflies everywhere in sky and cloud rising and falling, mixed with the lightning, and more intense than the stars."

Dateline: "BRANTWOOD, June 19th, 1889"

He never wrote again.

and for the PRE-RAPHAELITES

Ruskin's path first crossed those of the Pre-Raphaelite brotherhood in 1851 when he wrote to the *Times* defending John Everett Millais and William Holman Hunt against the paper's scornful criticisms. He wrote that:

"Pre-Raphaelitism has but one principle, that of absolute, uncompromising truth in all that it does, obtained by working everything, down to the most minute detail, from nature, and from nature only. Every Pre-Raphaelite landscape background is painted to the last touch, in the open air, from the thing itself. Every Pre-Raphaelite figure, however studied in expression, is a true portrait of some living person."

The move brought him the gratitude and friendship of the younger men; and then the plot thickened. See *E is for Effie*.

and for PROUST

The young Marcel Proust idolised Ruskin, and, despite his shaky grasp of English, was moved to translate two of Ruskin's books: *La Bible d'Amiens* (1900) and *Sesame et les Lys* (1906). The literary "affair", as one commentator has called it, lasted from 1899 to the spring of 1906, and passed through the phases of "infatuation, discipleship and disillusion" (the words of Richard Macksey, who also lists the various ways in which Proust and Ruskin were kindred souls: polymathic "foxes" who wished to be unifying "hedgehogs", both men were "plagued by demons of incompletion and digression..."). See Marcel Proust, *On Reading Ruskin*, translated and edited by Jean Autret, William Burford and Phillip J. Wolfe (Yale University Press, 1987).

and for PUBIC HAIR

The one thing that almost everyone knows about Ruskin is a myth. In the late weeks of 1999, for example, a newspaper previewer phoned the BBC producer Abigail Appleton to check details of the Radio 3 feature she and I were then making about Ruskin: "Just remind me", the journalist said, "He's the pubic hair man, isn't he?" Well, yes and no. It's true that the received version of the Ruskin yarn has it that he recoiled in horror from his wife on their wedding night, thinking her deformed because she had pubic hair - unlike the stone ladies made by classical sculptors.

It's true, too, that the marriage of Ruskin and Effie remained unconsummated, and was eventually annulled. But it's almost certain that Ruskin knew perfectly well what a naked woman looked like (his rowdier friends at Oxford had shown him pornographic drawings) and that there were other reasons for his recoil. One of his modern biographers, John Dixon Hunt, suggests that she was probably menstruating; in which case, P should be for *Period.*

The story has done great harm to Ruskin's reputation, not least among literary feminists: on which point:

Q is for QUEENS

Two Queens, in fact: the essay "Of Queen's Gardens", and *The Queen of the Air.*

In the 1970s and 1980s, following the publication of Kate Millett's *Sexual Politics,* which dealt harshly with him, Ruskin's name became mud in feminist circles. To some extent, it remains mud: there are still plenty of critics cultivating the Millett seed. Recently, however, scholars have begun to take a more balanced view, noting Ruskin's support for women artists and the keen interest he took in the education of girls (see *Y is for Young Girls*.) The most fertile text for this debate is *"Of Queen's Gardens"* (1865), an educational tract often given as a prize to promising schoolgirls well into the second half of the twentieth century.

The Queen of the Air is an extraordinary work even by the standards of late Ruskin: an enquiry into the body of Greek myths associated with the figure of Athena. See Dinah Birch, *Ruskin's Myths* (OUP, 1988).

R is for the RENAISSANCE

A Very Bad Thing, Ruskin ultimately came to believe: see, for example, his revealing phrase in *Praeterita*, "I had no idea then of the Renaissance evil in them...". The modern rot set in then, and has spread from the cellar to the attic of Western culture ever since.

It should be stressed, however, that Ruskin's definition of the Renaissance was unorthodox: he thought of the Quattrocento as being still part of the Middle Ages, and generally reserves the word "Renaissance" for the products of the sixteenth century.

and for ROSE LA TOUCHE

The Rose La Touche episode was the principal tragedy of Ruskin's later years. See below, *Y is for Young Girls.*

and for ROUSSEAU

Ruskin sometimes compared himself with Rousseau, and even entertained the idea that he might be Rousseau's reincarnated spirit; but when he made the comparison to his friends in later life ("Have I not often told you I was another Rousseau"), it was often by way of tactfully confessing his addiction to a certain solitary vice.

S is for SENTIMENTAL

"Thus, in a recent debate on the treatment of Canada, Sir C. Adderley deprecates the continuance of a debate on a question "purely sentimental". I doubt if Sir C. Adderley knew in the least what was meant by a sentimental question. It is a purely "sentimental question", for instance, whether Sir C. Adderley shall, or shall not, eat his mother, instead of burying her." - *Fors*, Letter XXXIV.

and for the SEVEN LAMPS OF ARCHITECTURE

Namely: Sacrifice, Truth, Power, Beauty, Life, Memory and Obedience. *The Seven Lamps of Architecture* was first published in May 1849, and - in partnership with *The Stones of Venice* - was to have an enormous effect on British architecture as an inspiration to the young men of the Gothic Revival. Ruskin, it should be stressed, heartily disliked a great deal of the work he was generally held to have inspired.

and for SHEFFIELD

Ruskin visited the town on many occasions, and founded a museum for working men there in 1875 - one of the Guild of St George's educational projects. Initially based at a cottage in Walkely, the museum boasted a handsome collection of geological specimens, engravings from Turner's *Liber Studiorum* and architectural drawings by Ruskin. (These were transferred to Meersbrook Park in 1900, and later integrated into the Sheffield Museum and Art Gallery.)

and for SOCIALISM

In the early pages of his autobiography, *Praeterita,* Ruskin declared himself "a violent Tory of the old school". So he was; and yet his influence on the early development of socialism in England was greater than that of any more obvious left-wing contender - greater, for example, than that of Marx. Asked to name the work which had most inspired them, the first generation of Labour Party politicians all plumped for the short work mentioned below in *U is for Unto This Last.*

T is for TODAY

Or, more exactly (see above, *J is for Dr Johnson*) for TODAY TODAY TODAY, the motto Ruskin chose for himself in 1863; though he reports having made a mental choice of the motto as early as 1854, explaining that it was intended to cure him of procrastination. (If there was really an interval of ten years between decision and adoption, the cure can't have been very effective.)

and for TOLSTOY

> "He was one of those rare men who think with their hearts, and so he thought and said not only what he himself had seen and felt, but what everyone will think and say in the future" - Tolstoy on Ruskin.

and for TRAVEL

Ruskin spent roughly half his life travelling. His most typical path, which he followed 26 times, was through France and Switzerland to Italy, a trip he took for the first time with his parents in 1835, when the family paid particular attention to Chamonix and Venice. (It's worth pointing out that quite a few of Ruskin's books are species of travel writing - *The Bible of Amiens* and *Verona and Its Rivers*, as well as *The Stones of Venice* - while his other books are full of remembered journeys.)

Ruskin lived to see his own writings backfire: inspired, particularly, by Volume IV of *Modern Painters*, British travellers began to tromp in their hordes around the remote alpine scenes he had evoked, Ruskin in hand. In fact, the Alpine Club, founded in 1857, enthusiastically recommended Ruskin's prose to would-be tourists. He struggled to be philosophical, but the gloom kept breaking through.

> "The influx of foreigners into Switzerland must necessarily be greater every year, and the greater it is, the larger in the crowd will be the majority of persons whose objects in travelling will be, first, to get as fast

> as possible from place to place, and, secondly, at every place where they arrive, to obtain the kind of accommodation and amusement to which they are accustomed in Paris, London, Brighton or Baden".

But not every tourist who followed in Ruskin's written trail was a soulless lout: see *P is for Proust.*

and for TURNER

In *Praeterita,* Ruskin wrote - uncertain of the exact date, but entirely certain of the event's significance - that "... on my thirteenth (?) birthday, 8th February, 1832, my father's partner, Mr. Henry Telford, gave me Roger's Italy, and determined the main tenor of my life."

More immediately, his engagement with Turner began in 1836, when *Blackwood's Magazine* ran an article ridiculing three recent pictures by Turner. "The review raised me to the height of "black anger" in which I have remained pretty nearly ever since...." By leaping to the defence of Turner's reputation, Ruskin established his own. *Modern Painters*, the huge work of art criticism, theory and polemic in five volumes on which Ruskin laboured between 1843 and 1860 (see above, *M is for Modern Painters*), was originally conceived as an attempt to explain to the British that they had among them a painter as great as any of the ancients.

Ruskin finally met his hero at a dinner in Norwood on 22 June 1840. In his diary he wrote:

> "Introduced to-day to the man who beyond all doubt is the greatest of the age; greatest in every faculty of the imagination, in every branch of scenic knowledge; at once the painter and poet of the day, J.M.W. Turner..."

His subsequent friendship with Turner was not altogether easy, and went particularly sour after a meeting at which Turner appears to have accused Ruskin of something dishonourable. On Turner's death in 1851, Ruskin was appointed one of the painter's executors, and set to work on the gargantuan task of cataloguing the 20,000 watercolours and drawings Turner bequeathed to the National Gallery. As part of his work, Ruskin took it upon himself to destroy a number of "obscene" drawings, probably of copulating lovers. Despite these discordant notes, the relationship of painter and critic was one of the most remarkable of all meetings of writerly and artistic talents.

U is for UNTO THIS LAST

Ruskin's short tract on economics and ethics: reviled or ignored on its first appearance in 1860, then gradually discovered and adopted as a visionary manifesto, not just by the Labour movement but by countless others. One night in 1904, a young lawyer was kept wakeful on his train journey between Johannesburg and Durban reading its lessons; and when he reached his destination, got off the train resolved to live his life in accordance with Ruskin's teachings. The lawyer's name: Gandhi.

and for (ST) URSULA

Late in life, Ruskin grew obsessed with Carpaccio's paintings of the life of St. Ursula; see *Y is for Young Girls*.

and for USURY

> "I know myself to be an usurer as long as I take interest on any money whatsoever. I confess myself such, and abide whatever shame or penalty may attach to usury, until I can withdraw myself from the system."
>
> - *Fors*, Letter XLIV.

V is for VENICE

A critic once remarked that Venice was to Ruskin what the Galapagos Islands were to Darwin - the city gave him a model for the growth and decay of cultures. True, *The Stones of Venice* (1853) does not quite rival *The Origin of Species* as a book which changed the world, but it did have unexpectedly far-reaching consequences both for architecture and - see above - politics.

When he wrote about the history of Venice, it is clear that he also had the history of his own sea-faring nation in mind. Indeed, he makes the connection explicit in the work's opening:

> "Since first the dominion of men was asserted over the ocean, three thrones, of mark beyond all others, have been set upon its sands: the thrones of Tyre, Venice, and England. Of the First of these great powers only the memory remains; of the Second, the ruin; the Third, which inherits their greatness, if it forget their example, may be led through prouder eminence to less pitied destruction."

In *Praeterita*, he points out that this involvement with Venice began more or less by accident: "But for that porter's opening, I should (so far as one can ever know what they should) have written, The Stones of Chamouni, instead of The Stones of Venice..."

"But Tintoret swept me away at once into the "mare maggiore" of the schools of painting which crowned the power and perished in the fall of Venice; so forcing me into the study of the history of Venice herself; and through that into what else I have traced or told of the laws of national strength and virtue."

and for VISIONS

Justifiably described or dismissed as "visionary" in the familiar, metaphorical senses of the word, Ruskin was also a man who quite literally saw visions later in his life, when in the grip of fever or mental distress, including one of his pet cat as the Devil. (He killed the poor beast.)

and for VIVISECTION

The immediate cause of Ruskin's resignation from his Professorship at Oxford was his moral outrage at the University's decision to have its life scientists practise vivisection: "I cannot lecture in the next room to a shrieking cat nor address myself to the men who have been - there's no word for it."

and for VOTING

> "I have never in my life voted for any candidate for Parliament, and... I never mean to." - *Fors,* Letter XXIX.

W is for WAR

Ruskin's lecture to the young soldiers of the Royal Military Academy, Woolwich, later published in *The Crown of Wild Olive,* contends that:

> "...all the pure and noble arts of peace are founded on war; no great art ever yet rose on earth, but among a nation of soldiers. There is no art among a shepherd people, if it remains at peace. There is no art among an agricultural people, if it remains at peace. Commerce is barely

> consistent with fine art; but cannot produce it. Manufacture not only is unable to produce it, but invariably destroys whatever seeds of it exist. There is no great art possible to a nation but that which is based on battle."

and for WHISTLER

If the "pubic hair" incident was the major sorry farce of Ruskin's early years, then the Ruskin-Whistler trial was its counterpart in his later years. Briefly put, the story runs like this:

Ruskin attacked a painting by Whistler - a "nocturne in black and gold" representing "the fireworks at Cremorne" in *Fors Clavigera* for 2 July 1877:

> "I have seen, and heard, much of cockney impudence before now; but never expected to hear a coxcomb ask two hundred guineas for flinging a pot of paint in the public's face."

Whistler took him to court, claiming £1,000 in damages; and, like the "flinging a pot of paint" phrase, some of the words spoken in the court have passed into folk-lore. As Whistler recalled the episode in *The Gentle Art of Making Enemies*, the Attorney-General asked him how long it had taken him to "knock off" his nocturne. About a day, Whistler eventually replied, after twitting the man for his use of the term "knock off":

> "Only a day?"
> "Well, I won't be quite positive; I may have still put a few more touches to it the next day if the painting were not dry. I had better say, then, that I was two days at work on it."
> "Oh, two days! The labour of two days, then, is that for which you ask two hundred guineas!"
> "No; - I ask it for the knowledge of a lifetime."

General applause. Whistler won, but was awarded damages of precisely one farthing; he took to sporting the coin on his watch-chain.

If history remembers Ruskin as the fool in this episode, then, once again, history may well have got it wrong.

and for WEALTH

At the end of *Unto This Last,* Ruskin wrote:

> "I desire, in closing the series of introductory papers, to leave this one fact clearly stated. THERE IS NO WEALTH BUT LIFE. Life, including all its powers of love, of joy, and of admiration. That country is the richest which nourishes the greatest number of noble and happy human beings; that man is richest, who, having perfected the functions of his own life to the utmost, has also the widest helpful influence, both personal, and by means of his possessions, over the lives of others."

X is for XENOPHON

One of Ruskin's many educational schemes was the publication of a series of books that he felt ought to be on the shelves of every working man. As one might expect, his choice was far from conventional: high on the list was a work on economics by Xenophon.

Y is for YOUNG GIRLS

Let it be stressed from the outset for our wary twenty-first century sensibilities: Ruskin was not a paedophile, never ill-treated or behaved in a sexually abusive manner towards any child, male or female. He did, though, take an extraordinarily keen interest in young girls: he loved to tell them stories, teach them, join in their games; and he seems to have found sexually immature girls at once more fascinating and less disturbing than older girls, let alone grown women. In middle age, he became a regular visitor to Winnington Hall girls' school, where he taught lessons in drawing and mineralogy and scripture - *Ethics of the Dust* is a reasonably faithful dramatisation of such sessions. The school became a refuge for him, and one of his recovered Edens, and his time there seems to have done little harm, either to him or to the girls. At roughly the same time, however, he had a more fateful encounter with a little girl.

Rose La Touche is by far the most important presence of Ruskin's later life. He met her in 1858, when she was nine and he almost forty, and about to undergo his "unconversion". Before long, he was besotted with her, and in 1866, when she was 16, asked her to marry him. She put him off for six years, and finally refused him in 1872. In all, the sorry episode lasted for more than fifteen years, and blighted both his life and hers; she succumbed to religious mania and other afflictions, and eventually died on 25 May 1875; "Rose has gone where the hawthorn blossoms go", Ruskin wrote to Susan Beever. He never quite recovered from his grief; on the contrary, his preoccupation with her grew more powerful. He attempted to contact her spirit at séances and became ever more deeply obsessed with Carpaccio's cycle of paintings representing the life of St Ursula, and particularly "The Dream of St Ursula", which he inspected at close quarters in September 1876 and spent months copying in watercolour. Ruskin's own dreams and waking reveries were dominated by his notion that St Ursula and Rose were one. Rose haunts Ruskin's writing, in many guises: Guy Davenport observes that "His Ariadne was named Rose, whose name he finds, and conceals, everywhere in the text of *Fors*." In his last decade, his mind gave way as Rose's had, and he retreated into almost complete silence.

Z is for ZOOLOGY

Ruskin's observations of the natural world were not confined to plants and stones and rivers and clouds. He was also fascinated by animals, and wrote about them at length, especially about snakes and birds. Ruskin shuddered at snakes - "the running brook of horror on the ground", he called the serpent in a memorable outburst - but his sense of dread did not keep him from precise observation:

"That rivulet of smooth silver - how does it flow, think you? It literally rows on the earth, with every scale for an oar; it bites the dust with the ridges of its body. Watch it, when it moves slowly: - a wave, but without wind! a current, but with no fall! all the body moving at the same instant, yet some of it to one side, some to another, or some forward, and the rest of the coil backwards; but all with the same calm will and equal way - no contraction, no extension; one soundless, causeless, march of sequent rings, and spectral procession of spotted dust, with dissolution in its fangs, dislocation in its coils. Startle it; - the winding stream will become a twisted arrow; - the wave of poisoned life will lash through the grass like a cast lance."

The Queen of the Air

In his later life, Ruskin suffered from frightening dreams of snakes, and though it might seem crass to read such nightmares as sexual, some of his accounts are hard to gloss in any other way.

Ruskin's fascination with birds reached its fullest expression in his late work *Love's Meinie* (see above, *M is for Menial*), surely one of the most idiosyncratic works of ornithology ever written, mingling exact observations of feather structure and polemics about the mechanics of flight with quaint etymological speculations and proposals for an entirely new system of classification. Sir Kenneth Clark was understandably beguiled by one of its definitions, that of the swallow:

> "It is an owl that has been trained by the Graces. It is a bat that loves the morning light. It is the aerial reflection of a dolphin. It is the tender domestication of a trout."

Love's Meinie also belongs to that unofficial category of books which defers reference to its own title until the final sentence; Ruskin concludes the work with a lyrical protest against the practice of killing animals in the name of sport, and brings his plea home with a quiet vision of paradise, by proposing that

> "... the inhabited world in sea and land should be one vast unwalled park and treasure lake, in which its flocks of sheep, or deer, or fowl, or fish, should be tended and dealt with, as best may multiply the life of all Love's Meinie, in strength, and use, and peace."

During his final decade of silence, Ruskin continued to live by just such a treasure lake, Coniston, and was free to walk in his private version of the paradise park. He once wrote - and it is possibly his most famous single maxim - that the highest of all mortal powers is the power of sight:

> "The greatest thing a human soul ever does in this world is to *see* something, and tell what it saw in a plain way. Hundreds of people can talk for one who can think, but thousands can think for one who can see. To see clearly is poetry, prophecy and religion, - all in one."

Though the old Ruskin no longer spoke very much, and would shy away from pen and paper as if startled, we must hope that this power did not fail him, and that he was still able to see as few other people have been able to see. Marcel Proust, writing his notice of Ruskin's death, set at the very end of his piece the words Ruskin had used in his obituary of Turner:

> "And through those eyes, now filled with dust, generations yet unborn will learn to behold the light of nature."

Worple Press is an independent publisher specialising in poetry, art and alternative titles. It is part of The Worple Company Ltd (Registration No 3829499) **Worple Press** can be contacted at:

12 Havelock Road, Tonbridge, Kent TN9 1JE
Email theworpleco@aol.com.

Titles include:

Choosing an England - Peter Carpenter
(ISBN 0 953094707)

'In an honest, considered and moving selection he has tied some new marriage-knot around post-modernist and mainstream verse'
David Morley

'this consistently entertaining collection'
Sophie Hannah

At The End of The Day
(A Dictionary of Received Footballing Wisdom)
(ISBN 0 953094715)

'Little gems lurk' *Time Out*

'A well-aimed harpoon into the great footballing whale' *The Independent*

The Falls - Clive Wilmer
(ISBN 0 953094731) April 2000

'An utterly English faith in the language's passionate reticence' Ruth Padel

'An enduring probity, a craftsman's soul'
PN Review

Looking in All Directions - Peter Kane Dufault
(ISBN 0953094758) October 2000

'He is a nature poet for grown ups. We need him' P.J. Kavanagh

'Every poem has a surprise. So fresh and new... Wonderful stuff' Ted Hughes

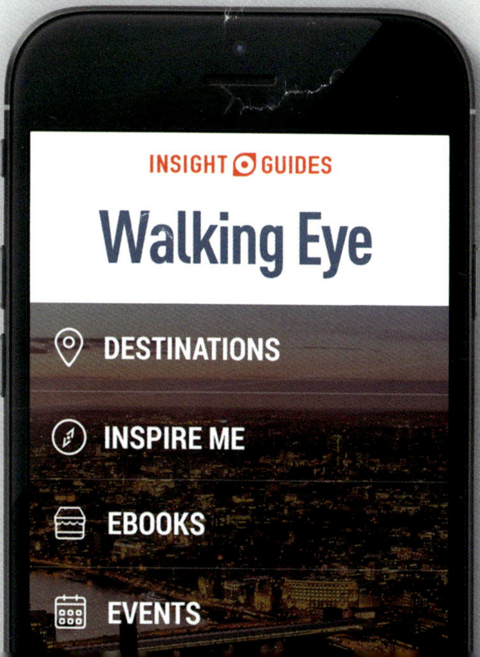

TOP 10 ATTRACTIONS

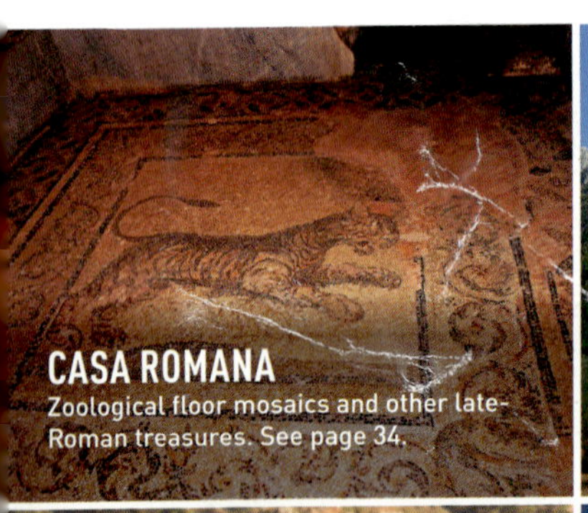

CASA ROMANA

Zoological floor mosaics and other late-Roman treasures. See page 34.

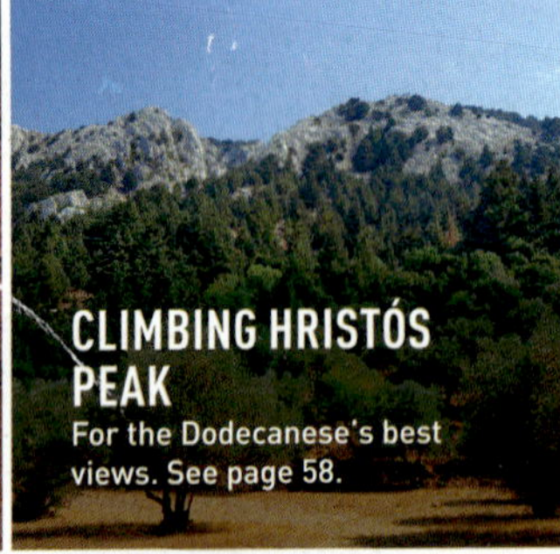

CLIMBING HRISTÓS PEAK

For the Dodecanese's best views. See page 58.

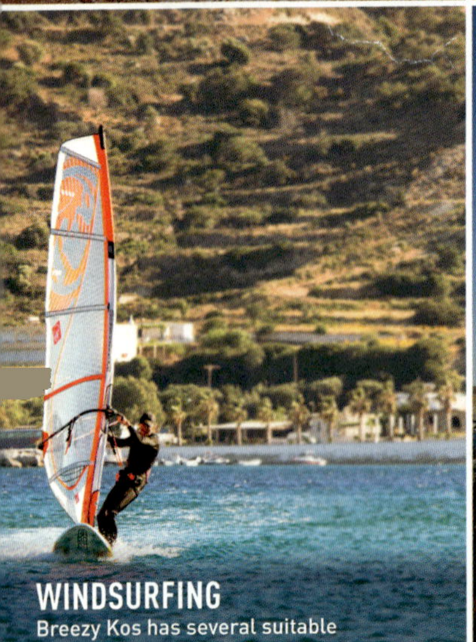

WINDSURFING

Breezy Kos has several suitable shorelines. See page 85.

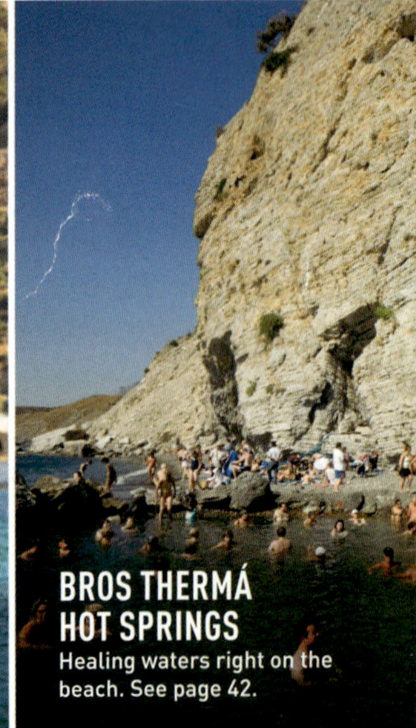

BROS THERMÁ HOT SPRINGS

Healing waters right on the beach. See page 42.

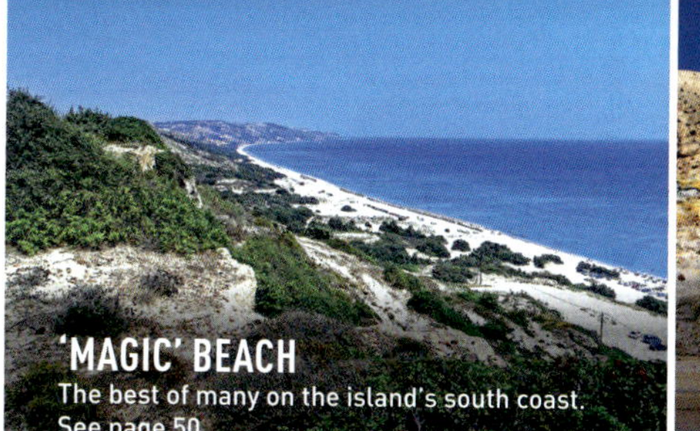

'MAGIC' BEACH

The best of many on the island's south coast. See page 50.

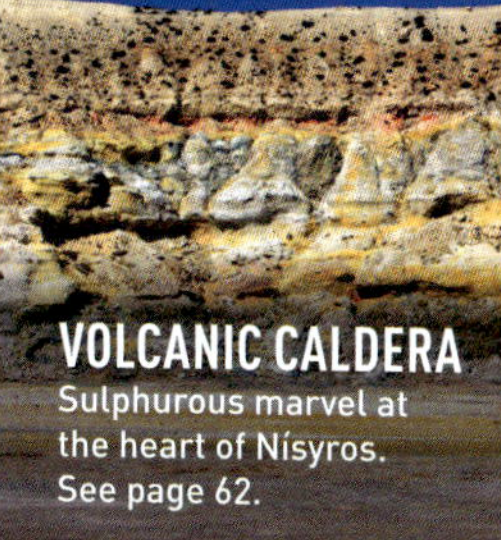

VOLCANIC CALDERA

Sulphurous marvel at the heart of Nísyros. See page 62.

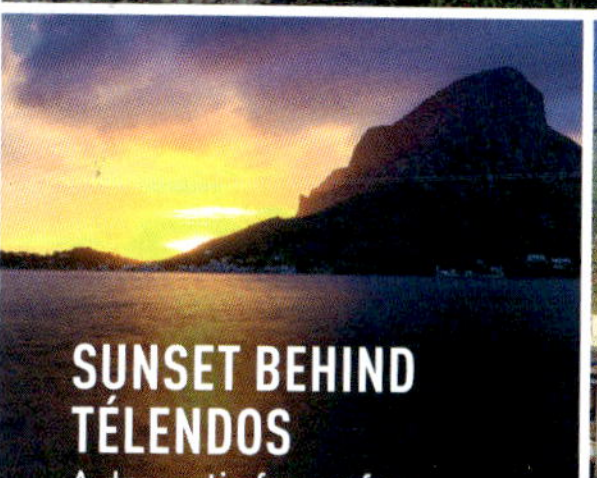

SUNSET BEHIND TÉLENDOS

A dramatic frame for spectacular sunsets. See page 71.

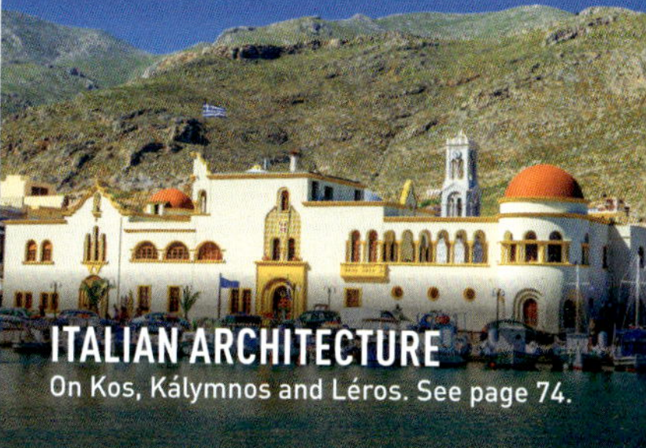

ITALIAN ARCHITECTURE

On Kos, Kálymnos and Léros. See page 74.

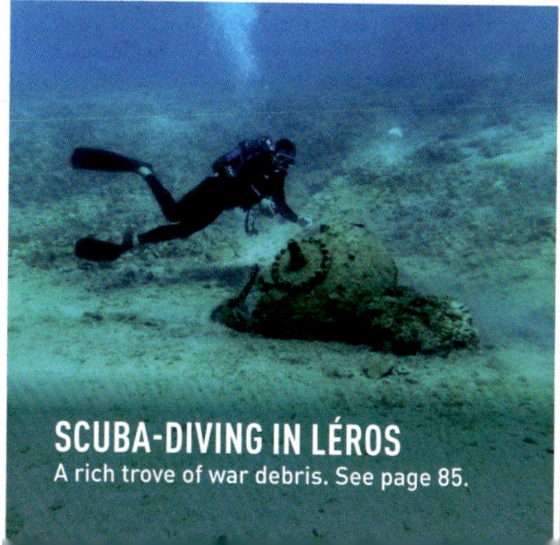

SCUBA-DIVING IN LÉROS

A rich trove of war debris. See page 85.

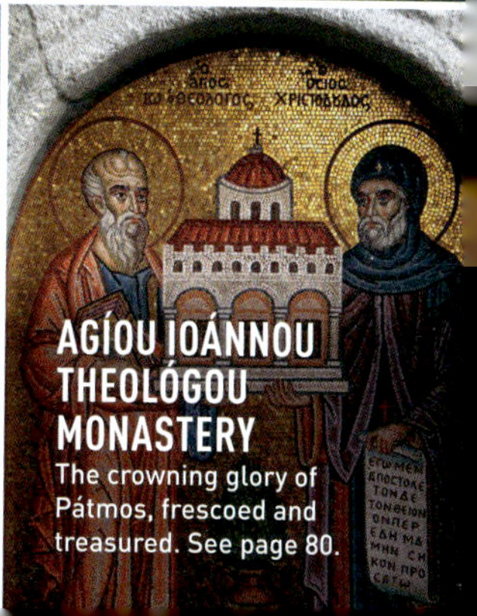

AGÍOU IOÁNNOU THEOLÓGOU MONASTERY

The crowning glory of Pátmos, frescoed and treasured. See page 80.

A PERFECT TOUR

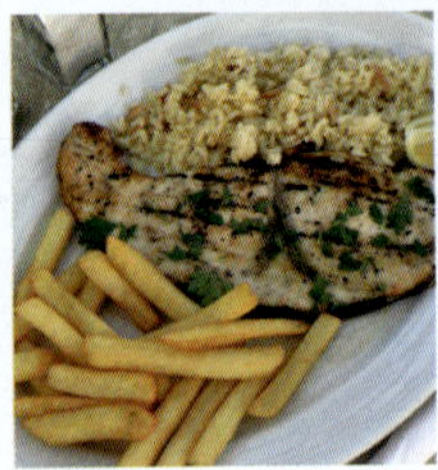

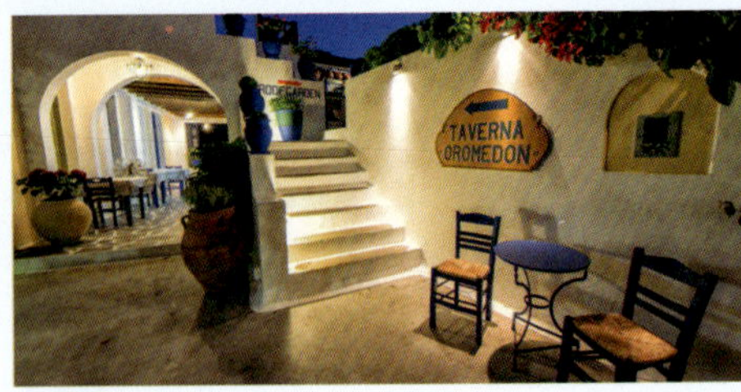

Day 1

First swim

At Kos airport, pick up your hire car and head straight to Kardámena for some fresh seafood. Have a cooling swim off Polémi or Psilós Gremós beach before hotel check-in at Kos Town, Psalídi or Ágios Fokás.

Day 2

Kos Town

Explore the Archaeological Museum and the Casa Romana museum in the morning. Swim near Tingáki or Marmári before lunch in or near Tingáki. Visit the hillside Asklepion in the late afternoon, before dinner at a Plátani taverna.

Day 3

Southwest coast

Ogle 1920s–30s Italian architecture before driving across Kos, visiting Andimáhia's castle before lunch at Mastihári. Continue to the far southwest around Kéfalos, perhaps stopping to windsurf at Kamári. Spend sunset on a pre-booked, north-coast horseback ride from the Salt Lake stables. Dinner is at Ambeli Taverna, outsideTingáki.

Day 4

A climb and a soak

Try more advanced windsurfing near Cape Psalídi, before lunch at Old Pyli taverna in Amanioú. Afterwards, see Lagoúdi village's frescoed church before climbing Khristós peak in the late afternoon. Dinner at Ziá's Oromedon taverna; then drive to Bros Thermá hot springs to soak away aches and pains.

Day 5

Nísyros

Take a morning excursion boat to Nísyros, where you overnight. On a scooter, tour the entire island besides its famous volcanic caldera – Pahiá Ámmos beach, the archaeological museum, two castles, two inland villages. Have lunch in Emboriós, dinner in Mandráki or Pálli, and visit the thermal bath-house.

OF KOS

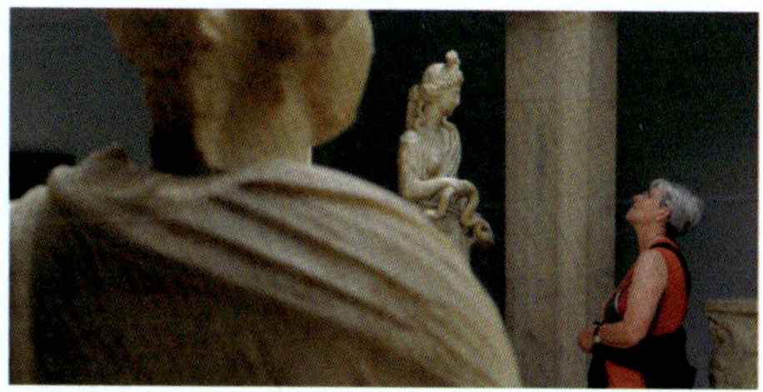

Day 7

Tiny Psérimos

Take the daily caique from Póthia harbour to Psérimos islet, with its idyllic beaches and laid-back pace; lunch at Avlákia port. Evening return to Kálymnos, with dinner in Póthia.

Day 6

Kálymnos

Board the catamaran from Nísyros to Kálymnos, arriving at lunchtime. From your Póthia base, head for Myrtiés by bus or scooter and take a little boat to peaceful Télendos islet. Return to Kálymnos to enjoy the sunset from a west-coast taverna at Melitsáhas.

Day 8

Léros

Pop into Póthia's Archaeological Museum before getting the catamaran to Léros, arriving for lunch at Pyrofanis, after hiring a scooter. After an afternoon swim and a look at Lakkí's Italian monuments, head up to the Knights' castle above Plátanos for superb sunset views. Dinner near your hotel in Krithóni, Álinda, or Vromólithos.

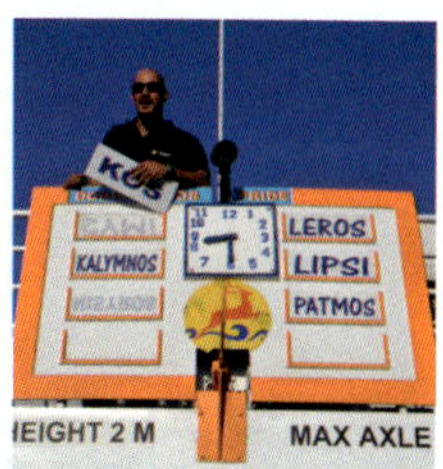

Day 10

Back to Kos

Take the morning catamaran from Pátmos to Kos, arriving in time for your afternoon or evening flight home. Spend any spare time in Kos Town.

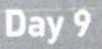

Day 9

Pátmos

Visit the Álinda Historical/Folklore museum before mid-day catamaran to Pátmos, with a swim and lunch at a beach and then an atmospheric evening pilgrimage to Hóra's magnificent monastery. Dinner at Votris in Skála.

CONTENTS

INTRODUCTION 10

A BRIEF HISTORY 15

WHERE TO GO 29

Kos Town 29
Neratziá Castle 30, Hippokrates' plane tree and the Loggia Mosque 31, The ancient town 32, Archaeological Museum 34, The Casa Romana 34, The Ottoman old town: Haluvaziá 35, Italian monuments 36, Platáni and the Asklepion 38, The Asklepion 39

The Northeast Coast: Lámbi to Bros Thermá 41
Bros and Píso Thermá 42

Northwest Coast Resorts: Tingáki To Mastihári 43
Tingáki and Marmári 44, Mastihári 45

Andimáhia, Kardámena And Pláka 46
Kardámena 48, Pláka forest 49

South-Coast Beaches: Polémi To Kéfalos 49

Kéfalos – the wild west 52
The Kéfalos peninsula 52

Around Mt Díkeos 54
Pylí: new and old 55, Lagoúdi 57, Evangelístria and Zía 57, Ascent of Hristós peak 58, Asómatos and Haïhoútes 60

Excursions 60
Nísyros 61, Kálymnos 66, Brostá: the west coast 70, Télendos 71, Psérimos 72, Léros 74, Álinda and around 76, Remote sites 76, Léros museums 77, Pátmos 78, Beaches 81, Bodrum (Turkey) 82

WHAT TO DO 85
Sports 85
Shopping 89
Entertainment 94
Children's Kos 96
EATING OUT 98
A-Z TRAVEL TIPS 114
RECOMMENDED HOTELS 136
DICTIONARY 143
INDEX 175

FEATURES

Refugees and Kos 12
Hippokrates, father of medicine 17
Historical landmarks 27
The Linopótis massacre 36
The Jews of Kos 38
Italian architecture in the Dodecanese 74
The Battle of Léros 78
The genuine icon 88
Wine varieties and tasting 93
Calendar of events 97
Non-alcoholic drinks 104

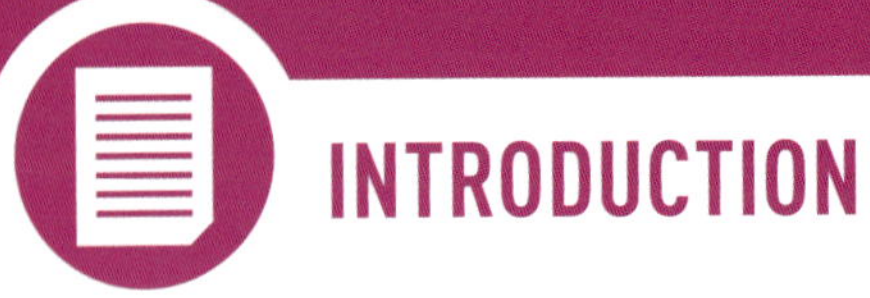

INTRODUCTION

It is impossible not to feel the weight of history when you arrive in Kos. The marble of Hellenistic and Roman sites, the sandstone of medieval churches and castles, are all tangible legacies of a long history. However, to imagine that Kos only appeals to archaeology buffs would be a mistake. With long, hot summer days, a balmy sea lapping numerous beaches, and lots to do, the island is a holidaymakers' paradise.

Kos belongs to the Dodecanese, an archipelago scattered in the southeastern Aegean Sea between Greece and Turkey. Originally made up of twelve major islands (*dódeka nisiá* means 'twelve islands' in Greek) that coordinated action against Ottoman repression during the late 19th and early 20th centuries, the group is now an administrative sub-region of Greece comprising nearly 40 islands and islets, though only twenty have permanent inhabitants.

Kos ranks third among the Dodecanese in size – but second in population at about 35,000 – and has been settled since ancient times, thanks to wide fertile plains, and a good harbour opposite Asia Minor, just three nautical miles away. The island is roughly 40km/24.7 miles long, 11km/6 miles across at the widest point, 287.2 sq km/111 sq miles in area, and orientated northeast to

The melon island

Near Linopótis, roadside stalls sell melons. The island has always been famous for watermelons especially, formerly exporting them in quantity to other parts of Greece. Old-timers on barren nearby islets remember, as children, eagerly awaiting the arrival of the summer watermelon boats from Kos.

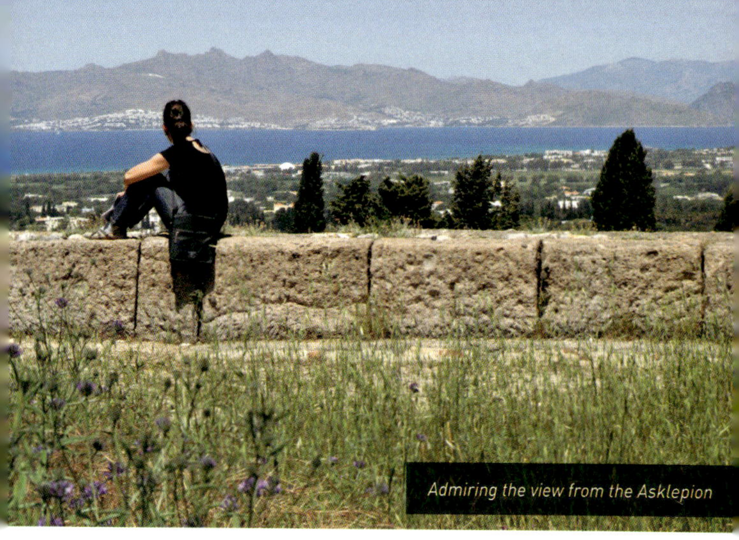
Admiring the view from the Asklepion

southwest on its long axis. Its coastline, a mix of sheer cliffs or beach, measures 112km/70 miles. Sand dunes are stabilised by important groves of strictly protected sea juniper *(Juniperus macrocarpa)*, in Greek *kédros* and thus invariably, wrongly, translated as 'cedar'. There are more junipers, and pines, up on the central mountain. Geologically, Kos is of partly volcanic origin (in the southwest), and rose from the seabed in stages between 1 million and 158,000 years ago. There are important wetlands at Alykí and Psalídi, which attract dozens of species of migrating birds annually.

Kos has always been a 'breadbasket' island, with a very limited maritime tradition, and could still be agriculturally self-sustaining should the need arise. In antiquity, Kos was renowned for its silk and wine; the silk industry is long gone, but wine-making has recently revived with a bang, and tasting local bottlings should be part of any visit. Unlike many holiday islands, farming has not completely been elbowed aside – herds of cattle grazing amidst wire-bound bales of hay are still very much part of the landscape, and local cheese is quite esteemed.

Kos was never strong enough to rule itself, but desirable and strategically located enough to be coveted by every east-Mediterranean empire or nearby state. It has, by turns, been part of the Dorian Hexapolis, the Achaemenid Persian Empire, Athens' Delian Confederacy, ancient Karya, the Alexandria-based Ptolemaic kingdom, the Roman republic and empire, Byzantium, Crusader principalities, the Ottoman Empire, the Italian 'Islands of the Aegean', and only since 1948 the modern Greek state. Each of these possessors, from the Ptolemies onwards, have left their mark on the island. Uneasy relations with adjacent Turkey mean that Kos has been heavily garrisoned by Greece since the 1950s, and you shouldn't be surprised to see tanks or armoured vehicles exercising in the volcanic badlands and ravines near the airport,

REFUGEES AND KOS

Kos spent 2015 in the media spotlight as one of the destinations for some of the 200,000 migrants who arrived in Greece by sea that year. At one point there were 7,500 refugees – mostly Syrian, but also Iraqi and Afghan – on Kos, some housed in disused hotels but otherwise sleeping rough. Every day, hundreds more landed on the island. Greece overall, and Kos in particular, was unable to cope – mid-economic crisis, the country simply didn't have the resources to help, and received scant assistance from the EU. On Kos (andelsewhere), sympathetic foreigners brought in supplies or took up local collections to feed and clothe the refugees, many of them women and children. Some 2,000 are currently housed in a former Italian facility near Pylí.

or parked in ranks at nearby military bases. Of late, better relations, and Greece's budgetary distress, mean that the military presence is scaled down – and you are as likely to see Turkish civilian holidaymakers as any other.

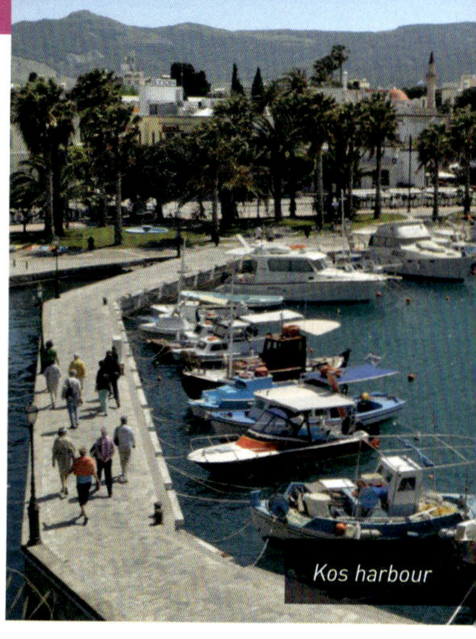
Kos harbour

KOS OF THE TOURISTS

The Italians built the first hotel on Kos in 1928, but British mass tourism arrived (at Kardámena) only during the 1970s, something observed wryly in John Ebdon's out-of-print but easy to obtain *Ebdon's Iliad*. The Dutch 'pioneered' northern Kos Town, as well as the 'bar lanes' at Mandráki, during the 1980s, and to some extent have remained loyal to it. Italians, Belgians and Germanophones were next; an increasing orientation towards the family and convention markets was signalled by the opening of many all-inclusive resorts around the millennium. Russians appeared next, but their numbers have now dropped as sanctions against Putin's regime shred the ruble's value. Cross-border tourism is increasingly significant, with potential Turkish visitors helped by the fact that the crossing from Bodrum opposite is the cheapest and most reliable for any of Greece's frontier islands.

For much of the 1980s and 1990s, Kos had a bad press, derided for being flat and boring – the centre of the island is indeed so low-lying that the peak of Nísyros can be glimpsed above it from Kálymnos to the north – as well as for its alleged

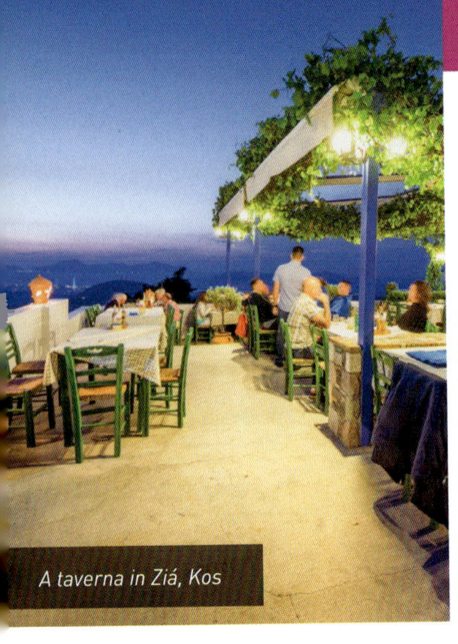
A taverna in Ziá, Kos

lack of architectural or culinary distinction. Clearly those detractors hadn't seen forested central Mt Díkeos or the rugged Kéfalos peninsula, Kos' unique Italian architectural heritage, or tasted the – by Greek island standards – highly idiosyncratic local cuisine, dishing up everything from Turkish-style kebabs to candied tomatoes to wine-marinated cheese to pork brawn.

In fact Kos has a lot to boast about: tourism has long been handled uncharacteristically efficiently on Kós, courtesy of a well-developed infrastructure: the urban bus service is a marvel, cyclists and the disabled are actively catered for with a network of marked bicycle lanes and wheelchair ramps in and around Kos Town, and proudly signposted biological sewage plants at Psalídi and Kardámena have preserved island seawater quality.

Twenty-first-century Kos remains one of the most popular islands with package holidaymakers, thanks to its many fine beaches, castles, and nightlife, as well as strong air links to northern Europe. With no university faculty (unlike many other large Greek islands) and no industry to speak of, tourism is the linchpin of the local economy. This is even more critical now given the country's economic tailspin in other respects, and you will be warmly welcomed.

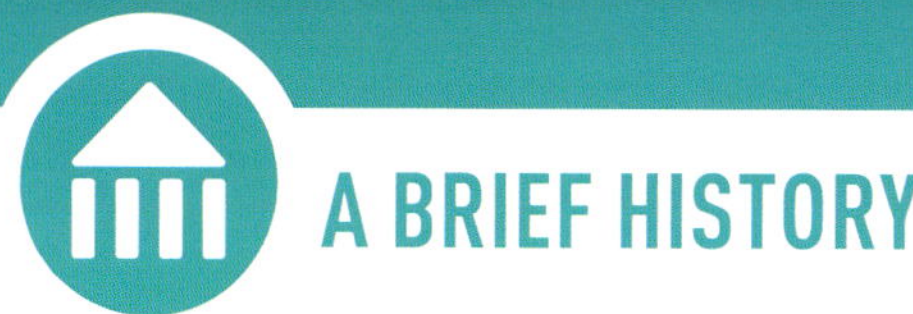

A BRIEF HISTORY

PREHISTORIC BEGINNINGS

The earliest habitation on Kos, at the Asprí Pétra cave, dates to 3400 BC; Kalymnian caverns hosted Neolithic man 2,000 years earlier. Early and Middle Bronze-Age settlers preferred Kos's fertile plains, with the exception of a Minoan expedition which founded the Seraglio site near the only natural harbour. After the Minoan civilisation collapsed around 1400 BC, Mycenean colonists occupied the Seraglio, staying until the arrival of the 'Sea Peoples' from beyond the Black Sea three centuries later.

The Seraglio was re-inhabited in about 900 BC by Argolid Dorians, who introduced the worship of Asklepios. Soon Kos entered history as a member of the Dorian Hexapolis, a federation of six cities on Rhodes, Kos and Anatolia opposite.

PERSIANS TO ROMANS

The Achaemenid Persian Empire under Cyrus the Great conquered Anatolia soon after 546 BC; Kos came briefly under Persian control, towards 500 BC. After Greek victories over the Persians at Plataea and Mykale in 479 BC, the island joined the Athenian-dominated Delian Confederacy. Kos got caught up in the Peloponnesian War of 431–404 BC, between Athens, Sparta and their respective allies; despite being Dorian, it did not join the Spartan side until 412 BC. Athens retaliated with a punitive expedition, but Kos again revolted in 407, before returning to the Athenian fold in 378. A civil war between pro-Spartan and pro-Athenian factions on Kos was only averted by the 366 BC founding of a new city, near Seraglio, and the political subservience or abandonment of other island towns.

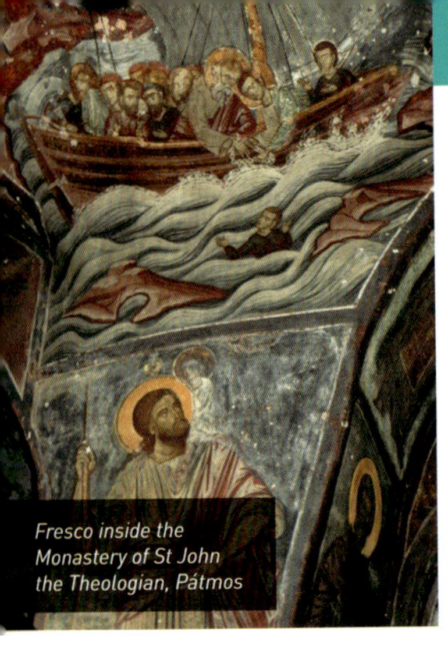
Fresco inside the Monastery of St John the Theologian, Pátmos

Kos city, with its excellent harbour near the main Aegean sea-lane, prospered. After brief rule by Halikarnassos opposite, both cities were taken by Alexander the Great's general, Ptolemy I, in 333 BC, and for the next 150 years Kos had strong links to the Ptolemaic capital, Alexandria.

Kos supported Rome during its 215–190 BC campaigns on the Greek mainland to crush the last Macedonian kings, and became a prominent banking centre. In 88 BC, Mithridates of Pontus sacked Kos; in revenge Kos provided a fleet to Rome, and was thus conspicuously favoured under both the Roman Republic and Empire, when it served as a popular resort for cures at the Asklepion.

BYZANTIUM AND CHRISTIANITY

The declining Roman Empire was divided into eastern and western empires. In 330 AD, eastern Emperor Constantine moved his capital to Byzantium, renaming it Constantinople (modern İstanbul) after him. While the last western emperor was deposed by Goths in 476, this eastern portion became the dominant east-Mediterranean power until 1025.

By 393, Christianity was the state religion; its liturgies and New Testament were written in *koine* Greek, based on Alexandria's Hellenistic dialect. Byzantine authorities eradicated any traces of pagan Hellenism, most obviously by recycling temple masonry when building churches.

Christianity came early to the Dodecanese. Kos, plus many smaller islands, have ruined basilicas with elaborate floors, invariably from the fifth or sixth century, often built atop pagan temples; these basilicas were either levelled by a severe earthquake/tsunami in 554 AD, or by the Saracen raids of the following century.

The 600s saw Constantinople besieged by Persians and Arabs, but the Byzantine Empire survived, losing only Egypt. From the ninth through the early eleventh centuries, in the Byzantine

HIPPOKRATES, FATHER OF MEDICINE

Hippokrates (c.460–370 BC) is regarded as the father of scientific medicine, and still influences doctors today through the Hippocratic oath – which he probably didn't compose, and scarcely resembles its original form. Hippokrates was definitely born on Kos, probably at ancient Astypalaia, but other details of his life are obscure. He was certainly a great healer who travelled throughout Classical Greece, but spent part of his career teaching and practising on his native island. Around seventy medical texts have been attributed to Hippokrates, only a few of which could he have personally written. *Airs, Waters and Places*, a treatise on the importance of environment for health from about 400 BC, is reckoned to be his, but most others were probably a compilation from a Kos library, which later surfaced in Ptolemaic Alexandria during the second century BC. This emphasis on good air and water, and the holistic approach of ancient Greek medicine, seems positively modern. His native island duly honours him today, with a tree, a street, a park, a statue and an international medical institute named after him.

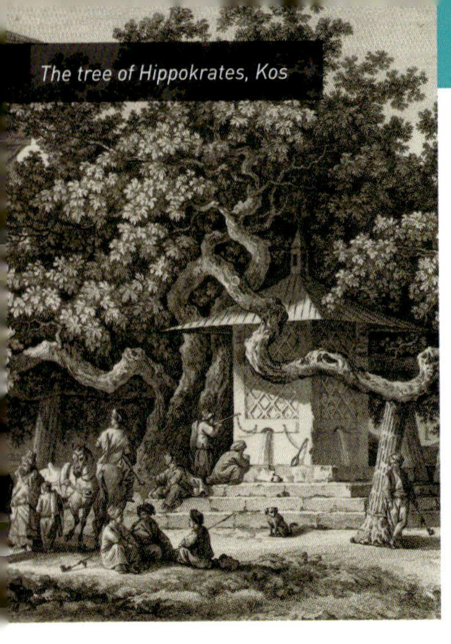
The tree of Hippokrates, Kos

heartland, Orthodox Byzantine faith exhibited a spiritual confidence, seeing Constantinople as a 'new Jerusalem' for the 'chosen people'. This prompted disastrous diplomatic and ecclesiastical conflict with the Catholic West, culminating in the 1054 schism between the churches.

Meanwhile, the Dodecanese became a backwater subject to periodic pirate raids, figuring little in history except for the 1088 foundation of Agíou Ioánnou Theológou monastery on Pátmos, a previously insignificant island granted to Abbot Khristodoulos by the emperor.

CRUSADER AND OTTOMAN CONQUEST

In 1095, Norman crusaders raided the Dodecanese en route to Jerusalem. Worse followed in 1204, when Venetians, Franks and Germans diverted the Fourth Crusade, sacking and occupying Constantinople. Latin princes and their followers divided up choice parts of the empire. Byzantium was reduced to four small peripheral kingdoms *(despotates)*; none was based in the islands, though Rhodes and Kos were held by Leo Gabalas, a Byzantine aristocrat, for four decades.

In 1261, the Paleologos dynasty, provisionally based at Nicaea, recovered Constantinople but little of its former territory and power. Their only Latin allies were the Genoese, whose support came at a price: extensive commercial privileges in the capital, and the ceding, at various moments up to 1355, of many Aegean islands to assorted Genoese families.

Genoese adventurers had seized Rhodes and other Dodecanese islands by 1248, but in 1309 the crusading Knights Hospitallers of St John, expelled from Palestine and dissatisfied on Cyprus, conquered Rhodes. Genoese Kos fell to the Knights in 1314, after which their possession of most of the Dodecanese was guaranteed. Astypálea, Kárpathos and Kásos stayed Venetian, while Pátmos remained Orthodox monastic territory. Knightly citadels, either purpose-built or adapted Byzantine castles, appeared on most islands.

The Byzantines faced a much stronger threat than the crusaders in the expanding Ottoman Turkish Empire. Weakened by internal struggles, they proved no match for the Turks. On 29 May 1453, Constantinople fell to Sultan Mehmet II after a seven-week siege.

From their strongholds, the Knights engaged in both legitimate trade and piracy, constituting a major irritant to the expanding Ottoman Empire. Attempts to dislodge them from Kos in 1457 and 1477 failed; it took the six-month siege of Rhodes in 1522 by Sultan Süleyman the Magnificent to compel their surrender and cession of all their Dodecanese islands.

Under Ottoman rule, the Dodecanese lapsed into a conservative mode of village life. Only larger islands with flat, arable land, like Rhodes and Kos, attracted extensive Muslim colonisation and

Calming effect of Kos

The Fourth Earl of Sandwich, doing his 1738 Grand Tour, noted that 'the Turks of Kos are... endued with more affability than the Mahometans in any other part of the Levant,' while an 1815 visitor observed that 'the Turks are by no means rigid or savage, and marry with the Greeks by civil contract.'

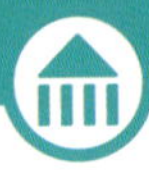

garrisoning, primarily in the largest towns, where non-Muslims were forbidden residence in the strategic central citadels. Taxes and discipline were imposed through imperial judges, tax collectors and military personnel, but local notables retained large enterprises or estates. Generally, insular Ottoman government was lackadaisical; 18th- and 19th-century travellers reported extensive neglect on Rhodes, including discarded weapons and unrepaired damage from the 1522 siege.

Greek identity was preserved through the Orthodox Church, which, despite occasional enforced conversion and intermarriage, suffered little interference from the Ottomans. All Orthodox peoples, Greek or otherwise, were considered one *millet* (subject nation), their patriarch responsible for his flock's behaviour, tax collection and administering communal and inheritance law. Monasteries organised primary schooling – and on Pátmos, a distinguished secondary academy.

Smaller islands enjoyed significant autonomy and special concessions (particularly tax exemption) under Ottoman rule. These privileges were honoured even after the establishment of a Greek state in 1830, withdrawn incrementally only after 1874. Barren maritime Dodecanesian islands made fortunes either through sponge-diving, transporting Anatolian goods with their own fleets, or building boats on Turkish commission. Until the 18th century, the Ottomans never acquired much seamanship, relying instead on Aegean crews and shipyards.

ITALIAN RULE AND WORLD WAR II

The Dodecanese were seized by Italy in a brief, spring 1912 campaign, the sequel to an autumn 1911 war which expelled the Ottomans from Libya. At first Greek Orthodox islanders acclaimed the Italians as liberators, who promised not to outstay their welcome. Early in World War I, however, Italy remained neutral, and was only persuaded to join the Entente by being promised, among other things, that its sovereignty over the Dodecanese would be recognised. Between 1915 and 1923, international conferences agreed that (except for Rhodes) the Dodecanese would be given to Greece, but after the collapse of Greece's Asia Minor invasion, and the rise of Italian Fascism, this became unlikely.

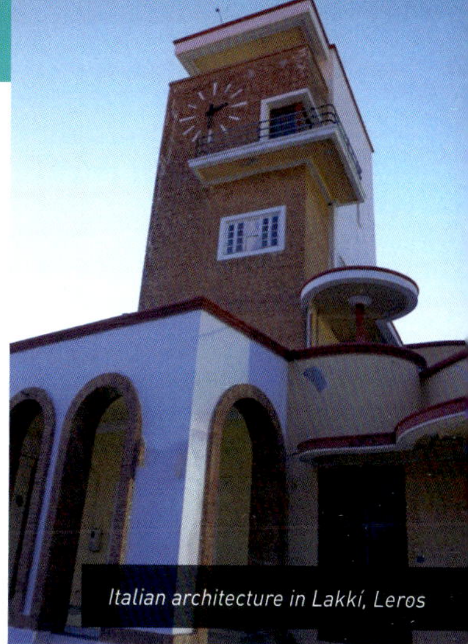

Italian architecture in Lakkí, Leros

In 1923, Italy definitively annexed the Dodecanese as the *Isole Italiane del'Egeo*, embarking upon gradual, forced Latinisation. During the term of first Governor Mario Lago, land was expropriated for Italian colonists and intermarriage with local Greeks encouraged, though only Catholic ceremonies were valid. A puppet Orthodox archbishopric was set up, and when this failed (except for three collaborationist bishops), the Orthodox rite was suppressed completely. Italian was introduced as the compulsory language of public life in 1936, when ardently Fascist Cesare Maria de Vecchi replaced Lago and accelerated assimilationist measures. These provoked riots on Kálymnos (with stone-throwing women in the front line).

The Dodecanese were never part of metropolitan Italy: islanders were awarded, en masse, 'lesser' Italian nationality, with no obligation for military service (and no civic rights), while 'major' or full Italian citizenship was granted to those who collaborated conspicuously with the authorities. Emigration was possible on

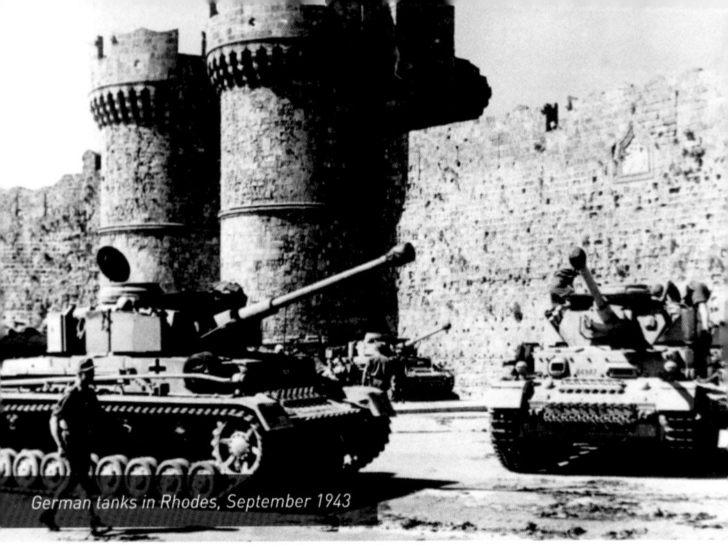

German tanks in Rhodes, September 1943

a 'minor' passport, and indeed by 1939 the Greek population of many islands had halved, which the Fascists probably intended. Expatriated Dodecanesians formed pressure groups in New York, Egypt, Australia and England to lobby any interested audience about the Greekness of the Dodecanese.

On larger islands, massive public works were undertaken to make them showcases of this 'Italian Aegean Empire'; roads, monumental buildings and waterworks were constructed (often using forced Greek labour), sound and unsound archaeological work was embarked upon, and accurate mapping done. The first hotels rose on Rhodes and Kos; tourists arrived by boat or seaplane. However, smaller islands, except for militarised Léros, were neglected.

Using a submarine dispatched from Léros, the Italians torpedoed the Greek cruiser *Elli, anchored at Tínos,* on 15 August 1940. This outrage went unanswered, as Greece was unprepared for war; but when Mussolini's troops overran Albania, and on 28 October sent an ultimatum demanding passage for them through Greece, Greek dictator Metaxas responded to the Italian ambassador in Athens with the apocryphal *"óhi"* (no). (In fact, his answer, in mutually understood French, was *"Alors, c'est la guerre"* – a gesture still celebrated as a national holiday).

Greece was defeated in April 1941 and a tripartite German-Bulgarian-Italian occupation imposed; little changed in the Dodecanese, except that Governor De Vecchi – hated even by many Italians – was replaced by Admiral Inigo Campioni.

When Italy capitulated on 8 September 1943, a brief free-for-all ensued on the Greek islands it had controlled. Churchill considered the Dodecanese easy pickings, but was denied assistance by the US, reluctant to endanger its precarious advance through Italy. The British occupied Kos and Léros, but insufficiently to repel German counterattacks; Kos fell on 3 October, Léros on 16 November, with considerable losses. German troops imprisoned and executed their erstwhile Italian allies, particularly on Rhodes, Léros and Kos. The Germans captured Campioni and handed him over to the Salo Republic, which executed him in May 1944 for refusing to fight for the Axis.

The British gradually took the Dodecanese from September 1944 onwards, picking off islands one by one, though Rhodes, Kos and Léros were too strongly defended and only abandoned by the Germans after their May 1945 surrender to the Allies, signed on Dodecanesian Sými. Along with western Crete, these were the last territories they held.

The British stayed for 22 months from May 1945, causing considerable unease in the Greek government, which suspected that they meant to set up a Cyprus-style colony or (worse) hand some or all of the Dodecanese back to Turkey. However, the British claimed they intended to cede these islands to Greece once it

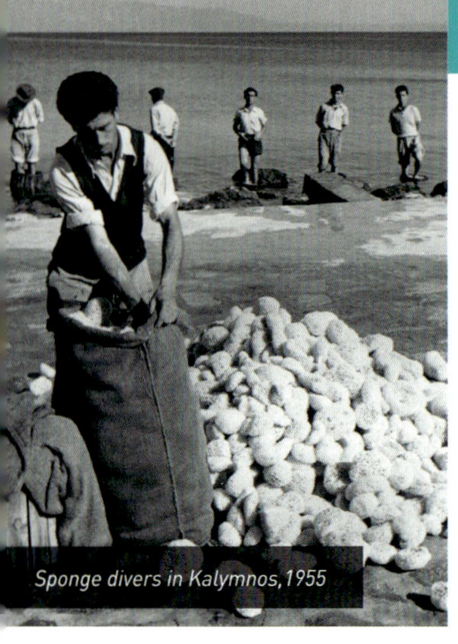

Sponge divers in Kalymnos, 1955

became clear the central government would prevail against communist rebels on the mainland, and were also awaiting the result of Italian-Greek peace treaty negotiations.

The negotiations' main sticking points were Greek demands for war reparations versus Italian claims of compensation for 'improvements' to the Dodecanese (eventually Italy paid a reduced sum of $105 million) and, more seriously, the fate of native Italians, and Greeks with 'major' Italian nationality. Metropolitan Italians, including those married to islanders, were given a year from February 1947 to choose between Greek or Italian nationality; if the latter, they were obliged to leave for Italy (a large number stayed). Native islanders who enjoyed 'major' Italian citizenship had their cases examined minutely; those who had adopted this status enthusiastically were also deported to Italy.

Once the treaty was ratified, the Greek Army assumed control on 31 March – a date responsible for the half-true assertion that the Dodecanese were united with Greece in 1947. A military governor presided over a ten-month lustration regime, evaluating the cases of 'major' Italian subjects, and winkling out any communists. Once this was completed, the Dodecanese were officially annexed by Greece on 9 January 1948, and the first civilian governor appointed.

UNION WITH GREECE: 1948 TO THE NEW CENTURY

A demoralised, impoverished Greece entered the American/NATO orbit during the 1950s. This and the next decade also saw wholesale emigration abroad or internally to larger cities. In the Dodecanese, many inhabitants of Kos and Kálymnos especiallyheaded off to Australia or Canada, both countries with labour shortages and less bothered about left-wing political affiliation than the US. As relations with neighbouring Turkey worsened after 1954, the resulting sense of insecurity on border islands accelerated depopulation.

Tourism saved some islands from complete desertion, though it began gradually. Kálymnos, Léros and Pátmos saw significant tourism only from the late 1980s onwards. The centre-left PASOK government, first elected in 1981 and in power almost uninterruptedly until 2004, tended to favour remote islands (which voted accordingly), and the infrastructure on Kos improved notably. An unusually stable local administration also helped, with an effective mayor re-elected repeatedly.

THE BAILOUT YEARS

PASOK defeated centre-right Néa Dimokratía (ND) in the early October 2009 elections, with George Papandreou becoming prime minister. In April 2010 the first bailout from European and international lenders was solicited. By late 2011, despite imposition of the harshest austerity measures seen in post-1945 Europe, Greece's economy and Papandreou's position had both become untenable; Papandreou resigned on 11 November in favour of a six-month technocratic government of national unity.

Successive May/June 2012 elections produced hung parliaments, with ND the top-finishing party in both. A coalition was assembled from ND, PASOK and centre-left DIMAR, specifically excluding new upstart leftist party SYRIZA. By late 2014, the result was clear: a collapsing economy with droves of small and medium-sized businesses bankrupted, overall unemployment reaching 27 percent, a 57-percent youth unemployment rate, and massive emigration of young, skilled individuals.

In the constitutionally-mandated parliamentary elections of 25 January 2015, SYRIZA, headed by Alexis Tsipras, gained a plurality but not a majority of seats. Nevertheless the old ND-PASOK duopoly was finished.

Negotiations resumed with Greece's creditors for a third bailout and possible debt restructuring. Talks halted in late June, just before PM Tsipras announced a 5 July referendum on the terms of a proposed bailout, and ordered Greece's banks shut for three weeks and withdrawal limits imposed to prevent them from collapsing.

The referendum went massively (61.3 percent) against accepting a third bailout on creditor terms. Despite this, Tsipras soon caved in and accepted another bailout even harsher than the one rejected. Battling rebels within his own party, he only secured approval of this €86 billion deal with opposition support. Added to existing debts of €317 billion, Greece would now owe over €400 billion with no hope of ever paying it off.

Meanwhile on Kos, a 20 July 2017 Richter 6.6 earthquake caused severe damage to the town and castle; two foreigners died in a collapsed club.

SYRIZA suffered major losses in the May 2019 Euro-elections, and then lost a parliamentary vote in July, when ND was able to form the first non-coalition government since 2011.

HISTORICAL LANDMARKS

3400 BC Neolithic settlement at Asprí Pétra, Kos.

1620 BC Minoans colonise Seraglio site, Kos.

850 BC Kos becomes a member of the Dorian Hexapolis.

460–370 BC Hippokrates's approximate lifetime.

366 BC Ancient Kos built on site of present town; Asklepion founded.

Late 3rd century BC – early 2nd century BC Kos is ruled from Ptolemaic Alexandria.

88 BC Pro-Roman Kos sacked by Mithridates of Pontos.

554 AD Severe earthquake and tsunami wrecks Kos.

c. 1314 Knights Hospitaller of St John assume control of Kos, Nísyros, Kálymnos and Léros from the Genoese.

1523 Knights evacuate peacefully following the successful Ottoman siege of Rhodes.

1912 Italians oust Ottomans from Kos and all other Dodecanese isles.

1923–43 Systematic archaeological excavations on Kos; Italian urban renewal and monuments on Kos, Kálymnos and Léros.

1933 Severe earthquake levels much of Kos Town.

1940 Italy attacks Greece; Léros is a vital Italian base.

1943 Germans seize control of the Dodecanese from the Italians, and defeat the British in the battles of Kos and Léros.

1945 Germany surrenders Kos, Léros and Rhodes to the British.

1947 British cede the Dodecanese to a Greek military governor.

1950s–60s Large-scale emigration to Australia and Canada.

1970s Beginning of Kos mass tourism.

2009–14 Incoming government discovers Greece is bankrupt; EU-brokered bailouts begin but economy shrinks 25 percent.

2015 SYRIZA-dominated coalition government elected; third bailout. Numerous refugees arrive on Kos.

2017 Severe July earthquake causes major damage in Kos Town, especially to the castle, Defterdar Mosque and port.

2019 SYRIZA lose Euro elections, then are defeated in national polls by ND.

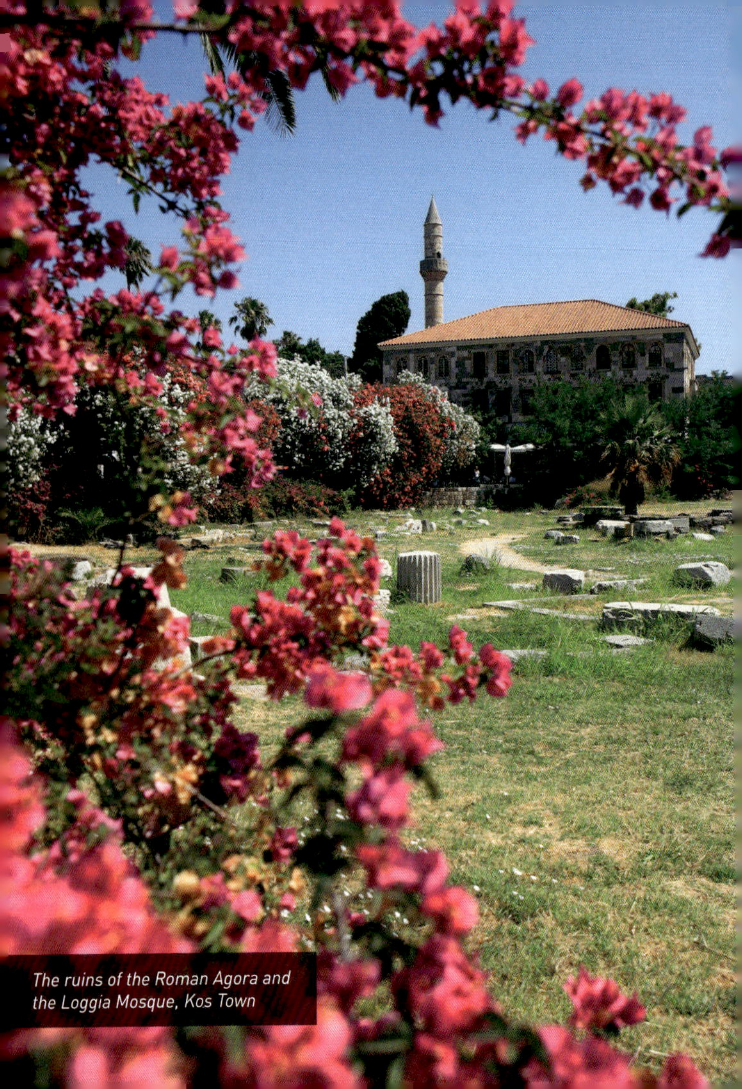

The ruins of the Roman Agora and the Loggia Mosque, Kos Town

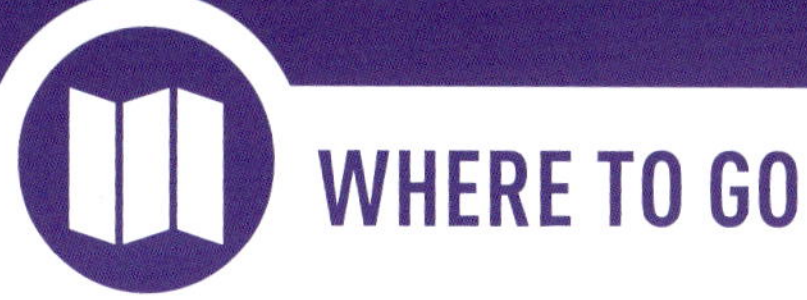

WHERE TO GO

Kos is an easy island to explore, with good public transport for independent sightseeing, as well as abundant outlets for renting cars, scooters or push-bikes. There's absolutely no need to take an organised tour.

This guide explores Kos Town first. Next there's a tour around the island, starting with Platáni and the nearby Asklepion, then continues around the coastline before forays into the interior. Finally there are excursions to (or more rewardingly, overnight stays on) a half-dozen smaller nearby islands.

KOS TOWN

Minoan settlers were attracted by Kos's only good natural harbour, opposite ancient Halikarnassos (modern Bodrum), and despite regular, devastating earthquakes throughout its history, **Kos Town** ❶ has remained there, prospering from seaborne trade. The contemporary city spreads in all directions from almost landlocked Mandráki port. Apart from the imposing Knights Hospitaller's castle, the first thing visible arriving by sea, its most compelling attractions are abundant Hellenistic and Roman ruins, many only revealed by a 1933 earthquake, and some quirky Italian architecture.

Despite a population of nearly 20,000 – well over half the islanders – Kos Town feels uncluttered, thanks to its sprawling, flat layout. Areas of open space alternate with a hotchpotch of archaeological zones, surviving Ottoman quarters, and Italian-built mock-medieval, Rationalist and Art Deco-style buildings, designed in two phases (1926–1929 and 1934–1939) either side of the earthquake by architects Florestano di

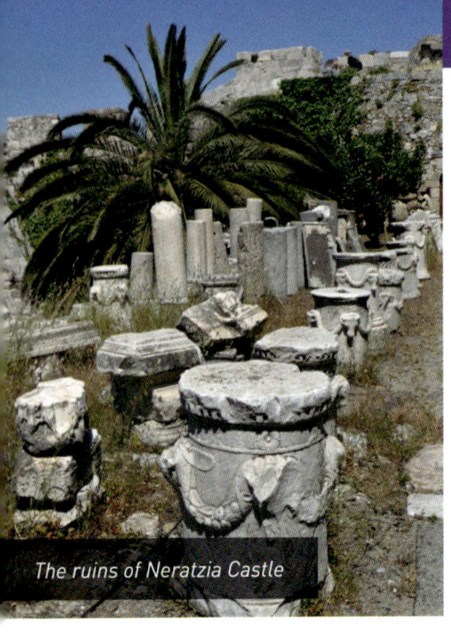
The ruins of Neratzia Castle

Fausto, Rodolfo Petracco and Armando Bernabiti. Plans incorporated, as always, a Foro Italico, the Italian administrative complex close to the castle, and a Casa del Fascio (Fascist Headquarters), with the inevitable speaker's tower for haranguing party rallies gathered on the central square below. The maze-like Ottoman core aside, this is a planned town, with pines and shrubbery planted by the Italians now fully matured, especially in the garden suburb extending east of the centre, its worker and officer housing mostly the work of Mario Paolini.

NERATZIÁ CASTLE

An obvious first stop, if it re-opens, is **Neratziá Castle (Castle of the Knights)** Ⓐ (closed indefinitely owing to earthquake damage), reached by a causeway over its former moat. The moat was long ago filled and planted with palms *(fínikes)* – thus the avenue's Greek name, Finíkon. The original Knights' castle which stood here from 1314 until 1450 has vanished without trace, replaced by the existing inner castle (1450–78). This nestles within an outer citadel, built to formidable thickness between 1495 and 1514 to withstand advances in artillery technology following unsuccessful Ottoman sieges in 1457 and 1477. The fortification walls make an excellent vantage point for photographs over **Mandráki**.

A fair proportion of ancient Kós, as masonry fragments and tumbled columns, has been incorporated into the walls of both strongholds or, more recently, piled up loose in the southeast forecourt. Escutcheons and coats-of-arms on various walls and towers will appeal to heraldry aficionados, as the period of construction spanned the terms of several Grand Masters and local governors of the Knights. The south corner of the older castle, for example, bears two Grand Masters' escutcheons, best admired from the massive, most technically advanced southwest bastion, identified with Grand Master Fabrizio del Caretto, who finished the job. Dozens of cannonballs lie about, few if any fired in anger, since this castle surrendered peacefully in accordance with the terms ending the marathon 1522 siege of Rhodes.

HIPPOKRATES' PLANE TREE AND THE LOGGIA MOSQUE

Steel scaffolding has replaced the ancient pillars that once propped up sagging branches of **Hippokrates' plane tree**, immediately opposite the Neratziá castle causeway. At seven hundred years of age, this venerable tree has a fair claim to being among the oldest in the Mediterranean, though it's not really elderly enough to have seen the great healer himself. The trunk has split into four sections, which in any other species would presage imminent demise, but abundant root-suckers promise continuation. Adjacent stand a hexagonal Turkish pillar fountain, another fountain

Signs of Life

The biggest explosion that ever occurred at Neratziá castle was orchestrated for the finale of Werner Herzog's black-and-white first feature film, *Signs of Life* (1968), in which a low-ranking Wehrmacht soldier goes berserk in 1944 and torches an ammunition dump inside the castle.

draining into an ancient sarcophagus (neither running now), and the imposing 1786-built mosque of Gazi Hasan Pasha, better known as the **Loggia Mosque** B after its covered northern portico. The upper stories are locked and window tracery still evinces wartime bombardments. The ground floor – like that of its contemporary (1780) the now minaret-less **Defterdar Mosque** on nearby Platía Eleftherías – is occupied by tourist-orientated shops. This is not sacrilegious, but common Ottoman practice: shopkeepers' rent helps maintain the mosque overhead.

Just east of the Loggia stands the **Apothíki Alatíou Hamam (Salt Depot Baths)** C (Wed–Mon 8.30am–4pm, free), excellently restored and labelled to reveal its function as a women's bath-house from the mid-17th century until 1948, after which it briefly served as a salt warehouse (thus the name). The changing room has a footbath in the middle and niches for stowing footwear. Ten bathing stations each have their own carved basin, while twelve complete or partial domes admit light through glass inserts. The largest room has a platform, right over the heating system, for massage; nearby steps lead up to the edge of a cold plunge pool.

THE ANCIENT TOWN

The largest excavated section of ancient Kos is the **agora** D, a sunken zone (unrestricted access) reached from either Ippokrátous or Nafklírou streets. The latter, a pedestrian lane (and lately much-subdued nightlife mecca), is separated from Platía Eleftherías by the **Pórta tou Fórou** E, all that remains of the outer city walls which the Knights erected between 1391 and 1396. It has been scaffolded since the 2017 quake, pending repairs.

What you see is confusing and jumbled owing to successive earthquakes in 142, 469 and 554 AD; the most salient items are the foundations of a massive double Aphrodite sanctuary roughly in the centre of the site, some columns of a Hellenistic stoa near the Loggia Mosque, plus two re-erected columns and the architrave of the Roman agora itself, on the far west.

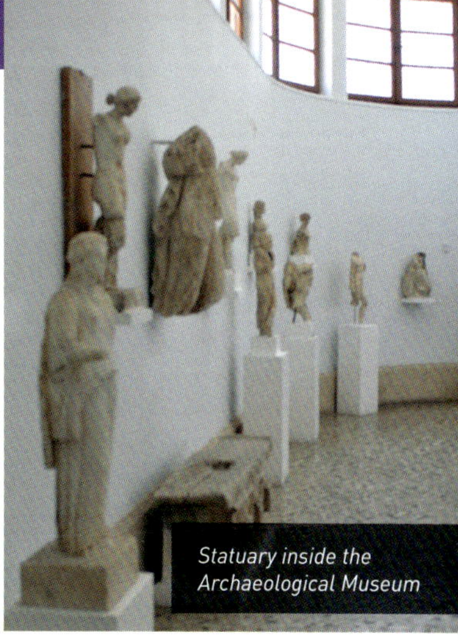
Statuary inside the Archaeological Museum

Another, more comprehensible section of the ancient town, the **western excavations** **F** (unrestricted access), abuts the ancient acropolis – where Platía Diagóras lies today. Intersecting marble-paved **Roman streets** (Cardo and Decumana), dating from the third century AD, lend definition to this area, as does the **Xystós**, or colonnade, of a covered running track. Inside the Xystós the hulking brick ruins of a bath squat alongside the original arch of its furnace room. South of the Xystós stands the restored door-frame of a baptistry belonging to a Christian basilica erected above the baths after 469 AD. The floor of the basilica, as well as that of an unidentified building at the northern end of the excavations, retain well-preserved mosaic fragments, although the best have been carted off to Rhodes. What remains tends to be under several inches of protective gravel or off-limits to visitors, like the famous **Europa mosaic** house to the north of Decumana street – though it, plus others nearby showing gladiators, a boar being speared and sundry gods or muses, can be viewed from a distance.

Secreted in a cypress grove across Grigoríou tou Pémptou Street is a fourteen-row **Roman odeion** **G** (open

all day; free), which in ancient times hosted musical events associated with the *Asklepieia* festivals (see page 40); it was re-clad in new marble during 1999–2000 and again is a popular concert venue. The best bit, open and illuminated for visitors, is the undercroft.

ARCHAEOLOGICAL MUSEUM

The north side of Platía Eleftherías is dominated by the refurbished **Archaeological Museum** ❽ (Apr–Oct Wed–Mon 8am–8pm, Oct–Apr earlier closure; charge), designed and built in 1935 in severe Rationalist style by Rodolfo Petracco. The Italians' original choice of exhibits was a none-too-subtle propaganda exercise, with a distinct Latin bias. Four ground-floor galleries containing good, if not superlative, statuary are grouped around a central atrium where a Roman mosaic shows Hippokrates welcoming Asklepios to Kos. The most famous exhibit, a statue thought to portray Hippokrates, is in fact Hellenistic, as is a vividly coloured, fragmentary fish mosaic at the rear of the atrium. But most of the other highly regarded works – Hermes seated with a lamb, Artemis hunting, Hygeia offering an egg to Asklepios' serpent, a boxer with his arms bound in rope, statues of wealthy townspeople – are emphatically Roman. An upper, post-renovation storey exhibits smaller treasures.

THE CASA ROMANA

The **Casa Romana** ❾ (Apr–Oct Wed–Mon 8am–8pm, earlier closure Oct–Apr; free), at the south edge of town, re-opened in 2015 after a five-year refit, well worth the wait; it now effectively functions as a museum of domestic, late-Roman (3rd–4th centuries AD) life. During World War II it served as an Italian infirmary – until 2010 you could still see faded red crosses painted on the exterior to deter Allied bombers.

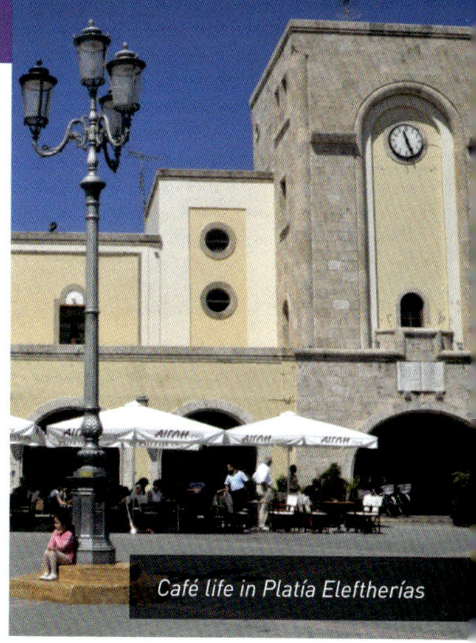
Café life in Platía Eleftherías

The structure, devastated by the 554 AD earthquake but abandoned long before, was clearly the villa of a wealthy family, arrayed around three atria with third-century tessellated marble or **mosaic floors**. The mosaic closest to the ticket booth shows a lion and a leopard respectively mauling two stags; the largest courtyard to the south is flanked by rooms, on opposite sides, depicting another panther and a tiger; while the third atrium's pool is surrounded by dolphins, fish and two leaping leopards, plus a damaged nymph riding a horse-headed sea-monster, possibly a representation of Poseidon. Standouts amongst the small finds displayed are a *nekrodeipno* (funerary banquet) relief with the goddess Kybele presiding; a figurine of Venus adjusting her sandal; and elaborate 'Knidos-style' oil-lamps.

THE OTTOMAN OLD TOWN: HALUVAZIÁ

Kos's medieval 'old town', the former Muslim district of **Haluvaziá** ❶, lines either side of a pedestrianised street running from behind the Italian-era market hall on Platía Eleftherías as far as Platía Diagóras and the orphaned minaret of the earthquake-tumbled Yeni Kapı Mosque overlooking the western excavations. It was long considered an undesirable area, but while all the rickety townhouses nearby collapsed in the 1933 earthquake, the sturdily built stone dwellings and shops here survived. Today, they are crammed with superfluous tourist boutiques, cafés and tavernas; one of the few genuinely old things here is a dry fountain with an Ottoman inscription, found where the walkway cobbles cross Venizélou. Another juts out from the wall of the barber shop at the corner of Hristodoúlou and Passanikoláki, next to the minaret-less but still-functioning **Atik Mosque** (refurbished in1892), whose name means 'Mosque of the Agile One'.

ITALIAN MONUMENTS

On Kos, the seafront Foro Italico extending southeast from Neratziá castle, erected during 1927–29, comprises the local **administration building**, now the police station; the adjoining courthouse, still in use; the graceful **Albergo Gelsomino** Ⓚ, restored and serving in its original role; the mayor's

THE LINOPÓTIS MASSACRE

Amnós tou Theoú was originally the chapel of the surrounding Catholic cemetery, which contains a memorial honouring Italian officers executed by the Germans on 6 October 1943. The British seized Kos on 14 September and with the Italian garrison resisted German attacks until being overwhelmed on 3 October. Taken prisoner were 148 Italian officers. Seven opted to fight again, 38 escaped to Turkey and the remaining 103 were marched across a field between Linopótis and the Tingáki salt-lake, mowed down by machine-gun and buried where they fell. In 1946, the German commander of Kos was convicted for his Cretan war crimes, and executed.

residence, today the municipal cultural centre; the **Italian officers' club**, now the Avra Lounge Bar; and inland opposite **Evangelismós Church** ⓛ, originally the Catholic cathedral of Agnus Dei. From the same era, but on the far side of the harbour entrance, stands the crenellated power plant, with the town hall found en route, behind Aktí Koundouriótou.

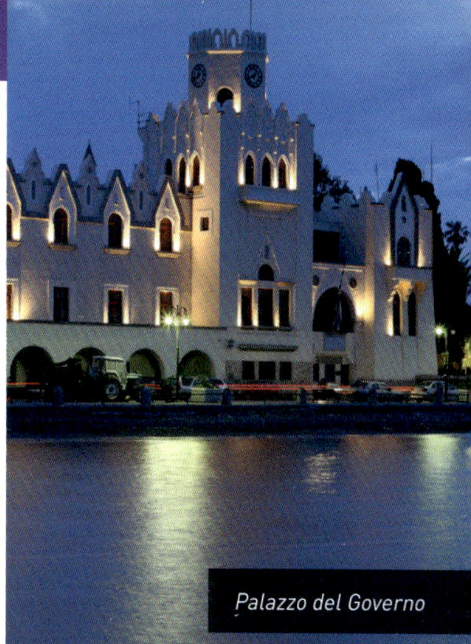

Palazzo del Governo

Post-earthquake monuments are more scattered, dating mostly from 1934–35. Notable ones include the **Casa del Fascio** Ⓜ (today part-occupied by the winter Orfeas cinema) with its prominent clock-tower/speaker's balcony; the **covered market** Ⓝ or *dimotikí agorá*, a fun if expensive place to souvenir-shop; and the aforementioned archaeological museum – all flanking focal Platía Eleftherías. Further afield are the exceptionally eclectic **synagogue** Ⓞ at Alexándrou Diakoú 4; the round-fronted, seafront **primary school** Ⓟ, at the base of Kanári; the **Fascist Youth building** Ⓠ at the corner of Venizélou and Koraí, now a branch of Pireos Bank; and the circular 1937 **Amnós tou Theoú** Ⓡ (Agnus Dei) Catholic church. Many other mixed-use buildings pop up around town, with shops on the ground floor and residences upstairs. Much of the fun in strolling around is spotting them – there's a particularly extravagant one at the corner of Venizélou and Vasiléos Pávlou.

PLATÁNI AND THE ASKLEPION

The Greek–Turkish village of **Plátani** ❷ lies 2km (1.2 miles) southwest of Kós Town, on the road to the Asklepion, served in tourist season Mon–Sat by city buses 3, 3A and 4 from 8am until 9pm (last return slightly before that). Until 1971 it was commonly known as Kermédes (*Germe* in Turkish), and the Turkish community had its own primary school, but in the wake of the successive Cyprus crises and the closure of the Greek theological seminary in Istanbul, the village was officially renamed and education provided only in Greek. Subsequent emigration to Anatolia has caused Turkish numbers on Kos to drop from about 3,000 to around 700; mainly those Muslims owning real estate and businesses have stayed. Relations between them and their Greek Orthodox neighbours are cordial, and even intermarriage occurs.

Plátani's older domestic architecture is strongly reminiscent of styles in rural Crete, from where many of the village's Muslims came between 1896 and 1912, speaking Greek rather than Turkish; Crete during that period was an autonomous region within the Ottoman Empire, but Cretan Muslims

THE JEWS OF KOS

Jews had lived on Kos since antiquity, although the Knights of St John exiled most of this community to Nice. Following the Ottoman conquest, Sephardic Jews settled here, their dwindling numbers reinforced after 1922 by co-religionists from İzmir in Anatolia. On the road between Kos Town and Plátani, a Jewish cemetery lies in a dark conifer grove. Dates on the headstones stop ominously in 1940. The remaining local community of about 140 was shipped to Auschwitz in 1944. Just one Koan Jew, who died early in the 1990s, survived the war.

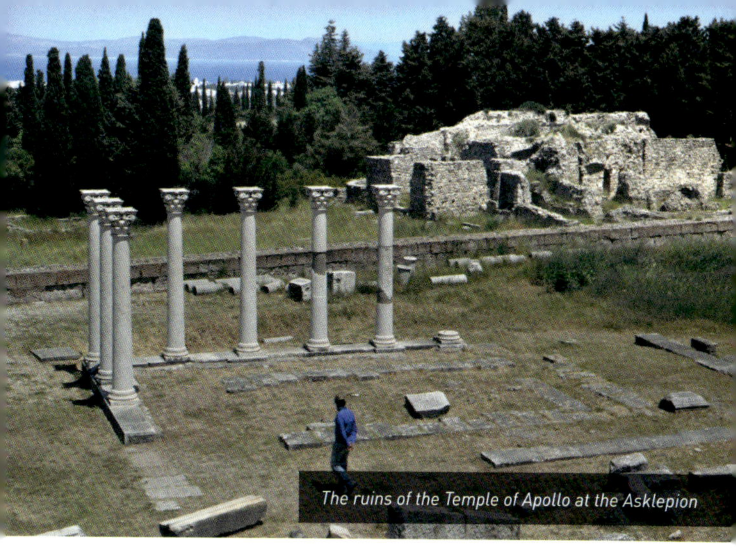
The ruins of the Temple of Apollo at the Asklepion

could see that their island would eventually join Greece and that there would be no place for them in the new order. Kos and Rhodes were the closest, similar Ottoman-held islands to which they could flee.

At the main crossroads, with a functioning Ottoman fountain nearby, are several Muslim-owned tavernas, the main reason outsiders stop here, as well as for superior ice cream at the Paradosi sweet shop (which now has a branch on Avéroff in Kos Town).

THE ASKLEPION

The Hellenistic **Asklepion** ❸ (summer daily 8am–8pm, winter Wed–Mon 8am–3pm; charge), 4km (2.4 miles) south of town, is one of just three in Greece. The site was first excavated in 1902–05 by islander Iakovos Zaraftis and the German Rudolf Herzog; digging resumed under Italian archaeologists Luciano Laurenzi and Luigi Morricone.

Urban bus number 3, or a mini-train make the trip via Platáni between 8.30am and 5.30pm; otherwise you can attempt the steep-ish bicycle ride, perhaps pausing for lunch in Platáni en route.

The Asklepion (pronounced *asklipíon*) was actually founded just after Hippokrates's lifetime, but presumably the methods used and taught here were his. Both a shrine of Asklepios and a curative centre, its magnificent setting on three hillside terraces overlooking Anatolia reflects early recognition of the importance of the therapeutic environment. Two fountains provided the site with clean, fresh water – one still dribbles slightly – and extensive stretches of clay piping are still visible, embedded in the ground.

Today, very little remains *above* ground, owing to periodic earthquakes and the Knights' pilfering of site masonry for their castle. The lower terrace in fact never had many structures, being instead the main venue for the *Asklepieia* – quadrennial celebrations and athletic or musical competitions in honour of the god. Sacrifices to Asklepios were conducted at an **altar**, the oldest (c. 340 BC) structure here, whose foundations lie near the middle of the second terrace. Just to its east, some Corinthian columns of a second-century AD **Roman temple** were re-erected by Laurenzini and Morricone. A monumental **staircase** flanked by *exedrae* (display niches) leads from the altar up to the second-century BC **Doric temple** of Asklepios on the topmost terrace, the last and grandest of a succession of the deity's shrines at this site, though only foundations remain.

Asklepios

Kos's Asklepion honours the Greek god of healing Asklepios, who according to legend was the son of Apollo and the nymph Koronis. His cult developed from the early Classical era onward, with a half-dozen combination shrines and therapy centres (the biggest at Epidauros) all over the Hellenic world.

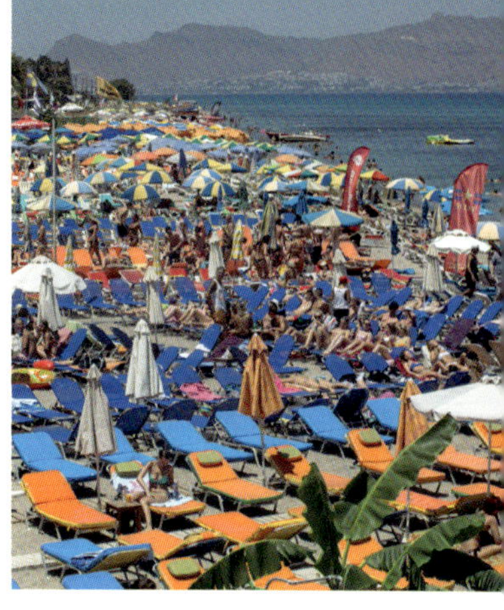
Busy summer beach near Kos Town

THE NORTHEAST COAST: LÁMBI TO BROS THERMÁ

Kos Town is flanked by two areas of seafront development. **Lámbi** ❹ immediately north is essentially a suburb, albeit one devoted almost entirely to tourism, fringed by a long, east-facing beach (thus the Ottoman name Kumburnu or 'Sand Point') liberally sown with beach bars and sunbed concessions. Their biggest concentration is along Aktí Andoníou Zouroúdi, which extends almost up to Mylos, a recommended windmill beach-bar beyond the urban grid. Don't try to walk or pedal past it all the way to the end at **Cape Skandári**, as this is an off-limits military base.

The coast road southeast from town, starting at the yacht marina, curls around the northeastern tip of Kos, passing en route much of the island's luxury accommodation. **Psalídi** ❺ can be said to start at the few spiral-fluted columns of the fourth-century AD basilica of **Ágios Gavriíl**, just inland from the road in a marshy area. There are a few indifferent public beaches nearby, with sunbed-and-umbrella concessions, but most coastline here is the domain of hotels (aside from near our recommended windsurf schools beyond **Cape Loúros**).

Once past the last resort hotel on the strip – Okeanis – Ammos beach bar signals the start of an excellent, much more protected stretch of sand and pebbles extending for over 1,000m (0.6 miles) south to **Cape Ágios Fokás** ❻, with its military watchtower. While there are no facilities aside from Ammos, this patch is popular with locals who come prepared with picnics and umbrellas to enjoy the clean sea here. Discreet naturism is practiced where low cliffs shield the beach from prying eyes up on the road. It's easy enough to pedal out here on a clunker bike, being only 6km (3.7 miles) from town, mostly on designated, flat cycle path.

The next decent beach is beyond the cape, between it and a final cluster of hotels. There's another beach-bar here, somewhat regimented, but the shore just east, where some tamarisks lend shade, is protected from most winds. Urban buses numbers 1 and 5 serve this route from dawn until midnight, with nine (between 9.15am–5.15pm, last return 5.35pm) continuing to the start of the dirt track down to Bros Thermá.

BROS AND PÍSO THERMÁ

The unusual, remote hot springs of **Bros Thermá** ❼ emerge from volcanic cliffs about 3km (2 miles) beyond Cape Ágios Fokás. They are most easily reached by rented vehicle (or for the very fit, multi-speed mountain-bike); the final approach lies along a dirt track heading down and left at a drinks stall just before the end of the asphalt, where buses leave you. Track roughness varies depending on the preceding winter; rent a jeep to guarantee passage. Parking is very limited and you may have to leave four-wheelers a good 300m/yards shy of the springs, certainly no further than the sunbed/snack bar concession which serves the small pebble beach at the bottom of the steep grade.

Scalding, odourless springs (45°C/113°F at source) issue from a tiny grotto at the base of the palisades, flowing through a trench to mingle with the sea at comfortable temperatures inside a giant corral of boulders. Winter storms disperse the boulder wall, re-fashioned every April, so the pool changes shape from year to year

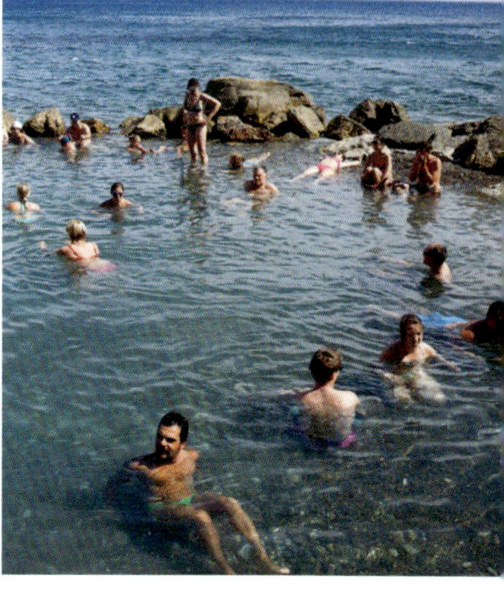
Enjoying the warm waters of Bros Thermá

– but always has a maximum depth of about three-and-a-half feet. Despite periodic threats of development as a spa, it remains free of access, and immensely popular with tourists and locals alike, especially during the cooler months or on moonlit nights – and under a full moon, it's truly magic (provided your pool companions aren't too rowdy!).

About halfway between Bros Thermá and Kardámena, maps show another coastal hot spring at a spot marked **Píso Thermá** ❽, or Agía Iríni after the chapel there. The normally authoritative Greek-language hot-springs guide *Ta Loutra tis Ellados* claims you can walk there along the shoreline with some difficulty from Bros Thermá in two hours, as does the municipal website www.kos.gr. The Píso Thermá springs were once hotter (47°/117°F) and stronger-flowing than Bros Thermá, but during the 1970s a boulder-fall blocked their main outflow, leaving just a few warm seeps emerging from the seabed. Today people mostly go by boat from Kardámena, especially for the saint's day (May 5) pilgrimage.

NORTHWEST COAST RESORTS: TINGÁKI TO MASTIHÁRI

Scattered along the northwest-facing coast of Kos, the resorts of Tingáki, Marmári and Mastihári share an exposure to prevailing summer winds, and great Aegean views. The profiles of (west to east) Kálymnos, Psérimos and the Turkish Bodrum peninsula on the horizon make for spectacular scenery, especially at sunrise or sunset.

TINGÁKI AND MARMÁRI

Tingáki ❾ (sometimes 'Tigáki'), the shore annexe of the Asfendioú hamlets (see page 55), lies 9km (5.5miles) west of Kos Town, whether via Zipári and the main trunk road, or by more relaxing back roads preferred by cyclists. It's a busy, somewhat higgledy-piggledy resort popular with Brits, with most of its accommodation scattered inland among fields and cow pastures. The long and narrow, white-sand beach, fringed at the back by jujube and tamarisk trees, improves, and veers further out of earshot from the frontage road, as you head southwest from the focal seaside T-junction/plaza, with the best patches to either side of the drainage from Alykí salt lake.

Just west of the plaza, **Artemis Hamam** (daily; www.artemishamam.com), is Kos's only public, non-hotel-affiliated answer to those across the way in Bodrum. All the usual massages and therapies are available, best enjoyed in discounted packages (€55–120). There's also a shop with genuine Turkish-made hamam products plus Western lotions and oils.

The traditional coastal annexe of Pylí village, **Marmári** ❿, 15km (9.3 miles) from Kós Town along the island trunk road, has a smaller built-up area than Tingáki; its beach is broader and arguably better, especially the section signposted as **Píthos**. To the west, the sand forms mini-dunes sheltering the odd naturist. A grid of paved rural lanes, popular with cyclists, links the inland portions of Tingáki and Marmári. Arriving along the main road, you turn off just past the little duck-pond and derelict buildings at **Linopótis**, which began life as the Italian agricultural colony Anguillara. Marmári is most popular with Germanophone and Italian visitors.

Tingáki and Marmári are separated by the **Alykí salt pan** ⓫, which becomes a brackish lake lasting until next autumn after wet winters. Recent years have indeed been rainy, with flamingos (and the odd swan) arriving as early as October and staying until early June; almost 450 flamingos were counted wading over one week early in 2015. If they aren't visible here, chances are the wind has diverted them to the smaller, brackish pond near the cape at Psalídi.

Western striped-neck terrapins *(Maremys caspica rivulata)* often congregate near the seasonal lake's outlet to the sea, a sluice with a narrow road bridge over it; if they come ashore, feed them bread at your own risk – they have strong jaws capable of inflicting nasty wounds, or even severing fingers.

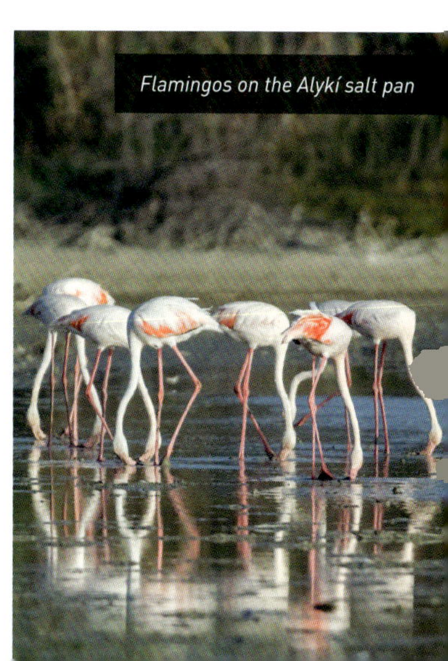

Flamingos on the Alykí salt pan

MASTIHÁRI

Although it has nearby its share of mega-all-inclusive complexes and Kos's biggest water-park, three-street-wide **Mastihári** ⓬, draped over a slope rising from the harbour and beach, remains one of the island's more low-key resorts; it was a permanent village long before

tourism times, as well as the historic summer quarters of Andimáhia, 3km (1.8 miles) inland.

Mastihári, 25km (15.5 miles) from Kos Town, is also the ferry port for the shortest crossing to Kálymnos; most of the year there are morning, mid-afternoon and early evening ro-ro sailings (in summer up to 6 daily), keyed more or less to the arrival times of flights from Athens – KTEL buses between airport and town make a stop in Mastihári en route, dovetailing with the comings and goings of the ferry. Three days weekly during summer there is a useful speedboat link from here to Psérimos islet.

While shorter than those at Marmári or Tingáki, the local beach extending southwest is broader, with dunes (and no sunbeds) towards the far end. The early sixth-century basilica of **Ágios Ioánnis** ⓭ (fenced but unlocked) lies about 1.5km (1 mile) down this beach, following the shoreline promenade (look for the enclosure near the Hotel Ahilleos). The basilica is fairly typical of the island's numerous early Christian monuments, with a row of column bases separating a pair of side aisles from the nave, a tripartite narthex and a baptistry tacked onto the north side of the building. It was excavated during the 1950s by the great Byzantinologist and architect Anastasios Orlandos, but regrettably its intricate floor mosaics are covered in protective gravel.

ANDIMÁHIA, KARDÁMENA AND PLÁKA

Visitors inevitably pass through blufftop **Andimáhia** ⓮, immediately northeast of the airport, but few stop in the village itself as there are no conventional attractions aside from an old restored windmill, kitted out as a museum with sails rigged (turning again since 2014). This **Mýlos tou Pappá** is the last surviving mill of

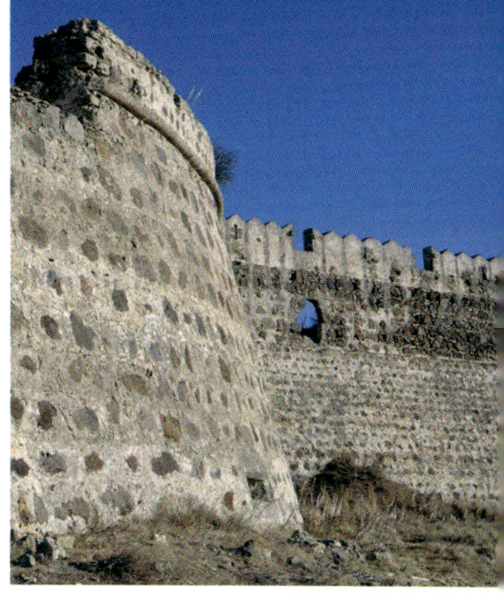
Andimáhia castle fortifications

more than thirty which once dotted the ridges here and at Kéfalos. You can inspect the inner workings (daily 9am–5.30pm; charge).

More compelling is **Andimáhia castle** ⓯, about 4km (2.4 miles) southeast of the village, mostly by a diffidently signposted if paved side-road beginning at an army camp. Enormous when seen from afar, this triangular stronghold of the Knights Hospitaller overlooks Nísyros and Tílos, and would have been a vital signalling link between those islands and the Knights' castle at present-day Bodrum in Turkey. The originally Byzantine castle was initially used by the Knights as a prison, then modified during the 1490s in tandem with improved fortifications at Kos port citadel.

The fortifications (unrestricted entry) prove less intimidating close up – except for a rather pathetic old man, dressed in mainland evzone costume the likes of which has never been worn on Kos, who accosts all visitors with a loud, barked '*Tradizionale*!' and demands money to be photographed. A less authentic or edifying spectacle cannot be imagined; nearby villagers are embarrassed by him but, since he is breaking no law, there is nothing to be done about it.

Once past the fake evzone and through the imposing double north gateway, surmounted by the arms of Grand Master Pierre d'Aubusson dated 1494, you can follow the well-preserved west

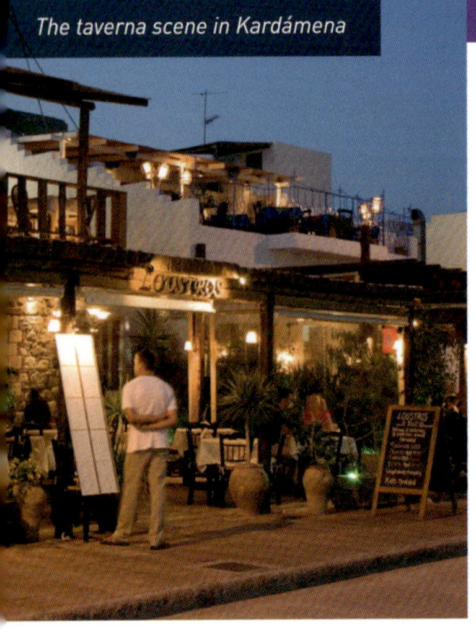
The taverna scene in Kardámena

parapet. The badly crumbled eastern wall presides over a sharp drop to ravines draining towards Kardámena. Inside the walls stand **two chapels** (open): the westerly, dedicated to Ágios Nikólaos, retains a fresco of Ágios Hristóforos (St Christopher) carrying the Christ Child, while the eastern one of Agía Paraskeví, though mostly devoid of wall painting, sports fine rib vaulting springing from half-columns. Gravel walkways, illumination and a ticket booth were installed in 2001 – and never really used except when there's a summer concert here, arguably the best time to visit.

KARDÁMENA

Some 5km (3 miles) southeast of the airport, **Kardámena** ⓰ is the closest resort to it, just pipping Mastihári, and the largest (1,926) coastal settlement outside of Kos Town. Good beaches stretching on either side, plus a seafront promenade and *platía* with minor Italian-era buildings, comprise its daytime charms. A lively bar and club scene prevails after dark, though nothing like Kardámena's 1990s heyday as designated party resort for younger Brits. Visitors lately – especially Russians, young couples and families – form a broader profile, and bars with naughty Brit-centric names like 'Ten Toes Up, Ten Toes Down' or 'Slug and Lettuce' are now extinct.

Northeast of the resort centre, the best patch of **beach** from the standpoint of amenities, no-hassle parking, good sand and access to exceptionally clean sea free of reef or sharp-edged pebbles is in front of Atlantis Taverna, about 1.5km (1 mile) out of town, which rents sunbeds and parasols affordably.

Beaches southwest of Kardámena tend to be scrappier and monopolised by mega-hotels. One can drive back to the main road directly along here without retracing your steps via the airport, but between the Robinson Club and defunct Lakitira resorts, a stretch of rough, steep dirt road is best tackled with a jeep, especially after hard winters.

PLÁKA FOREST

Just west of the airport on the main island trunk road, signs indicate an initially paved turning to 'Pláka'. The road soon becomes dirt (but always passable) as one descends into the densely forested **Pláka** ⓱ dell. The main attraction here, besides welcome shade, is a thriving population (c. 30) of wild but camera-friendly peacocks – shrieking, flying up into the trees and marching lines of their offspring around. Local feral cats have learned, presumably after some well-aimed pecks from the parents, to leave the chicks alone. It's a great outing for kids, as the peafowl are not otherwise aggressive.

SOUTH-COAST BEACHES: POLÉMI TO KÉFALOS

Climbing out of Pláka valley back up onto the main island road, and then heading southwest, drivers soon see profuse signage pointing left (south) and down – sometimes sharply down – to the best beaches on Kos. This is essentially one giant, 5km- (3-miles) strip of sand up to Cape Tigáni, but subdivided into separate patches with individual access roads, whose Greek

and touristic-English names co-exist on placards. Beyond Ágios Stéfanos and Kastrí islet, Kéfalos Bay extends along another 3.5km (2.2 miles) of sandy beach.

The beach sections, described below from east to west, are all provided with sunbeds, a rudimentary snack/drinks-bar and often a jet-ski franchise. **Magic** ⓲, officially Polémi, is the longest, broadest and wildest section, with a full-service taverna above the car park (see page 109), no jet skis and a nudist zone (**Exotic**) at the east end. **Sunny**, officially signed as Psilós Gremós and easily walkable from Magic, has another taverna and jet-skis. **Langádes (Markos)** ⓳ is the cleanest and most picturesque section of beach, with junipers tumbling off the dunes almost to the shore. **Paradise**, alias Bubble Beach in boat-trip jargon owing to volcanic gas vents in the shallows, is overrated; the sandy area is too small for the crowds descending upon its wall-to-wall sunbeds and tavernas, while boats attached to paragliding and banana-ride outfits, plus the inevitable jet-skis, buzz constantly offshore. **Camel** (Kamíla) ⓴ is the shortest and loneliest of these strands, flanked by weird rock formations (but no humped beasts) and protected somewhat from crowds by the very steep, unpaved drive in past its hillside taverna; the shore here is fine sand, with no jet skis and good snorkelling on either side of the cove.

Uninterrupted sand resumes at **Ágios Stéfanos** ㉑ peninsula, with beaches to either side; the left-hand (easterly) one, with sunbeds, is backed by a now-abandoned Club Med complex. The sparsely marked public access road to Ágios Stéfanos begins near a bus stop on the highway, cutting through the Club Med grounds. Two triple-aisled, late-fifth-to-early sixth-century **basilicas** occupy the peninsula. Once the premier early-Christian monuments on Kos, they are now in disgraceful condition. All of the columns have been toppled by vandals since the 1980s, and the rich mosaics which cover the entire floor have either been damaged or covered in a thick layer of protective sand. You'll need a plastic beach trowel or a thick brush to uncover two peacocks perching upon and drinking from a goblet, or (in the north basilica, next to the baptistry) two ducks paddling about. All that said, Ágios Stéfanos is still the best preserved such complex on the island, and a wonderfully atmospheric spot.

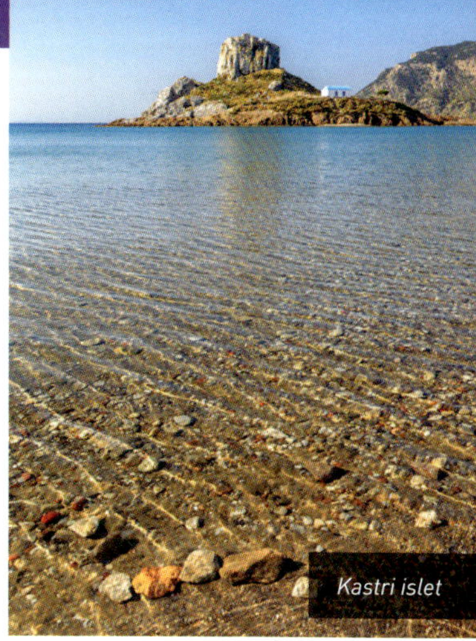
Kastri islet

The basilicas overlook tiny, striking **Kastrí** islet, sporting a chapel and a distinct volcanic pinnacle. From the sandy cove west of the peninsula it's just a short swim away; in spots, you can even wade. The shallow sea here warms up early in the year and stays that way into November, offering the best snorkelling on an island not otherwise known for it, owing to rock formations cutting across the generally sandy seabed. As at Paradise beach, gas bubbles up from the ocean floor.

The main road southwest from here runs behind a serviceable but not spectacular beach, of equal interest to windsurfers and bathers. Resort development here is modest, formerly pitched at budget-conscious Brits a generation or so older than at Kardámena, but clientele is now more mixed, including many Russians. The strip of scattered one- or two-star hotels, low-rise apartments, tavernas and bars ends at **Kamári** ㉒, the

far end of the bay and the fishing-port annexe of Kéfalos village overhead. Boat trips may be offered out of Kamári, but probably no further than Bubble Beach and certainly not to Nísyros.

KÉFALOS – THE WILD WEST

The extreme southwestern tip of Kos, a sparsely inhabited monster-head-shaped landmass, is a semi-mythical paradise for island foodies – literally a land of milk and honey, source of the best island cheese, honey and bread. There is just one inland village, **Kéfalos** ㉓, 43km (26.5miles) from the capital and the terminus for buses. Squatting on a flat-topped hill, looking northeast along the length of Kos, Kéfalos has little to recommend it other than a single ATM and a few basic snack bars. Even the **Knights' castle** here, downhill beside the Kamári road, is rudimentary – hardly more than a signalling tower – and unimpressive; the Knights abandoned it in 1504. But the village makes a natural staging point for expeditions south into the rugged peninsula that terminates at sheer Cape Kríkello.

THE KÉFALOS PENINSULA

The first point of interest is Byzantine **Panagía Palatianí**, 1km (0.6 miles) south of Kéfalos; a signposted dirt track (passable to ordinary cars) east from the roadside leads to a parking area by a modern church. Just below stands the fenced-off 9th- or 10th-century chapel, built entirely from masonry of an ancient temple.

Some 500m/yards beyond, there's contrastingly no signage for ancient **Astypalaia** ㉔, the original capital of Kos until abandoned in 366 BC. Your clue is the large, roadside parking area with a dry fountain, opposite an unlocked gate. It's a two-minute path-walk down to a late Classical **amphitheatre** with two rows of seats still in place, enjoying a fine prospect over

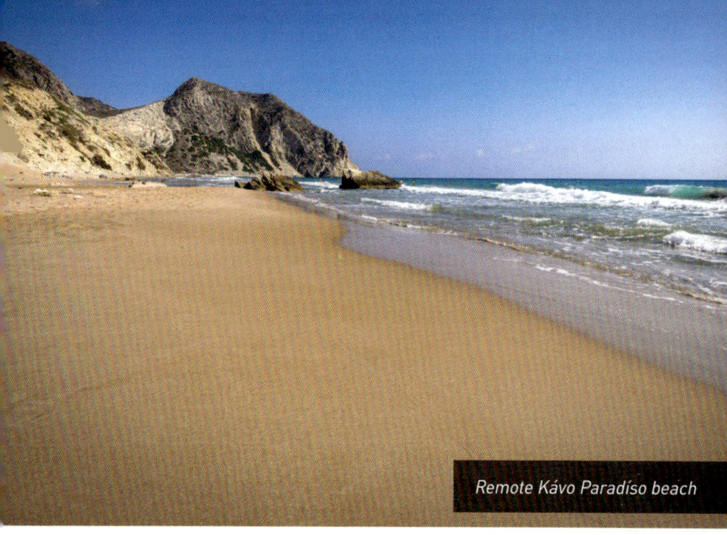
Remote Kávo Paradíso beach

the curve of Kéfalos Bay – a lovely, pine-shaded spot despite the scanty remains of this once-important city.

Immediately past Astypalaia, a paved side-road leaves the ridge road and heads west towards **Ágios Theológos** ㉕ beach, 6km (3.7 miles) from Kéfalos. Besides the saint's chapel, there's an eponymous taverna which takes full advantage of its local monopoly – just stop in for dessert and a drink perhaps. Forays along the dirt tracks to either side – a jeep or dirt-bike is advisable – will reveal secluded sandy coves below low cliffs.

Appealing **Ágios Ioánnis Thymianós monastery** ㉖ (6.5km/4 miles from Kéfalos), reached by following the paved road to its end, is almost the end of the line for non-4WD vehicles (jeeps can reach Ágios Mámas, 4.5km/2.8 miles beyond, almost at the cape). Set on a natural balcony under assorted trees, with extensive pebble mosaics, the church is locked except during the festival on 28–29 August; it's a fine picnic spot at other times.

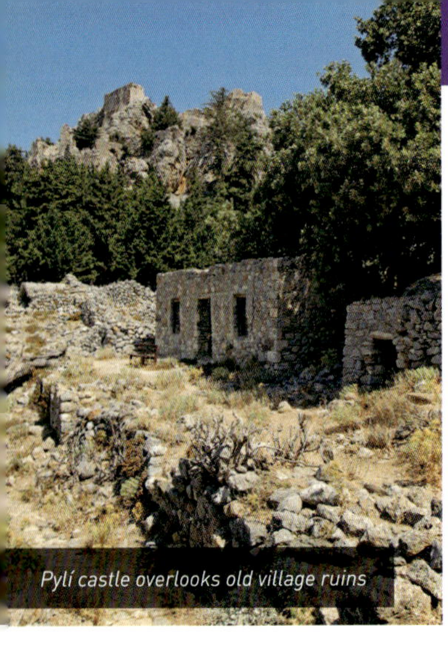
Pylí castle overlooks old village ruins

The dirt track heading straight south beyond the monastery goes 1.8km (1.1 miles) to a crossroads; turn hard right here and head another 2km (1.2 miles) down to the island's remotest beach, **Kávo Paradíso** 27 (officially **Halandríou**). Jeep drivers will feel more confident – after a harsh winter one could ground a saloon car in the deep ruts along the last kilometre, though with extra care plenty of small cars make it through. Kávo Paradíso, a vast expanse of sand and clean (if often surfy) sea with a dramatic mountain for a backdrop, is worth the effort; clothing is optional and most years a drinks bar with sunbeds operates June–Sept (bring your own food).

The only other notable beaches around Kéfalos are up on its north shore. **Limniónas** 28 (sometimes Limiónas) is 4km (2.4 miles) due north of the village by good road; there are actually two protected sandy coves here (one with sunbeds), separated by an isthmus leading to the little fishing anchorage. **Kohylári**, further east along the same coast, is too exposed to interest folk other than kitesurfers; see page 85 for details.

AROUND MT DÍKEOS

The main interest of inland Kós resides in the hamlets on the north slope of **Mount Díkeos** (the ancient Oromedon). This cluster of settlements, collectively called **Asfendioú**, nestles amid the island's only natural forest and provides a glimpse of what Kos looked like before tourism and concrete took hold. They can be reached from the island trunk road via the extremely curvy side road from Zipári, 7.5km (4.6 miles) from Kos Town; a minimally signposted but paved, straighter minor road to Lagoúdi starting about 1km (0.6 miles) further west; or the shorter access road to Pylí from Linopótis pond.

PYLÍ: NEW AND OLD

Just over 13km (8 miles) from Kos Town along the main highway, **Linopótis** is a sunken, spring-fed pond, alive with ducks and eels. From the junction here, a good road leads southeast to contemporary **Pylí** ㉙, which divides into two districts. In the upper neighbourhood, 150m/yards west of the main square and church, Pigí district comprises a lush oasis with a recommended taverna (see page 109) and a giant, sixteenth-century cistern-fountain, the *pigí* of the name, with four lion-head spouts – the water is excellent and constantly collected by locals.

Pylí's other monument is the so-called **Harmýlio** (Tomb of Harmylos), signposted near the top of the village en route to Kardámena as 'Heroön of Charmylos', a mythical ancient king of Kos. This consists of a subterranean vault (fenced off) with twelve niches, probably a Hellenistic family tomb. Immediately above it, ample masonry of an ancient temple, perhaps dedicated to demigod Harmylos, has been incorporated into the medieval **chapel of Stavrós**.

Paleó Pylí

Paleó (Old) **Pylí** ㉚, just under 3km (2 miles) southeast of its modern descendant, was the Byzantine capital of Kos, inhabited from about the tenth century until the Ottoman conquest. Head there

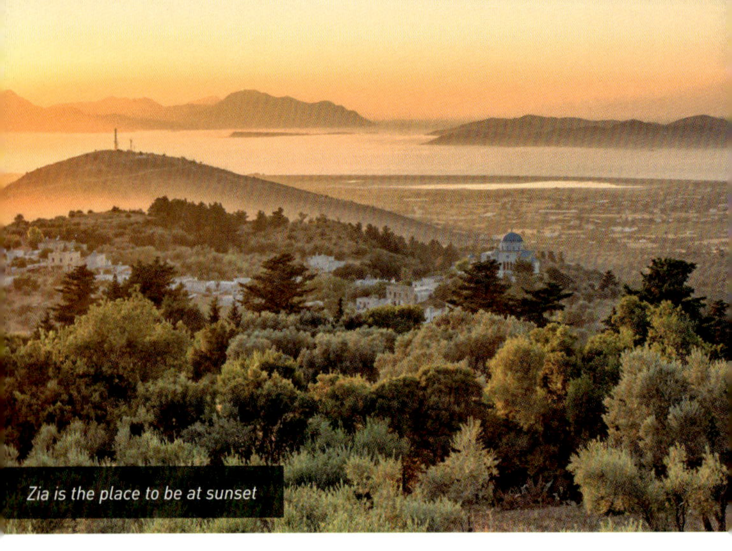
Zia is the place to be at sunset

via Amanioú, keeping straight at the junction where signs point left to Ziá and Lagoúdi. The road continues up to a wooded canyon, dwindling to a dirt track beside a trough-spring for local livestock. Some five minutes' walk uphill from the spring along the track are the remains of a **water mill** in the ravine just west.

From opposite the trough, a stair-path leads within fifteen minutes to an 11th-century **Byzantine castle**, whose partly intact roof affords superb views. En route you pass the ruins of the abandoned village, as well as three fourteenth- or fifteenth-century **churches**. That of **Arhángelos**, the first encountered, retains substantial fourteenth-century frescoes, particularly numerous scenes from the life of Christ on the vaulted ceiling, including a fine *Betrayal* in the north vault. Unfortunately it is usually locked following 2012 restoration, but should it be open, make it a priority to pop inside. Outside are the remains of a graceful Latin arcade of a type usually only seen on Rhodes or Cyprus. Rectangular **Ágios Nikólaos** (unlocked), just south of the route to the citadel, has a *Communion of the Apostles* in the apse, while **Ypapandí**, the largest church and nearest the castle, is almost bare inside but impresses with its barrel vaulting supported by re-used ancient columns.

LAGOÚDI

From Paleó Pylí, return to the junction in Amanioú and turn right (east) through **Konidário**, an abandoned Muslim village that's now a forest reserve and picnic grounds. After 3km (2 miles) you reach picturesque **Lagoúdi** ㉛, with the prominent **Génnisis Theotókou church** at the village summit. Its interior shelters vivid 1980s frescoes by reclusive iconographer Nikos Vlahogiannis. If he's still living adjacent, friendly Father Kyriakos will greet you.

EVANGELÍSTRIA AND ZÍA

The first Asfendioú village encountered, either heading east from Lagoúdi or going up the curvy side-road from Zipári, is **Evangelístria** ㉜. Beyond the eponymous parish church extends a neighbourhood of low, whitewashed houses, now mostly abandoned following the stampede down to the coast; the remainder have been bought up and restored by outsiders.

Further up the twisty road from Evangelístria, **Ziá**'s ㉝ spectacular views and sunsets make it the hapless target of numerous tour buses each evening. Just six people still dwell full-time in the

Mt Díkeos the Just

'Díkeos' means just or righteous in Greek, and local legend asserts that the mountain assumed this demotic name (versus the ancient Oromedon) because it is 'just' in directing its abundant waters to flow usefully north to the island's villages and fields, rather than pointlessly south into the sea.

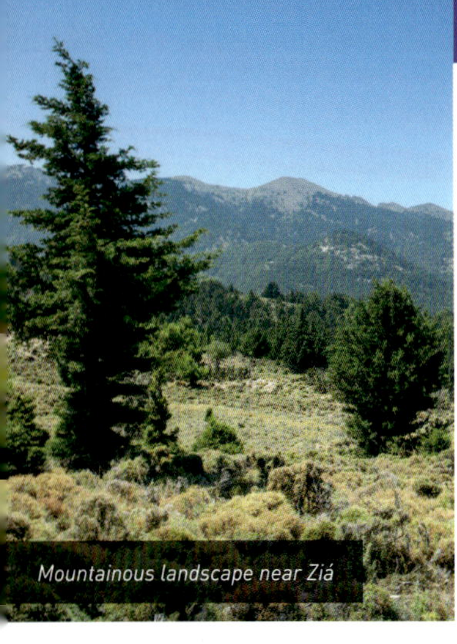
Mountainous landscape near Ziá

village, but otherwise any building on the main street that isn't a taverna is a souvenir shop. The only sight is the preserved water-mill on the grounds of the recommended Neromylos Café (see page 109).

ASCENT OF HRISTÓS PEAK

Ziá is the classic trailhead for the ascent of 840-metre (2756ft-) high **Hristós peak** ㉞, by a paltry three metres (10 ft) the second highest point of the Díkeos range. Taking rather less than half a day, this is within the capabilities of any reasonably fit, properly shod person, and offers arguably the best views in the Dodecanese. Except on the date (6 August) of the annual pilgrimage climb, you will see few or no other hikers.

At Ziá's upper Platía Karydiás, with its fig tree in a round masoned enclosure and Neromylos Café, find the step-path indicated as 'Dikaios Mountain Kefalovrisi'. Some five minutes up this, you'll pass the seldom-open Kefalovrisi Taverna, and then onto a dirt track for a few minutes more to **Isódia tís Theotókou** chapel with its vaulted roof, covered porch and bomb nose-cone hung as the bell. Bear right at the junction behind it – blue arrows guide you, and the surface underfoot is briefly cemented – and head west past Ziá's last house.

Some fifteen minutes from Platía Karydiás, you pass **Ágios Geórgios** chapel, locked to protect its frescoes (some visible through the door window). The rough onward track, just passable to vehicles, curls gradually south past one large and one small rural cottage; beyond Ágios Geórgios, a section of path marked by cairns shortcuts a wide bend in the track (though it takes time to get through a wire-fastened gate across the path).

Thirty-five minutes above Platía Karydiás, you'll reach the true trailhead amidst a juniper grove. The spot is fairly obvious; boulders flanking the path have blue paint dots and the word 'Dikeos'. There's also a triangular metal sign in Greek Byzantine script ('Xpictóc'), and just uphill stone cairns and more paint marks.

The distinct trail zigzags eastwards up the mountainside, leaving the junipers within twenty minutes and arriving just over an hour out of Ziá at the ridge leading northeast to the summit. The grade slackens, and several shattered cisterns, once used by shepherds, are seen north of the path.

From the moment the ridge is attained, it's another twenty minutes maximum to the peak along the watershed, usually just to its north. The little pillbox-like chapel of **Metamórfosi tou Sotírou**, visible most of the time, stands about 40m/yards northeast of the altitude survey marker; there's also a small bad-weather shelter nearby, possibly a roofed-over cistern. Just north of this, you can ponder the esoteric symbolism of a giant crucifix fashioned from PVC sewer pipes and filled with concrete.

Turkey's Knidos Peninsula dominates the **view** to the southeast; Nísyros, Tílos and Hálki float to the south; Astypálea closes off the horizon on the west; Kálymnos and, on a good day, Léros, are spread out to the north; and the entire west and north portions of Kós are laid out before you.

The south flank of Mt Díkeos takes a steep dive towards the Aegean; those intent on visiting remote Theológos chapel down this slope should engage a qualified local guide. The ridge continuing northeast to the true summit (843m/2740ft) can only be

tackled by technical climbers – there are too many knife-edge saddles and arêtes. So the sole feasible descent involves retracing your steps, which takes just ten minutes less than the climb, owing to the rough surface. Allow two hours thirty minutes minimum walking time for the out-and-back trip from Ziá – three-plus hours inclusive of photo and rest stops.

ASÓMATOS AND HAÏHOÚTES

The paved road east of Ziá threads through the densest forest on Mt Díkeos – mixed juniper and pine – and also passes two of the more interesting Asfendioú hamlets. **Asómatos**, with views rivalling Ziá's (but no amenities), is still home to perhaps thirty villagers plus a handful of foreigners and Athenians renovating houses. The place really only comes to life at the November 7–8 festival of the gaily painted central **Arhángelos church**, whose spacious courtyard (usually locked) features a fine pebble mosaic.

Haïhoútes ㉟, officially Ágios Dimítrios but increasingly referred to by its Ottoman name, lies 2km (1.2 miles) further. It was abandoned entirely during 1967–74, when the villagers departed for Zipári or further afield. Today, there are signs of revival, with eight residents, old-house renovations and a pleasant café (light meals served) operating just uphill from the reliable, potable fountain. In the narthex of the attractive central **church**, a small photo display documents a considerable population during the 1940s, when the village was a centre of resistance against the occupation.

The road continues another 6km (3.7 miles) to the Asklepion, completing your circuit of the island.

EXCURSIONS

Kos offers opportunities to visit several Dodecanesian neighbours on separate day-trips, or overnight stays. Scheduled catamarans make it possible to design your own itineraries without signing on to organised excursions available from boats moored at Mandráki port.

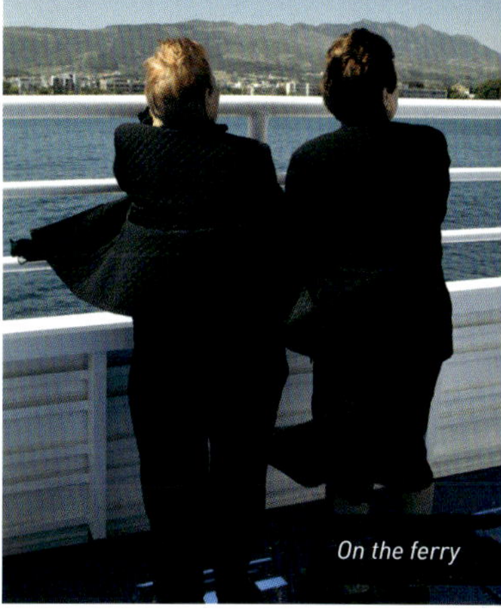
On the ferry

Closest is volcanic Nísyros on the south, with its caldera and photogenic villages. Northwest lies craggy Kálymnos, once a sponge-divers' island, and its sleepy satellite islets Psérimos and Télendos, ideal day-trip destinations from Kálymnos. Beyond Kálymnos, Léros merits a visit for a fine castle and 1930s Streamline Modern architecture. Last and remotest, the holy island of Pátmos beckons with its fortified summit monastery and the enchanting surrounding village. You can also pop over to Bodrum in Turkey, whose lights are clearly visible by night northeast of Kos.

NÍSYROS

In legend Poseidon, battling the titan Polybotes, tore a rock from Kos and crushed his adversary beneath it. The rock became **Nísyros** ㊱. Hardly less prosaic are the facts of a prehistoric eruption, when this volcano-island apparently blew its top Krakatoa-style. Notably fertile despite lacking water, Nísyros has proven attractive and wealthy enough to keep over 1,000 permanent inhabitants (down, though, from 5,000 in 1912, and 2,600 in 1947). While remittances from overseas (particularly New York) are vital, most income is derived from offshore **Gyalí** islet, a vast lump of

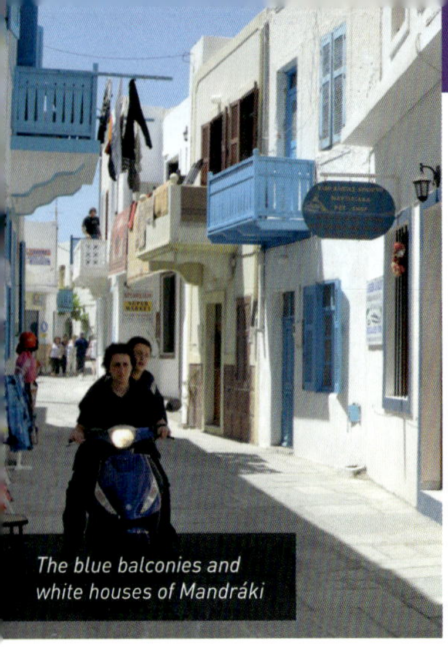

The blue balconies and white houses of Mandráki

pumice and perlite slowly being quarried by a score of miners. Rent collected by the municipality from the mining concession funds a public bakery, pharmacy and well-padded civil service. Accordingly, islanders bother little with agriculture besides keeping cows; hillside terraces meticulously fashioned for grain and grapes lie abandoned, and winemaking has ceased.

Day-trips from either Kardámena or Kos Town typically arrive at 10.30–11am, with passengers whisked immediately by coach up to the volcanic caldera in the interior before transfer back downhill for lunch and departure at 3.45–4pm. But visiting just for the day is a pity, as Nísyros fully deserves an overnight or two. Hire a scooter or car from Manos K (tel: 22420 31029) on the port, or trust public buses and your own feet. The most reliable boat from Kos Town is the Panagia Spiliani (http://gonisyros.gr/en/), which even takes a few cars.

Away from its harbour, **Mandráki** 37 proves an attractive, deceptively large capital, with blue patches of sea visible (and audible) at the end of narrow, cat-thronged streets. Brightly painted wooden balconies and shutters hang cheerfully from tall, white houses ranged around a central communal orchard. The well-labelled **archaeological museum** (Wed–Mon 8am–3pm; charge) does a gallop, over two floors, through local history, from Archaic grave goods to Roman stelae and Byzantine painted bowls. Overhead, a **Knights' castle** (best appreciated from Hohláki beach behind) shelters the earlier **Panagía Spilianí monastery** with its grotto-like church, built in accordance with instructions from the *Panagía* ('Mother of God') herself, who appeared in a vision to an islander. On the way up, the local **folklore museum** (unreliable hours May–Sept; charge), with traditional paraphernalia and archival photos, is worth a glance if open. During 1996–97, the Langadáki district just below was rocked by multiple earthquakes, damaging numerous houses (mostly repaired).

As a defensive bastion, the seventh-century-BC Doric **Paleókastro** (unrestricted access), a short walk out of Langadáki, is far more impressive than the Knights' castle, and one of the finest ancient forts in Greece. You can clamber up onto massive, polygonal-block walls, standing to their original height, using a broad staircase inside the still-intact gateway.

The volcanic zone

As you approach the **Lakkí volcanic zone** ❸❽ (12.5km/8miles from Mandráki), a rotten-egg stench greets you as vegetation gradually yields to lifeless, caked powder. The sunken main crater, **Stéfanos**, is an extraordinary moonscape of grey, brown and jaundice-yellow 260 metres (845ft) across; another, less visited double crater (dubbed **Polyvótis**), even more dramatic, awaits to the west, created between 1873 and 1888. Steam-puffing fumaroles in the craters accumulate little pincushions of sulphur crystals.

Standing on the floor of Stéfanos (stick to trodden areas, the crust is thin elsewhere) you hear mud boiling away below you – the groaning of trapped Polybotes, for some 45,000 years according to geologists. The most recent eruptions, which produced steam, ash and earthquakes, occurred in 1422, 1873, 1888 and 1933 – the volcano is merely dormant. The Greek power corporation made exploratory geothermal soundings

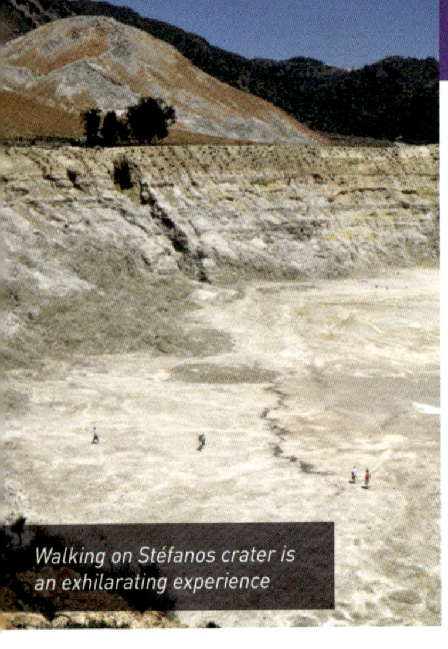
Walking on Stéfanos crater is an exhilarating experience

nearby until 1993, when it departed, stymied by islander hostility – though not before destroying the 1,000-year-old cobbled road down to Mandráki.

Four eucalypts shade a drinks kantína in the centre of the wasteland; a ticket booth flanking the access road charges admission to the area in season. The easiest path up to Polyvótis begins along the fence 20m/yards beyond the kantína.

Villages and walks

Two photogenic villages perch above Lakkí. Nearly abandoned **Emboriós** (pop. 27), with a tiny summit castle, is slowly being bought up and restored by outsiders, who often discover natural saunas in the basements of their crumbling houses; at the village outskirts there's a signposted public **sauna** the grotto entrance outlined in white paint. (Most Emboriots relocated to the fishing/yacht port of Pálli after World War II.)

Nikiá ❸❾, 13km (8 miles) from Mandráki's port, is busier, with 61 registered inhabitants and signs of some renovation activity. Its quirky round *platía* has one café and there's also a moderately worthwhile **Volcanological Museum** occupying the disused school (Mon–Thu 11.30am–6.30pm, Fri–Sat 10.30am–2.30pm; charge). For most visitors though, the unlocked chapel of **Agía Triáda**, with its 15th-century frescoes, will prove more tempting. To get there starting from the round platía, take the stair path down past the cemetery; 60m past its gate, look right to see a low-slung, unlocked building. Frescoes are damaged, but the following scenes are discernible: on the right wall, the Nativity and Presentation of Jesus; between the latter and the door, the Redemption of Eve; on the far side of the door, Adam Redeemed; on the ceiling by the apse, the Ascension with Christ in a mandorla; on the left wall, the Assumption, Transfiguration, Pentecost and Baptism.

Nísyros offers good **walks** through countryside green with oak or terebinth, on a network of fitfully marked and maintained trails; these are traced correctly on the recommended map. Autumn is a wonderful time, especially for the succulent local figs (the Turks called the island *İncirli*, 'Fig Place').

You can sample the best routes in a single day, by starting with a mid-morning bus ride to Nikiá. From beside the museum, follow a sign downhill, then right, towards eyrie-like **Ágios Ioánnis Theológos monastery**, then continue north 90min towards Emboriós (there's 1.3km/0.8 miles of unavoidable road-slogging). After lunch there, head west, starting near the little castle, for 45min to **Evangelístria monastery**, a major hikers' junction. Allow time for a detour (2hr return) up the well-marked path to island summit **Profítis Ilías** (698m/2268ft), with a chapel and views to rival those from Hristós on Kos. From Evangelístria, complete a long but satisfying itinerary by descending 40min to Mandráki.

Beaches and baths

Hohláki, reached by masoned pathway, lies 10min beyond Mandráki – a prime sunset-watching venue, but the sea can be choppy and the coarse pebbles aren't very comfortable. The sandy, gently shelving beach extending east from **Pálli** port is more user-friendly, with a few tamarisks for shade and a sheltering breakwater. Halfway between Mandráki and Pálli, the **Dimotiká Loutrá**

(Public Baths) were refurbished in 2015 with quality marble tubs (7–9.30am & 5–7.30pm; 20-min soak for a charge). Upstairs is a basic inn, and at the corner of the building a recommended mezedopolío. The only other **thermal pool** on Nísyros is in front of Mandráki's Haritos Hotel (charge for non-guests).

Nísyros's longest, best, cleanest and least windy beaches lie on the east coast, 9km/5.5miles from Mandráki. Sandy **Liés** marks the end of the road, with a summer (late June–early Sept) snack bar and parking area. From there a 15-minute trail past **Mouléri** beach and volcanic-ash cliffs leads to **Pahiá Ámmos** ⓸⓪ (Fat Sand), exactly that – 300m/yards of grey-pink stuff heaped into dunes behind, limited shade at the far end, and a constituency of naturists and free campers.

KÁLYMNOS

First impressions of **Kálymnos** ㊶, northwest of Kós, are of an arid, mountainous landmass with a decidedly masculine energy in the main port town of Póthia. The former dominant industry, sponge-diving, has now been supplanted by tourism and commercial fishing. But the island's prior mainstay is evident in home decor of huge sponges or shell-encrusted amphorae, and souvenir shops overflowing with smaller sponges.

Kálymnos essentially consists of two cultivated, inhabited valleys sandwiched between three limestone ridges, harsh in the full glare of noon but magically tinted towards dusk. The climate, especially in winter, is alleged to be drier and healthier than on its neighbours, since the quick-draining limestone strata, riddled with many caves, doesn't retain much moisture. Kálymnos's position and excellent harbours ensure that it has always been important – especially during Byzantine rule, which left many ruined basilicas here. Another Byzantine legacy is the survival of peculiar medieval names

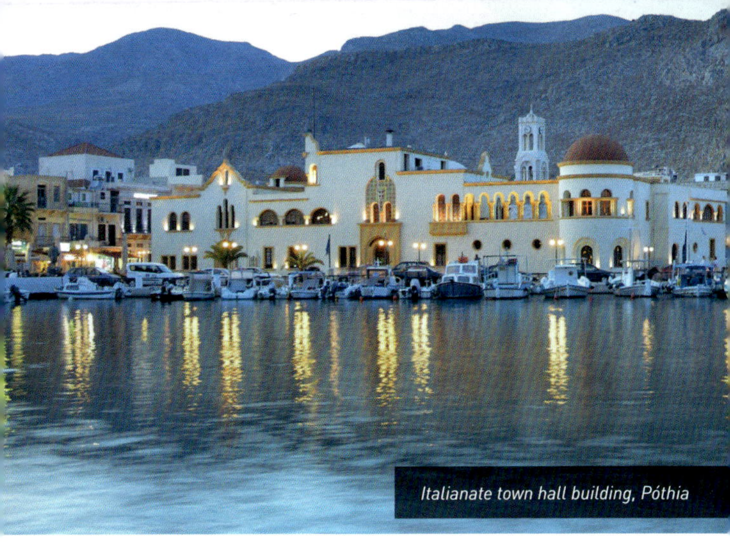
Italianate town hall building, Póthia

(Skévos, Sakellários and Mikés for men, Themélina, Petránda and Sevastí for women), found nowhere else in Greece.

Póthia and around

Póthia 42 itself (population 12,324), the third-largest town in the Dodecanese, is noisy and workaday Greek, its brightly painted houses rising in tiers up the flanking hillsides. Mansions and vernacular dwellings with ornate balconies and wrought-iron ornamentation (an island speciality) are particularly evident in Evangelístria district. Florestano di Fausto's 1926–28 administration building and Rodolfo Petracco's 1934 town hall and market complex, just seaward of Hristós church, deserve a look.

The most dazzling conventional attraction is the **Archaeological Museum** (early Apr–31 Oct Wed–Mon 8.30am–4pm; winter closed; charge). Stars of the displays include a huge Hellenistic cult statue of Asklepios; an unusual robed,

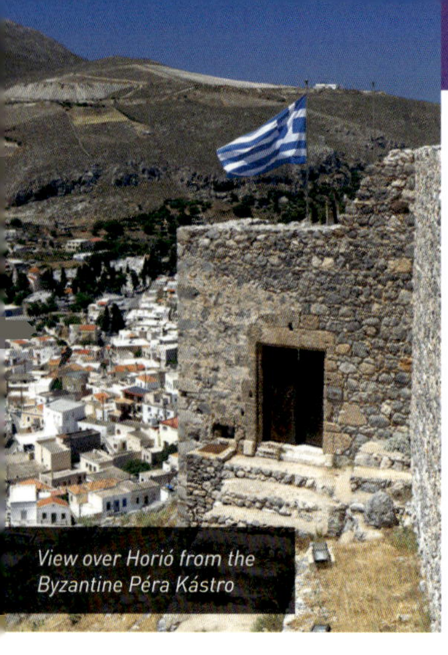
View over Horió from the Byzantine Péra Kástro

child-sized *kouros* (most were naked); and a life-size third- or second-century BC bronze of a clad woman with her right hand raised in admonition, retrieved by fishermen in 1994 and inevitably dubbed **'The Lady of Kálymnos'**.

The **Nautical and Folklore Museum** (no set hours owing to staffing issues; tel: 6977 092538 or 6946 629374 for admission), on the seaward side of Hristós cathedral, contains fascinating photos of old Póthia (no quay, jetty, roads, or sumptuous mansions in the 1880s) and equipment from seafarers' lives, including ingenious, dart-shaped nautical-mile logs, dragged off the stern; dangerously primitive divers' breathing apparati; and wicker 'cages' to keep propellers from cutting air lines, a constant hazard. Failing this, visit the **Kalymnian House** on the road to Vothýni (daily 9am–8pm; tel: 22430 51635 to be sure), where a guided tour (charge) elucidates wedding customs on this matrilineal island, the family sleeping platform (including cradle) and women's task of gathering firewood.

Northwest of Póthia loom two **castles** (daily all day; free): **Hrysoheriás**, the Knights Hospitaller stronghold adapted from a Byzantine fort, where the views appeal more than anything inside, and the purely Byzantine castle of **Péra Kástro** above Horió, Kálymnos' second town. Although this pirate-proof citadel was inhabited until the late 1700s, there are few intact structures inside besides several unlocked churches offering fragmentary 15th- or 16th-century frescoes.

West from Horió, some 200m/yards past the airport road, stand the two most intact, and easiest found, of Kálymnos' Byzantine basilicas. Whitewashed steps lead over a stone wall to **Hristós tis Ierousalím (Limniótissa) basilica**, in legend built by Byzantine Emperor Arkadios (395–408 AD) in gratitude for deliverance from a storm, though sixth-century construction is far more likely. The ornate apse with bishops' throne is fully preserved, as are sections of marble flooring; both incorporate inscribed masonry taken from a local Hellenistic Apollo temple. One field east, reached by a separate path from the road, is larger, three-aisled but less impressive **Agía Sofía basilica**; again the apse is most intact, used as a chapel after the rest of the church was destroyed during 7th-century Arab raids.

Vathýs and Beyond

The main sight northeast of Póthia is **Vathýs** ㊸, the island's main oasis, 11km/miles away by road. The first stretch is grimly industrial, passing a boatyard, a power plant, tank farms, quarries and a rubbish tip. None of this prepares you for a sudden road-bend and dramatic view to Vathýs far below, its green contrasting sharply with the mineral grey and orange uphill. This long, fertile valley, carpeted with walled orange and tangerine groves threaded by a maze of lanes, seems a continuation of cobalt-blue Rína fjord penetrating the landscape here. **Rína** is popular with yachties and thus has a clutch of overpriced tavernas at the head of the port, but no beach.

Without a vehicle, the best (and a popular) way to reach Vathýs is by **hiking** along the old **cobbled trail** from beside Agía Triáda church in Póthia's Evangelístria district, arrowed conspicuously on a wall as 'Italian path'. It takes an hour to reach the

Snail or princess?

Legend asserts that the mountainous bulk of Télendos, viewed at dusk fromMyrtiés, is the petrified reclining head of a princess, gazing out to sea following her unhappy affair with the mythical prince of nearby ancient Kastélli. The less romantically inclined will only see the silhouette of a snail.

pass (400m/1,312 ft elevation) in the ridge overhead, and another forty minutes downhill to Plátanos hamlet in the oasis.

Once at Plátanos, collect water from the potable spring under the namesake plane tree and ponder a continuation. You can loop back to **Horió** on a major trail around Profítis Ilías (676m/yards), descending a scenic gorge, or carry on from Metóhi hamlet with its frescoed Taxiárhis chapel to the start of the two-hour path to Arginónda (with some brief road-walking in the middle). Have lunch and a swim in coastal **Arginónda**, then catch a bus back to town – you may have to road-walk 5km (3 miles) to Armeós to get one. All these routes are detailed accurately on the recommended topographic map.

BROSTÁ: THE WEST COAST

The consecutive **beach resorts** on the west coast are referred to collectively by islanders as 'Brostá' (Forward), the leading side of Kálymnos, as opposed to 'Píso' (Behind), the Póthia area.

Kandoúni ㊹ attracts mostly Greek and local clientele, the latter owning summer villas here; the beach – 200m/yards of brown, hard-packed sand – isn't brilliant. Especially towards sunset, take the obvious coastal path southwest to the little monastery of **Ágios Fótis** (80min return hike), offering seascapes, cliffs and a ravine.

Smaller **Linária** cove, just north of Kandoúni bay, has better sand, tavernas and cafés, plus separate road access. Walk around the corner (or again distinct vehicle access) to **Platýs Gialós** beach, opposite Agía Kyriakí islet, with Kálymnos's best sand; a pity the sea is often turbid.

The main road, descending in zigzags, meets the sea again 8km (5 miles) from Póthia at **Melitsáhas** and **Myrtiés** ㊺, which share Kálymnos' much-diminished beach-tourism trade with **Masoúri** and **Armeós**, just north but reached by an upper bypass road, part of a circular one-way system. Melitsáhas and Myrtiés have the best beaches and cleanest sea, but these contiguous resorts have partly reinvented themselves to host spring and autumn rock-climbers.

Beyond Armeós, the road mostly hugs the coast en route to **Emboriós** ㊻, end of the line 20km (12 miles) from Póthia. This has average tavernas, a mixed bag of beaches to either side (some only path-accessible) and late-afternoon taxi-boat service back to Myrtiés. Buses beyond Armeós are rare, but Kálymnos is ideally explorable by scooter; a recommended rental outlet in Póthia is Spyros Kypraios near Ágios Nikólaos church (tel: 22430 24300, http://kipreosrentals.gr).

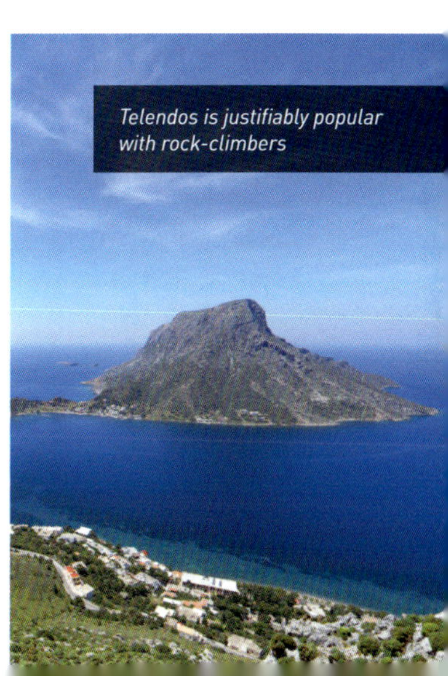
Telendos is justifiably popular with rock-climbers

TÉLENDOS

These resorts' most appealing feature is the striking islet of **Télendos** ㊼ opposite, which frames some of the Aegean's more dramatic sunsets. Home to 45 winter inhabitants,

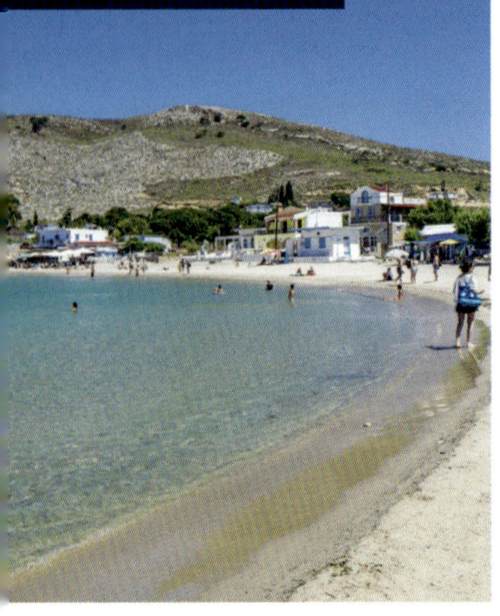
Avlákia Beach on Psérimos

Télendos is car-free and tranquil, though tourism (including rock-climbing) has certainly arrived, via little taxi-boats crossing the straits from Myrtiés jetty (daily half-hourly 8am–11pm). Télendos was sundered from Kálymnos by the cataclysmic 554 AD earthquake; remains of a submerged town lurk at the bottom of the channel, sixteen fathoms down.

The sole waterside hamlet huddles under **Mount Ráhi** (459 metres/1,506ft). Halfway up the north side of the mountain, an hour's trek away by paint-marked path, perches the fortified chapel of **Ágios Konstandínos**, with excellent views. Less energetic souls explore the ruined Byzantine basilicas of **Ágios Vassílios** and **Agía Tríada** at the northern and western edges of the hamlet.

Beaches vary considerably; a long, sandy, tamarisk-shaded one stretches north of 'town', while scenic **Hohlakás**, 10 minutes west, has coin-sized pebbles (and sunbeds) on two separate bays, as do three smaller coves beyond the sand beach, with usually clean water: **Pláka**, **Pótha** and **Paradise** (naturist, 20min away).

PSÉRIMOS

Kálymnos' other satellite islet, **Psérimos** 48 (permanent population 35), is an idyllic place once the daily crop of trippers leaves sandy Avlákia bay, with only cicadas in the huge communal olive grove to break the stillness. Excursion boats from Kos operate 'three-island' tours (€25–30) which spend just one hour at Psérimos before pushing on to nearby **Pláti** islet (one chapel, one villa) for more swimming before a rushed lunch on Kálymnos. We don't recommend these tours, and the only way to spend a whole day on Psérimos – well worth it – is to depart from Kálymnos daily at 9.30am on the little ro-ro ferry Maniaï, returning at 5pm (€10; 55min journey each way). The islanders themselves use this boat for shopping and administrative business; there is only a primary school on Psérimos. During mid-summer, one speedboat per day also calls from Mastihári on Kos.

West-facing **Avlákia**, the port and only village (including several tavernas), is fronted by a magnificent sandy beach where most trippers park themselves. For those with six hours to spend on Psérimos, there are two other, remoter beaches: clean **Vathý** (sand and gravel), a well-marked, thirty-minute path-walk east of Avlákia, or idyllic all-sand **Grafiótissa** beach to the northwest.

The path there starts from the northwestern-most house in Avlákia; go anticlockwise around its perimeter fence to see a light-green paint arrow pointing right towards an obvious trail, which passes between a prominent tree and a concrete survey marker, over a low ridge. The way becomes increasingly obvious, with more green- or white-painted arrows, dashes and blobs to dispel doubt. Allow just over half an hour to reach the ruined old church of **Panagía Grafiótissa** (festival 8 Sept), split in two by the sea, with just the apsidal half clinging to the low cliff. Nobody alive today on Psérimos can remember a time when it was intact. The modern replacement church just inland has a rain cistern with a bucket for water emergencies. The beach below – a vast expanse of blonde sand lapped by sea of a near-Caribbean hue – is the whole point. There's some reef offshore, but nothing that impedes entry; Pláti baffles the prevailing wind and occasional swell.

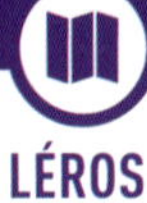

LÉROS

Well-vegetated **Léros** ❹❾, with its half-dozen deeply indented bays, looks like a jigsaw puzzle piece gone astray. **Lakkí** ❺⓿, the biggest, deepest inlet and large-ferry port, is graced by one of the world's largest Rationalist-Streamline Modern planned towns, designed as 'Porto Lago' by Rodolfo Petracco and Armando Bernabiti and erected during 1934–38 for the officers (and their families) of the huge nearby Italian naval base. The striking, photogenic, renovated buildings here include the round-fronted cinema (still used), the market hall with its clock-tower and circular atrium, the arcaded primary school, and the angular church of Ágios Nikólaos.

Lakkí's present population of 2,058 (a quarter of Léros' inhabitants) rattles around the underused streets; nautical flavour is imparted by yacht marinas and dry-docks, here and at adjacent Teménia. The atmosphere was long weighted by three hospitals for disabled children and mentally unwell adults, though these

ITALIAN ARCHITECTURE IN THE DODECANESE

Italian rule has left a significant architectural heritage here. During 1924–36, Italy attempted to form a generic Mediterranean architecture.

Kos and Kálymnos received a Foro Italico (administrative complex) in neo-Crusader style. Fascist theory also required a square for rallies (on Kos, Platía Eleftherías). 1936–41 was marked by intensified ideology and reference to the islands' Latin heritage. This entailed 'purification', removing orientalist ornamentation and replacing it with stone cladding. Additionally, severity and rigid symmetry – as in the Orthodox cathedral on Kos – was stipulated.

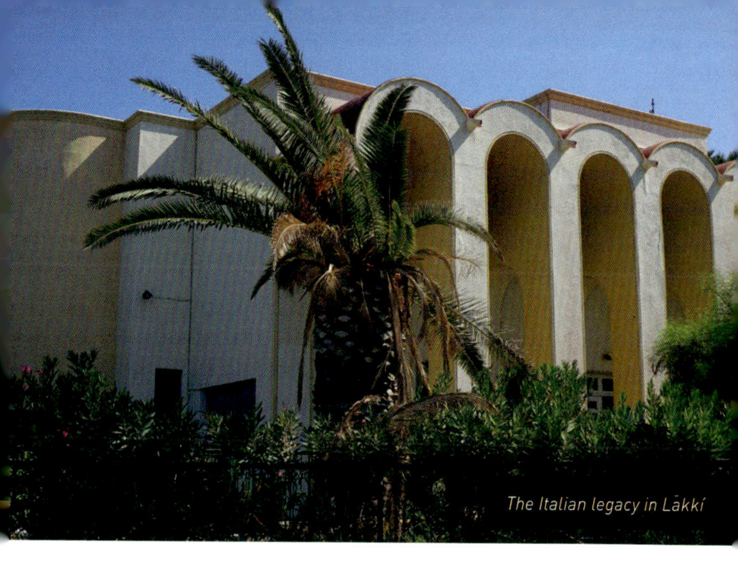
The Italian legacy in Lākkí

institutions have mostly closed and the facilities partly occupied by the University of the Aegean's nursing faculty.

The rest of Léros (easily toured by scooter) is more conventionally inviting, particularly the fishing/yacht port of **Pandéli**, with its fine-pebble beach and waterfront tavernas, just downhill from the capital of **Plátanos**, its pastel-hued vernacular houses draped over a saddle. Overhead looms a well-preserved **Byzantine-Knights' castle** (daily 8am–1pm and 4–8pm; charge) sheltering an excellent ecclesiastical museum (the English-speaking warden gives an engaging tour). The summit views, especially southeast at dusk, are superb. South of Pandéli, **Vromólithos** ❺❶, especially at southerly **Tourkopígado**, has the best easily accessible and car-free beach on an island lacking good, sandy ones. Elsewhere, sharp rock reefs must often be crossed entering the water. Southeast of Vromólithos, two sandy coves at **Ágios Geórgios** are less crowded.

Picturesque **Agia Marína** ⓬, beyond Plátanos, is the usual excursion boat and catamaran harbour (though adverse weather may force catamarans to dock at Lakkí). It has several tavernas and cafés, plus more whimsical Italian monuments like the market hall and customs house.

ÁLINDA AND AROUND

Álinda ⓭, 3km (2 miles) northwest along the same bay via **Krithóni**, is Léros' oldest established resort, with a long pebble beach right by the road – quieter swimming is available east around the bay at **Panagiés** and **Dýo Liskária** (3 coves, taverna-café). In a walled enclosure at Álinda's south end, a poignant, immaculately maintained **Commonwealth War Graves cemetery** contains 184 casualties of the Battle of Léros.

The other Álinda sight is the **Folklore and Historic Museum**, housed in the unmistakable Bellenis castle-mansion (May–mid-Sept Tue–Sun 9am–1pm and 6–8pm; charge). Many displays pertain to the battle: relics from the sunken Queen Olga, a Junkers bomber-wheel, a stove made from a bomb casing. There's also a rather grisly mock-up clinic and assorted rural impedimenta, costumes and antiques. One room is devoted to Communist artist Kyiakos Tsakiris (1915–98), interned locally by the junta, his works executed on stones, shells and wood. Photos recall vanished monuments: a fine market hall in Plátanos demolished in 1903, and a soaring medieval aqueduct at the Kástro destroyed during the 1943 battle.

REMOTE SITES

In antiquity Léros was sacred to Artemis, though her temple is lost somewhere near the airport – definitely not the sign-posted foundations of an ancient fort. Artemis' reputed virginity survives in the place-name **Parthéni**, past the airport: an infamous political prison during the 1967–74 junta, now a grim army base, as it was in Italian times. Things perk up beyond, at the hilltop chapel of **Agía Kiourá** 54 (always open), decorated by Tsakiris and two other junta-era prisoners with strikingly heterodox murals of Christ's Passion and the Evangelists, which the mainstream Church has always loathed – they are legally protected from further erasure. Just below, **Blefoútis** bay has a decent, shaded pebble beach and an excellent taverna.

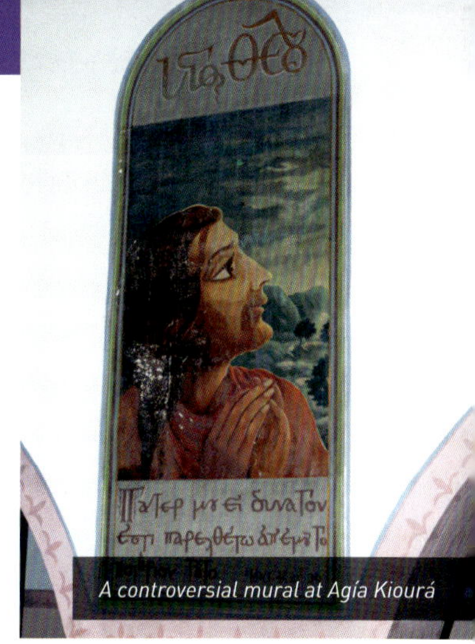

A controversial mural at Agía Kiourá

Other bays tend not to be worth the effort. West-facing **Goúrna** has a long, sandy and gently shelving (but also windy and often dirty) beach. Isolated, southerly **Xirókambos** refuses to face the fact that its scrappy beach hinders its chances of becoming a proper resort; caiques ply to and from Myrtiés (Kálymnos) daily in season, but it's better to continue to Pandéli (four times weekly). For more variety in swimming spots, take a **day cruise** (11am–7pm; €25–30) from Agía Marína to various islets northwest of Léros.

LÉROS MUSEUMS

The **Merikiá Tunnel War Museum** (daily 9.30am–1.30pm; charge), occupying the former Italian naval command centre, displays abundant, barely labelled documents and military

hardware; histrionically narrated archival footage tries to explain everything. Either Ioannis Paraponiaris' **Deposito di Guerra** (www.deposito-di-guerra.com) in remote Agía Iríni, or Tassos Kanaris' collection at the Eleftheria Hotel in Plátanos, makes better viewing. On a side street where Plátanos blends into Agía Marína, the one-gallery **archaeological museum** (Wed–Mon 8am–1pm; free), aided by good labelling, presents local finds from the late Neolithic to early Byzantine times.

PÁTMOS

Pátmos 55 has been synonymous with the biblical Book of Revelation (Apocalypse) ever since tradition placed its authorship here, in AD 95, by John the Evangelist. A volcanic landscape, with evocative rock formations and sweeping views, seems suitably apocalyptic. In 1088 the monk Hristodoulos Latrenos

THE BATTLE OF LÉROS

Across Léros bomb nose-cones and shell casings serve as gaily painted courtyard ornaments or gateposts – evidence of the 1943 **Battle of Léros**. Over 52 days from 26 September – when the destroyers Intrepid (British) and Queen Olga (Greek) were sunk at Lakkí – the Germans bombarded the island with 1,369 air-sorties from Rhodes and Greece's mainland. On 12 November, the Germans began landing both para-troops and fighters shipped to the northeast coast. German mastery of the air made resupply of the island impossible, and ensured the Allied loss of Léros. On 16 November, the British commander surrendered, with 8,500 Commonwealth and Italian soldiers taken prisoner and thousands of casualties on all sides.

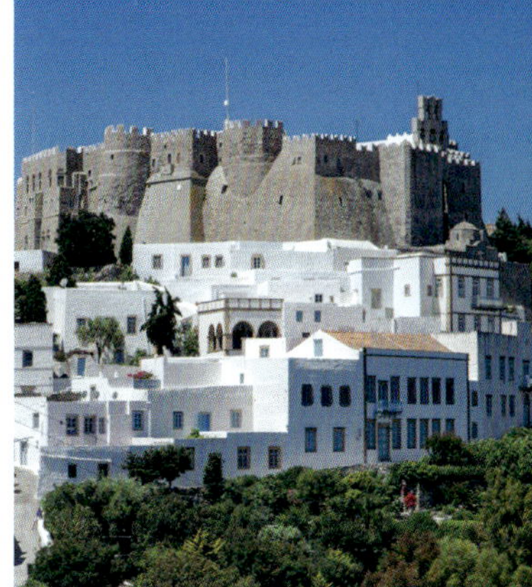
The Monastery of St John the Theologian on Pátmos

founded a Patmian monastery in honour of St John the Theologian (as John the Evangelist is known in Greek; Theologos is a common island male name), which soon became a focus of scholarship and pilgrimage. A Byzantine imperial charter granted the monastery tax exemption and the right to engage in trade, concessions respected by later overlords.

Although the monks no longer rule Pátmos, their presence tempers potential resort rowdiness. While there are some naturist beaches, nightlife is genteel, and the clientele upmarket (including the Aga Khan's family, plus various ruling or deposed royal families). Those who elect to stay overnight appreciate the unique, even spiritual, atmosphere that Pátmos exudes once day-trippers and cruise-ship patrons have departed.

Skála 56 is the port and largest village (1,415 out of 3,047 islanders), best appreciated at night when crickets serenade and yacht-masts glow against a dark sky. By day Skála loses its charm, but all island commerce is based here. The modern town dates only from the 1820s, when the Aegean had largely been cleared of pirates, but at the summit of the westerly rise, known as Kastélli (signposted), lie the extensive foundations of an ancient acropolis.

Buses leave regularly from the quay for the hilltop **Hóra**, but a 40-minute cobbled path short-cutting the road (or a longer trail shown on the recommended map) is preferable in cool

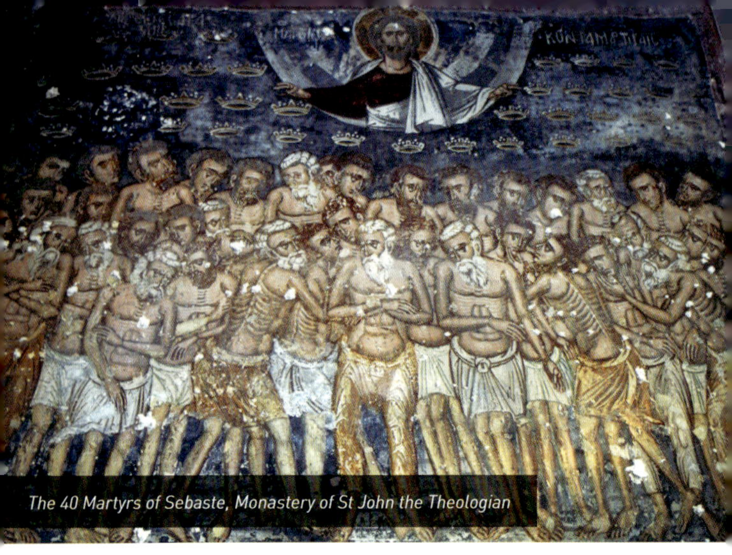
The 40 Martyrs of Sebaste, Monastery of St John the Theologian

weather, at least downhill. Hóra's core, protected by massive, pirate-proof fortifications and visible from a great distance, is **Agíou Ioánnou tou Theológou Monastery** (Monastery of St John the Theologian; daily 8am–1.30pm, Mon also 4–6pm, Tue, Sat also 4–7pm), hopelessly packed out when cruise-ship groups arrive – time visits accordingly. A photogenic maze of interlinked courtyards, stairways, chapels and passageways, it occupies the site of an ancient temple, duly admired by Hristodoulos and his work party before they demolished it to recycle its masonry. The Treasury (charge) houses the most impressive monastic collection in Greece outside Mount Athos. Among precious icons and jewellery, the prize exhibit is the edict of Emperor Alexios Komnenos granting the island to Hristodoulos. The narthex of the main church, to your left as you enter the monastery, has excellent late-medieval **frescoes** by Cretan painters, mostly scenes from the life and miracles of Hristodoulos.

Hóra 57 village grew up immediately outside the monastery from the 1280s onwards. Despite earthquakes and Italian demolitions to create open space, it remains architecturally homogenous, with cobbled, occasionally arcaded alleys lined by dozens of shipowners' mansions dating from Pátmos' 17th- and 18th-century heyday, purchased by wealthy outsiders decades ago. High, almost windowless walls and monumental wooden doors betray nothing of the opulence within: painted ceilings, pebble-mosaic terraces, flagstoned kitchens with carved cistern heads, antique furniture, embroidered bed-curtains.

Away from the principal thoroughfares and approaches to St John you stumble upon rarely disturbed passages, no wider than one person, lined with ruins or overgrown with fragrant marvel-of-Peru. On summer nights, when the monastery ramparts are floodlit to startling effect, Hóra ranks as the most beautiful settlement in the Dodecanese.

From **Platía Lótza** in the north you have one of the most sweeping views in the Aegean, taking in multiple land-masses: going clockwise, Ikaría, Thýmena, Foúrni, Sámos, Arkí, Lipsí and double-humped Samsun Dağ (ancient Mount Mykale) in Turkey.

Just over halfway down the path from Hóra to Skála, smaller **Apokálypsis Monastery** (same hours as main monastery) was built around the grotto where John had his Revelation. A silver band on the wall marks the spot where John lay his head, while the divine Voice spoke through a great cleft in the rock above.

BEACHES

Pátmos's remote beaches are surprisingly good, with islet-spangled seascapes offshore and (usually) excellent tavernas. Buses ply between **Gríkou** resort (**Pétra** beach immediately south is better) and northerly **Kámbos** bay. Scooters can be rented in Skála (try Billis, tel: 6974 100788). The biggest pure-sand cove is the

exposed but gently shelving **Psilí Ammos** ⑤⑧ in the far south, accessible by a half-hour marked trail-walk from road's end where scooters park; the southern third is favoured by naturists. Beaches north of Skála, most on the sheltered 'inner' coastline, include (in order) sandy **Melóï**, with Pátmos's oldest beach taverna; long **Agriolivádi**; sandy **Vagiá** beyond Kámbos, having the cleanest water; pebbly, double-cove **Lingínou**, popular with nudists; isolated **Livádi Geranoú** ⑤⑨, sand and gravel, with an islet to swim to; and finally **Lámbi** ⑥⓪, with irresistible, multi-coloured volcanic pebbles (it's forbidden to collect them).

Excursion boats from the northwest end of Skála quay offer **day-trips** (typically depart 9am, return at 5pm, to the islets of **Maráthi** ⑥①, **Arkí** ⑥② and **Lipsí** ⑥③ northeast of Pátmos. With a long sandy beach and two tavernas, Maráthi is a relaxing choice.

BODRUM (TURKEY)

Kos and its neighbours are close to Turkey's southwestern coast, so day-trips there are widely offered. You'll need your passport for entry/exit formalities, but unless you stay overnight, UK nationals do *not* require a visa. Although Turkey uses the Turkish lira, almost all transactions – particularly souvenir purchases – can be conducted (at a slight mark-up) in euro, dollars or sterling.

The nearest Turkish port to Kos is **Bodrum**, 20–40 minutes away depending on boat type. Three companies offer day-trips from the international quay, so competition is keen; day-return fares can be had for as little as €15–20 in shoulder season. Departures are typically at 9–10.15am, with returns from Bodrum at 4–5pm, allowing six hours in Turkey. Make sure your boat docks at the old central harbour, *not* the inconvenient new harbour.

Upon clearing old-port immigration, head straight to the nearby, massive **Castle of St Peter**, built by the Knights Hospitaller 1402–1522. This now houses the **Museum of Underwater Archaeology** (late Mar–Oct Tue–Sun 9am–4.30pm, www.bodrum-museum.com; charge), one of the best of its type, arrayed over several galleries. Unmissable are the Uluburun Glass Wreck Hall (Tue–Fri 9am–noon & 2–4.30pm), featuring treasures recovered from the oldest (14th-century BC) known shipwreck, and the Carian Princess Hall (same hours), exhibiting the remains and effects of a local 4th-century BC noblewoman, including a gold diadem, drinking cup and jewellery.

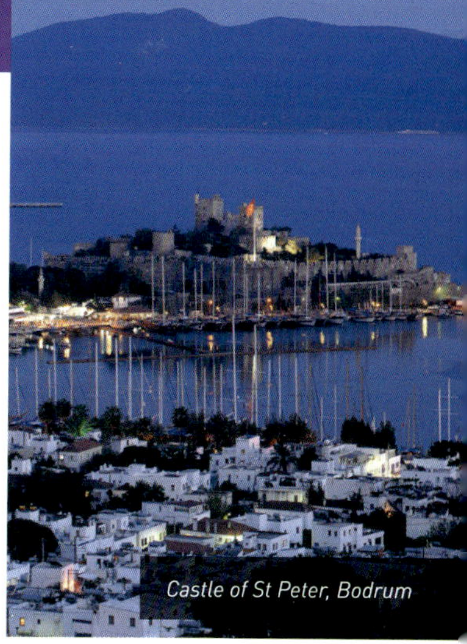
Castle of St Peter, Bodrum

Bodrum's other main attraction is its **bazaar** – a warren of lanes inland and northeast from the castle, either side of Cevat Şakir Caddesi. Mass-produced trinkets predominate, along with spices, leather goods, jewellery, beads, and shoddily made counterfeit designer apparel. Sales tactics are intense, and prices not necessarily cheaper than on Kos.

Allow time for strolling through Bodrum's residential districts, inland from the yacht anchorage. Come lunch-time, better value can be found away from waterfront establishments – for example at Otantik Ocakbaşı on Atatürk Cad 12/B, Kumbahçe, inland from the east beach, or Nazik Ana, at Eski Hükümet Sok 5 in the bazaar. Many menu items are the same as on Kos – only the name changes, and even then not always. Greeks and Turks have lived together for almost a millennium, and their cultures are more similar than some would admit.

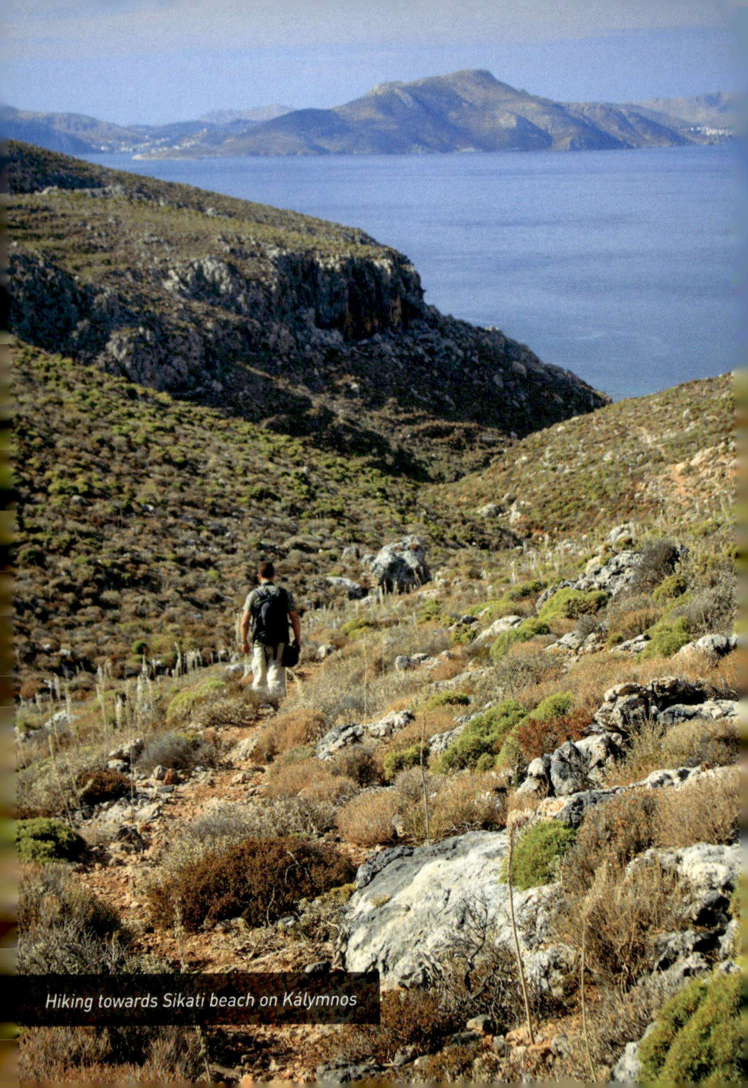

Hiking towards Sikati beach on Kálymnos

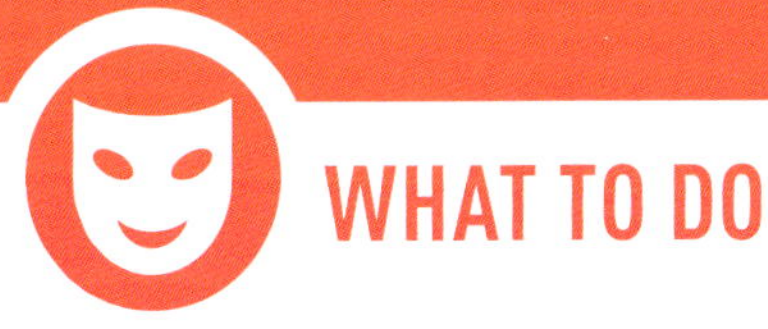

WHAT TO DO

Kos and its neighbours are not just excellent holiday destinations in terms of scenery, historical sites and museums – they offer assorted sporting, shopping and entertainment opportunities.

SPORTS

There are plenty of occasions for an active holiday on Kos or surrounding smaller islands, both on land and at sea. Beaches – whether sandy, pebbly or a mixture – and swimming are covered in the Where to Go section. Sea-surface temperatures attain 26°C/79°F in August/September; water cleanliness is usually among the best in the Aegean.

WATERSPORTS

Kos, as you'll soon notice, is a very breezy place, with reliable prevailing northwesterly winds. Accordingly, windsurfing and kitesurfing is avidly practiced. The best spots are around Cape Psalídi in the far northeast, Marmári and Kohylári on the northwest-facing coast, and southeast-facing Kéfalos Bay.

Established centres for instruction and equipment rental include Windzone, Psalídi (www.windzone-kos.gr, tel: 6939 117475 or 6979 723193); Big Blue Surf Center, Psalídi (www.bigblue-surfcenter.gr, tel: 6945 898232); Marmari Windsurfing, behind the Marmari Beach Hotel (www.marmari-windsurfing.com, tel: 6940 607280); Kohilari Kite Center, at Kohylári beach near Limniónas (www.kefaloskite.com, tel 69445 72567) and Kefalos Windsurfing, Kéfalos Bay (www.kefaloswindsurfing.com, tel: 6977 620316).

Scuba courses and dive trips are offered from Kos, but with principally sandy, shallow bottom there is little to see nearby; even

one of the dive centres admits that their emphasis is on certification, not expeditions. Conditions are better around Kálymnos, but the best diving in the region is to be had off Léros, which is surrounded by extensive military debris – German, Italian, Greek and British – from the autumn 1943 Battle of Léros, much of it between 30 and 60 metres deep. Thus only intermediate and advanced divers can visit the wrecks of the Greek destroyer *Queen Olga*; a British landing craft; a Junkers 52 transport airplane; an anti-submarine-net tender; and the submarine net itself. Shallower wrecks accessible to novice divers include a German landing craft; a Heinkel 111 bomber; and an Arado 198 seaplane.

Two reputable Kos dive centres are Kos Divers in Psalídi (www.kosdivers.com, tel: 6932 155422), with PADI Open Water certification courses from €310, and Arian Diving Centre in Kardámena (http://arian-diving-centre.com, tel: 22420 92264), with certification courses (5 half-days) at €450. Kálymnos has two centres, Divers Island (www.diversisland-kalymnos.gr, tel: 22430 48287) and Kalymnos Diving (https://kalymnosdiving.gr, tel: 6947 604120). On Léros, there is just one dive operator, Hydrovius in Krithóni (www.hydrovius.gr, tel: 2247026025), which offer 10-dive packages to qualified divers at an attractive price of €350, and Advanced Open Water courses for the same price.

HIKING

Kos does not have much of a path network – it's too cultivated and developed; the unmissable ascent of Hristós peak is detailed on page 58. Kálymnos by contrast has a good, well-documented network of paths, providing excellent walking during the cooler months. The same is true of Nísyros, and to a lesser extent Pátmos, where routes have been marked since 2010. With the exception of Pátmos (Anavasi map 10.39, scale 1:20,000; www.anavasi.gr), these islands are adequately

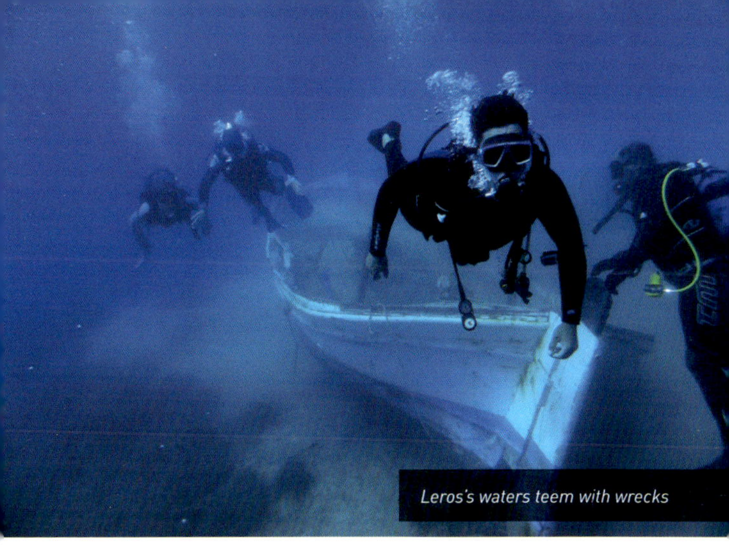
Leros's waters teem with wrecks

covered by Terrain maps (http://terrainmaps.gr) at scales of 1:20,000–1:25,000 (1:45,000 for Kos).

MOUNTAIN-BIKING

Kos may not be a hiking destination, but with numerous dirt-surface forest and ravine tracks of a moderate grade, it is fine for mountain-biking during the cooler months, as are adjacent Nísyros and Kálymnos. Kos Bike Activities in Psalídi (http://kosbikeactivities.com, tel: 6944 150129) offers guided tours four days weekly on Kos, once a week on Nísyros and once weekly on Kálymnos. Most itineraries, on Scott-brand bikes with other essentials supplied, are rated difficult and at least partially off-road.

ROCK-CLIMBING

The cliffs of Kálymnos and its satellite islet Télendos afford some of the most exciting big-wall climbing in Europe. Since the

late 1990s, the international climbing fraternity has effectively extended the tourist season on these islands back to March and forward into November, avoiding being baked to a crisp on the palisades during high summer. There are literally scores of routes, mostly from Masoúri north to Skália; two good sources of information are www.kalymnosclimbing.eu, affiliated with a particular climbing school, and the more disinterested https://climbkalymnos.com, with a guidebook available.

THE GENUINE ICON

Icons (Greek *ikónes*) are images of saints, prophets, archangels or apostles, or episodes in Christ's or the Virgin's life. They are not intended as naturalistic depictions of holy personalities, whose unvarying attributes – hairstyle, instruments of martyrdom, clothing – were fixed early in Christianity.

Icons form the heart of Orthodox worship, as a focus for prayer and a 'window' to the saint being petitioned. All are considered sacred; some reputedly possess miraculous powers. The oldest surviving examples date from after 843 AD.

Icon-painters created works for private clients as well as for churches, and they were popular souvenirs for Grand Tourists and religious pilgrims. However, modern production methods, including the use of thin canvas and synthetic colours, saw them lose favour. But traditional painting methods have been revived, both for church renovations and for commercial sale. Powdered natural pigments, vinegar and egg yolk are painstakingly mixed to form tempera, then brushed onto thick stretched canvas, wood, rock or a roof tile. Gold leaf is then applied, giving the whole image a unique patina. Such time-consuming work is exquisite and thus expensive.

HORSE-RIDING

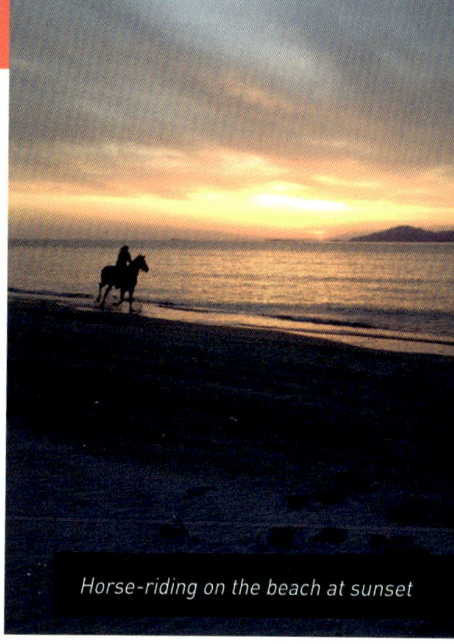
Horse-riding on the beach at sunset

There are several horse-riding stables on Kos, offering either foothill jaunts or beach itineraries. The oldest (since 1992) and largest stables, with Hungarian, French and Belgian horses, is Canadian-and-Greek-run Salt Lake Stables near Marmári, just southwest of said salt lake (www.facebook.com/horseriding.saltlakestables, tel: 6944 104446, May–early Nov), with small groups, young kids or novices catered for and full equipment provided. Sunrise/sunset and moonlight rides along the nearby beach are their speciality; budget €45–50 for a two-hour dawn/dusk ride, €50 for two hours after dark. They also offer swimming with horses (€60) – some Salt Lake horses love water and will take you into the sea.

SHOPPING

The Greek islands are not a shopper's paradise in the way that countries like Morocco, India and Mexico are, but there are still many things that make nice souvenirs or gifts.

Antiques. Very few genuine antiquities (officially classified as anything made before 1821) are sold. These are usually ceramics, jewellery or icons, and will require authentication certificates and an export permit – the dealer should be able to advise you in this process. For those whose budget does not

stretch to such items, there are many reproductions, of varying quality and price. Skála on Pátmos, where cruise-ship patrons come ashore, has a few shops stocking knick-knacks from a century ago, but don't expect any bargains.

Carpets and rag-rugs. Any oriental carpets sold on Kos are imported from Turkey, via Bodrum opposite. You may as well go on a day-trip and secure a rug in person, being mindful of regulations concerning duty-free import value (VAT may still be payable in Greece) – currently €430 worth of goods per adult. Obtain realistic invoices for the goods in Bodrum – Greek customs officials know the market.

Indigenous weaving traditions on Kos and its neighbours have all but died out. You might see – more likely in a homewares shop than a tourist boutique – brightly coloured *koureloúdes* (rag-rugs), which can be good value. Older ones have more subdued hues and tighter weave, and are thus priced accordingly. Tasteful new *koureloúdes* are currently sold at a few points (including the boat quay) on Télendos islet, off Kálymnos.Most of the cotton rugs and bathmats on display, with Aegean motifs such as dolphins framed by a geometric meander pattern, are mass-produced and imported from India. That said, such mats are cheap, hard-wearing and do not shrink much, but rot quickly if left wet.

Ceramics and sculpture. Kos still has a small pottery industry, with shops in Kos Town, Lagoúdi and Ziá. Plates, jugs, cups and bowls are produced in various patterns and colours. Skála on Pátmos is also promising for ceramics shopping. Prices vary according to the quality of materials and workmanship, which you will discern this after visiting different stores and closely examining the items.

Clothing. Kos has plenty of outlets for summery cotton or muslin trousers, tops, kaftans, and dresses. You will also find plenty of T-shirts, swimwear and beach footwear. The traditional

August sales now start in July, but you'll be lucky to find something in the most common sizes, which sell out instantly.

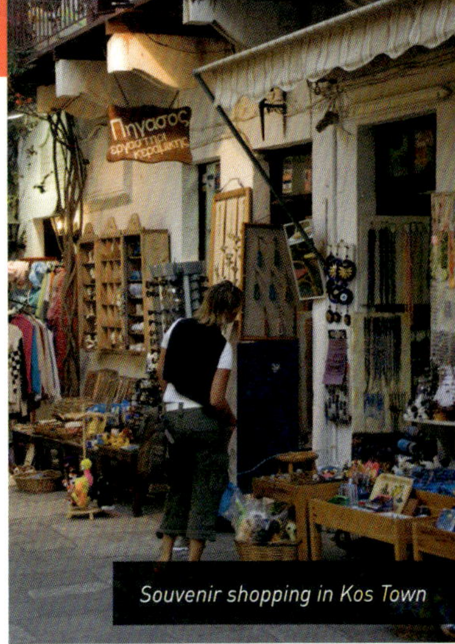

Souvenir shopping in Kos Town

Jewellery. You can choose as many carats in precious stones as your budget can handle. Gold and silver are sold by weight, with relatively little extra cost added for the workmanship. In the lower price ranges there is plenty of everyday jewellery such as ankle chains in metal or leather, navel studs and rings.

Leather items. Handbags, wallets and belts, of widely differing material and workmanship, are widely sold. A quality handbag that will last several years costs upwards of €40.

Olive wood items. Olive wood is laboriously carved or lathe-turned into practical souvenirs, ranging from coasters or flat-candle holders to large salad bowls, smaller cereal bowls or cutting boards, the latter fairly expensive (€20–35 for a board, €18–50 for a bowl). Pricier items are more likely (though not guaranteed) to be from fully cured wood, which resists cracking; green olive wood is more popular with craftsman because it's easier to work, but invariably develops fatal splits after a couple of years as it finishes drying in your home. Cutting boards should be one-piece, not glued sections. Protect your investment by oiling it occasionally with olive or linseed oil, and never leave it immersed in water.

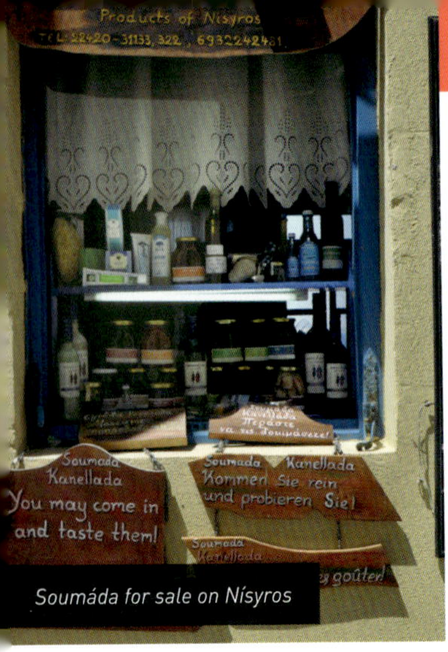

Soumáda for sale on Nísyros

Food and drink. Fruit – especially sour cherries, figs, plums and Seville oranges – are preserved in jars as *glyká koutalioú* or 'spoon sweets'. Nísyros is the place to score a jar of pickled caper greens, a great accent to any salad, or on their own.

Bees frequent aromatic hillside herbs on Kos, Kálymnos and Léros, producing delicious honey. Kalymnian honey is arguably the best available on the islands in this guide. But beware – there is no quality control of the industry, and adulteration is rife. Always taste first before buying, if possible. Much of what is touted as 'thyme (thymarísio) honey' isn't. Genuine thyme honey is dark and highly aromatic, and when a jar or can is opened the distinctive aroma should waft out. On Kos, supermarkets sell Papourakos or Papavasileiou thyme honey from Kéfalos.

Olives are preserved either in oil or brine, or made into unadulterated 'extra virgin' (first, cold pressing) oil for cooking and delicious salad dressings. Hatzipetros or Papadimitriou are the major bottlers on Kos, with their products ubiquitous.

A distinctively Greek drink to take home is anise-or-fennel-flavoured oúzo –the best comes from the islands of Sámos (Zarbanis or Frantzeskos brands) and Lésvos (too many distillers to list). Go for *apóstagma* (purely distilled). Many of the better Greek wines can be found at Marinos bottle shops (www.

marinossa.gr), with outlets on Kálymnos (Póthia waterfront, tel: 22470 22093) and on Kos (tel: 22420 41940).

On Nísyros, two non-alcoholic drink bases are made and sold. *Soumáda* is almond syrup, sadly no longer made from island almonds but imported ones. Diluted 4:1 with chilled water, it's supremely refreshing. Somewhat less so and more

WINE VARIETIES AND TASTING

Kos has at least three commercial wineries equipped for visits. Hatziemmanouil, on the trunk road just southwest of the main Tingáki turning (www.hatziemmanouil.gr, tel: 22420 68888; May–Oct daily 9am–7pm, otherwise by arrangement), is the most established, with six labels available. Best is their red Syrah (13.5 percent), aged one year in oak barrels; the Cabernet/Syrah blend (13.5 percent) is cheaper. They also make two whites, a rosé and a dessert wine. The Triantafyllopoulos winery nearby (www.koswinery.gr, tel: 22420 69860; May–Oct Mon–Sat 8.30am–5pm) has plusher tasting facilities, with views over vineyards to the sea. They offer nine labels, the most interesting being whites of *athíri-asýrtiko* or sauvignon blanc-*malagouziá* blends, an oak-aged red (13.5 percent) of blended Tempranillo, and Syrah and a great Grenache Rouge/Syrah Rosé. Hatzinikolaou (www.facebook.com/HATZINIKOLAOUwinery/, tel: 22420 68921) has minimal tasting facilities 1km east of Zipári, but their products (several reds, a white, a rosé) are widely available in local supermarkets; go for their dry, non-fruity Syrah/Cabernet Platananki rosé(13 percent) and Platanaki red (12.5 percent), a blend of Merlot and Mavrothílyko, an heirloom grape rescued from extinction on Nísyros.

cloying is local *kaneláda*, a red, cinnamon-laced syrup, a bit like dentist's mouthwash.

WINERY TOURISM

Commercial wine-making on Kos collapsed in 1998 with the bankruptcy of the Vinko co-operative. Since 2004, however, the slack has been taken up admirably by a handful of private wineries, some producing 50,000–80,000 bottles per year. Unusually for a Greek island, Kos excels particularly at dry red wines, made from legacy Greek grapes, imported varieties or blends. There are also newish wineries on Léros and Pátmos.

ENTERTAINMENT

MUSIC AND DANCE

The rich and varied Greek musical tradition goes back hundreds of years, originally based on Byzantine chant but in modern times featuring wonderful settings of popular poetry to music. Each region of Greece has its particular songs and dances; those of the southeastern islands, including Kos and its neighbours, are called *nisiótika*. Some tavernas or bars host live traditional music, typically on Wednesday, Friday and Saturday evenings. Genuine folk dancing is now

Summer cinema

Cine Orfeas, Fenaréti 3, Kos Town (www.cine-orfeas.gr, tel: 22421 16923; early June to late Sept/early Oct) is one of the loveliest outdoor cinemas in Greece. Screenings are nightly at 9pm or 11.15pm, sometimes 10pm. Sit back with a box of popcorn and enjoy last year's releases. Admission €7, €9 for 3D; Thursday is discount night.

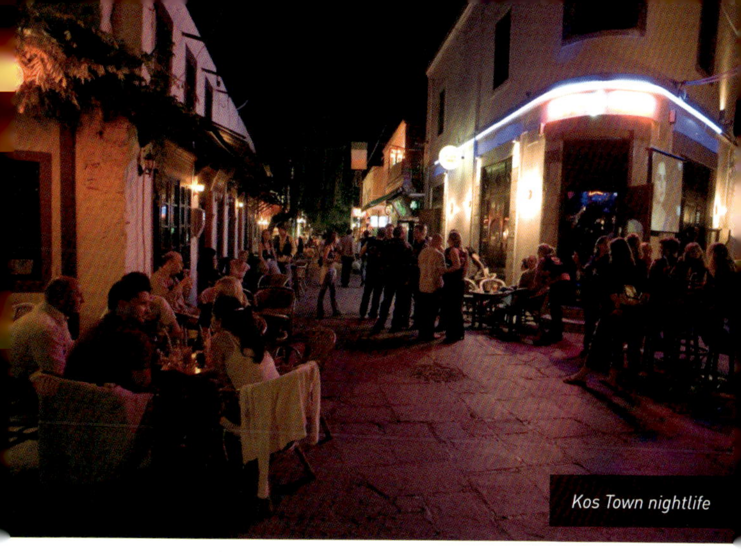
Kos Town nightlife

difficult to witness, but more likely at a private wedding or saint's day when performances occur in their true context.

NIGHTLIFE (AND DAYLIFE)

The best concentrations for lively bars on Kos are along Aktí Andoníou Zouroúdi, the main drag of the Lámbi seafront; the earthquake-damaged 'Bar Lanes' just in from Mandráki port; and the back-streets of Kardámena. On Nísyros, the Lefkandió waterfront in Mandráki is typically hopping after dark, while evergreen bars on Léros include Savana at Pandéli and Café del Mar at Vromólithos. The profile on Kálymnos and Pátmos is much more fluid at present. In terms of big, hi-tech clubs, Starlight at the edge of Kardámena has managed to survive dire economic conditions since 2014, with a popular beach-bar annexe.

A well-loved Greek institution are all-day beach bars with DJ'd music. They generally get going around noon and keep on until the small hours. On Kos, three good ones are Mylos on Aktí Andoníou Zouroúdi, Ammos in Psalídi (www.ammos-kos.gr/en/) and Aplo near Mastihári (www.aplo-beachbar.com; live blues/rock music some nights).

Kos has a summer (late June–Aug) festival, the Hippokrateia, but this has no website, Facebook page or printed advance programme – look out for posters instead. Events comprise re-enactments of folk customs, exhibits and concerts.

CHILDREN'S KOS

Kos and surrounding islands are great places to take kids. Greek society is very family-orientated, and children will be indulged in cafés and tavernas. Most Kos resort hotels have a range of child-friendly activities, including kids' clubs, designated swimming areas and playgrounds.

Since the Mediterranean has very little tide, and Kos and Pátmos in particular have many gently shelving bays, there are lots of safe places for children to paddle. Sandy beaches are more fun than pebbly ones for castle-building and hole-digging; our beach coverage distinguishes the two.

For older children, the Knights' castles on Nísyros, Kálymnos, Léros and in Bodrum will prove fascinating; the volcanic craters on Nísyros should also be a hit, as will the peacocks of Pláka Forest. The recommended Kos riding stable accepts all ages, with ponies for youngsters. Watersports are offered at most resorts across the island – standup paddle-boarding, kayaking, windsurfing – provide a more active challenge. For a fun family day out, try Lido Water Park near Mastihári (daily May–Oct 10am–6.30pm; www.lidowaterpark.com, tel: 22420 59241), with a multi-lane slide, lazy river, special kids area and several pools including a wave pool.

CALENDAR OF EVENTS

1 January: *Protohroniá*/St Basil's Day; traditional greeting is 'Kalí Hroniá!'
6 January: *Agía Theofánia*/Epiphany, the Baptism of Christ; young men dive into the sea to recover a crucifix cast by the local bishop.
7 March: 1948 Union of Dodecanese with Greece: parades, dancing.
Clean Monday: 48 days before Easter, Lenten fast (no meat or dairy) begins; kite-flying and countryside outings.
25 March: Greek Independence Day/Festival of the Annunciation.
Easter: the most important Orthodox holiday. Maundy Thursday eve features the moving Crucifixion Mass; on Good Friday, processions in each parish follow the flower-decked bier of Christ. The midnight Resurrection Mass on Holy Saturday concludes with fireworks and relaying of the sacred flame from officiating clergy to parishioners. On Sunday mageirítsa stew and roast lamb ends the Lenten fast.
1 May: *Protomagiá*/May Day: flower-gathering excursions to the country – and massive parades by the political Left.
May/June variable: *Agíou Pnévmatos*/Holy Spirit (Whit) Monday. National holiday concludes a three-day weekend; hotels fill for first time.
14–15 August: *Kímisi tis* Theotókou/Dormition of the Panagía. Processions and festivals wherever there is a church dedicated to this feast (some Marian churches celebrate 8 September or 21 November).
29 August: *Apotomí Timías Kefalís Prodrómou*/Beheading of John the Baptist; pilgrimage and celebration at his monastery near Kéfalos, Kos.
14 September: *Ýpsosi tou Timiou Stavroú*/Elevation of the Holy Cross, observed on Nísyros.
25–26 September: *Metástasi Ioánni Theológou*/Departure of St John the Theologian, at his monasteries on Pátmos and Nísyros.
28 October: *Óhi* (No) Day, commemorating Greek defiance of the Italian invasion in 1940.
25–26 December: *Hristoúgenna*/Christmas. The traditional symbol, in public squares, is an illuminated boat. Santa is an invasive species.
New Year's Eve: Adults play cards for money, and a cake (the vassilópita) is baked with a coin inside – bringing good luck to whoever gets that slice.

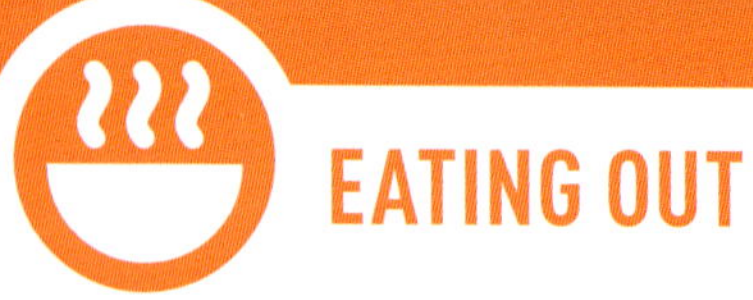

EATING OUT

Greek cuisine relies on seasonal ingredients at peak flavour and freshness, served raw, or cooked simply – on a grill, flash-fried or slow-baked. Greeks have long cherished staples like olive oil, cheese, yoghurt, wild greens, seafood and free-range meat, along with garden vegetables, fruit, pulses and nuts. The traditional Greek diet is among the healthiest in the world.

WHERE TO EAT

On Kos and its neighbours you find several types of eateries, each emphasising certain dishes; don't expect oven-cooked casseroles at a seaside grill, or at a mezedopolío. Many resort restaurants offer bland fare aimed at timid palates; for more authentic, good-value cuisine, refer to the recommendations section (see page 107).

The *psistariá* offers charcoal-grilled meats, plus a limited selection of salads and *mezédes*. The *tavérna* has a more elaborate menu, offering pre-cooked, steam-tray dishes known as *magireftá*, as well as some grills and salads.

A mezedopolío purveys not just anise (*glykániso*)-flavoured oúzo, or unflavoured tsípouro, but also the *mezédes* dishes that complement it. *Oúzo* and *tsípouro* are never drunk by themselves; octopus, olives, cucumber

Proper Greek chips

No taverna with any professional pride or hopes of courting local diners shrinks from the task of making hand-cut, fresh chips daily, as opposed to frozen pre-packed imports. Piping hot, regularly changed oil and thorough draining are obvious in the result.

slices, a bit of cheese, salami, or nuts are traditional accompaniments.

The *kafenío* (coffee shop) is traditionally an exclusively male domain, and still is in rural areas. Often very plainly decorated, they host political discussions and backgammon games. Usually only drinks are served.

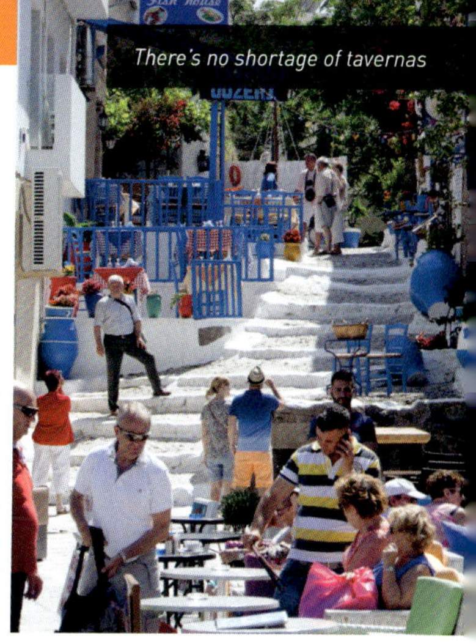

There's no shortage of tavernas

WHEN TO EAT

Resort tavernas open for lunch and dinner; some offer a full breakfast. Typically, Greeks don't eat breakfast – a coffee and a baked pastry is as much as they indulge in. English/American-style breakfasts are only available in tourist centres and fancier hotels. Lunch is taken between 2.30 and 4.15pm, before shops open again at around 5.30pm. Dinner is usually eaten from 9.30pm onwards; some establishments will take last orders after midnight.

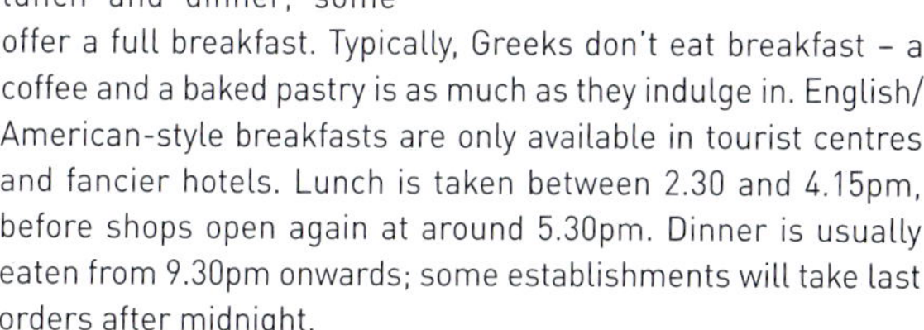

Tourist-orientated tavernas begin evening service at around 6.30pm. You will have your choice of table if you sit down before 7.30pm, but the atmosphere is definitely better later on when locals come out to eat.

WHAT TO EAT

Extensive, multilingual menus indicate available items with a price pencilled in adjacent. The menu is most useful for checking that the taverna is in your price range for items like meat or fish; a more reliable account of that day's offerings can be obtained from your waiter. Check also the steam-trays or chiller case to see what is fresh that day.

All restaurants levy a 'cover charge'. This is essentially for a serving of bread and is rarely over €1 per person – typically €0.75.

Appetisers

Carefully selected appetisers *(mezédes)* can constitute a full meal. Shared by the whole table, they are a fun way to eat – simply order as many platters as you want. *Mezedopolía* have no qualms about purveying *mezédes*-only meals, bringing ready-made choices out on a *dískos* or tray – though they also serve hot main courses to order *(tis óras)*.

The most common appetisers are *tzatzíki*, yoghurt dip flavoured with garlic, cucumber and mint; *florínes* or *piperiés kérates gemistés*, red or green peppers stuffed with cheese; *yaprákia*, vine leaves stuffed with rice, herbs and sometimes mince – which can be served hot (with *avgolémono* – egg-lemon sauce) or cold (with yoghurt); *lahanodolmádes*, cabbage leaves stuffed with rice and mince, often with *avgolémono* sauce; *taramosaláta*, cod-roe paste blended with breadcrumbs or mashed potato, olive oil and lemon juice (ideally beige and not

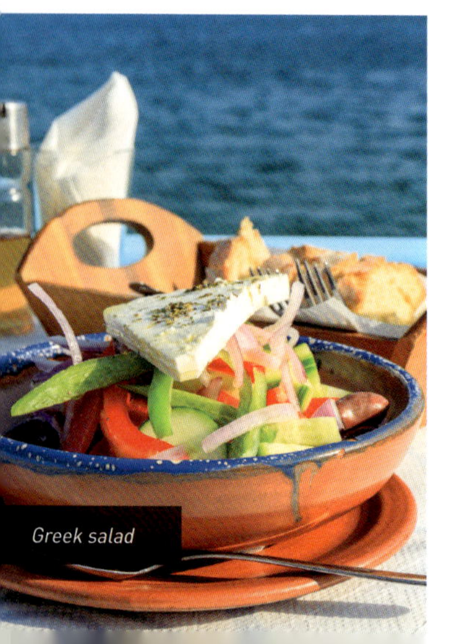

Greek salad

dyed pink); *melitzanosaláta*, aubergine purée, ideally without mayonnaise – ask; *anthí*, stuffed courgette flowers, often battered; *kolokythokeftédes*, courgette fritters; *kalamarákia gónos*, fried hatchling squid; *tyrokafterí* or *kopanistí*, two kinds of spicy cheese dips; *plevrótous*, grilled oyster mushrooms; *bekrí mezé*, diced pork in spicy sauce; and *hórta*, boiled greens (wild chicories or endive in spring/autumn, farm-raised *vlíta* or Amaranthus viridis in summer). *Saganáki* is yellow cheese coated in breadcrumbs and then fried, while *féta psití* is feta cheese baked with garlic, tomato and hot peppers.

Greek salad or *horiátiki saláta* (usually translated as 'village salad') consists of tomato, cucumber, onion, green peppers and olives topped with feta cheese. On Nísyros especially sprigs of brine-preserved caper leaves *(kápari)* often adorn Greek salads, which are portioned for two.

Cruets of olive oil *(ládi)* and wine vinegar *(xýdi)* are found with salt, pepper and napkins on the table. A January 2018 law, widely ignored, requires that tavernas provide individually sealed servings of oil (charged for) to diners.

Kos specialities

Kos has some 'indigenous' dishes which you won't find on other islands. *Pinigoúri* is bulgur wheat, by itself or as the basis of meat casseroles. *Pikhtí* is pork brawn, usually served cold, while *krasotýri* is hard goat cheese aged in red wine – pungent going on its own, better as a stuffing. Inferior versions illegally steep in *póssa*, which is wine sludge.

Fish

You choose from the fish displayed on ice. This is then weighed, un-prepared, before cooking – check the price as seafood is usually expensive. Frozen seafood (likely from July to September)

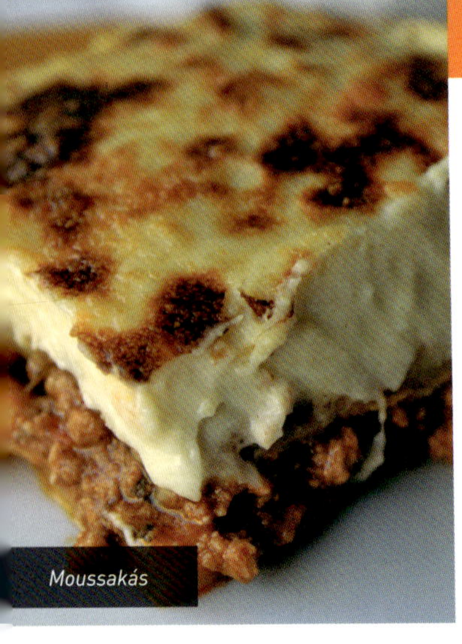

Moussakás

must be so indicated on the menu – though often cryptically with a 'k' or an asterisk. The idiom for wild, free-range fish is *alaniáriko*.

Larger fish are usually grilled and smaller fish fried, then served with fresh lemon and *ladolémono* (olive oil with lemon juice). Common species are *barboúni* (red mullet), *koutsoumoúra* (another mullet), *skorpína* (scorpion-fish, baked, in soup, or grilled), *koliós* (chub mackerel), *bakaliáros* (fresh hake, also rehydrated), *xifías* (swordfish), *tsipoúra* (gilt-head bream) and *fangrí* (bream) – the latter two often farmed. A Kos treat is *filipáki* (no translation), a blunt-headed, sand-bank-dwelling little fellow served fried, not very meaty but delicately flavoured. *Marídes/maridáki* (picarel), *gávros* (anchovy) and *atherína* (sand smelt) are also served crisp-fried by the portion, while *sardélles* (sardines) are often grilled. More elaborate seafood dishes include *soupiá* (cuttlefish) with rice in its ink or with fennel, *khtapódi xydáto* (marinated octopus salad), or *garídes saganáki* (prawns in cheese sauce).

Meat and Casserole Dishes

Meaty snacks include *gýros* (pork slivers cut from a vertical cone), and *souvláki* (small chunks of meat), either served with tomato, *tzatzíki* and chips in pitta bread. Whole chickens or bigger chunks of lamb and pork are rotisseried on a *souvlá* (skewer) as sit-down mains. Pork *brizóla* is a cutlet; veal chop is spalobrizóla; lamb or goat chops, however, are *païdákia*. *Pansétta* are spare ribs, the cheapest meat mains around besides *loukánika* (sausages). In these economically fraught times, *sykotákia arnísia* (lamb liver chunks) are inexpensive and popular, as are chicken livers *(sykotákia poulerikón)*.

Greece's most famous oven dish is *moussakás* –sliced potato, aubergine and minced lamb topped with béchamel sauce. It should be firm but succulent, and redolent of nutmeg. *Pastítsio* is another layered recipe with macaroni, mince and cheese sauce. Other common casseroles include *giouvétsi* (meat baked in a clay pot with *kritharáki* pasta – Italian *orzo*) and *papoutsáki* (eggplant 'shoes' stuffed with mince).

Hot vegetarian dishes include *gemistá*, tomatoes, or peppers filled with herb-flavoured rice; *melitzánes imám*, aubergine stuffed with tomato, onion, and garlic; or *briám/tourloú* (ratatouille). Vegetarian *yaprákia*, more common than meaty ones, are called *gialantzí* ('liar's'). Gluten (gluténi) intolerance is catered to in Greece.

Cheeses

Greek cheeses (*tyriá*) are made from cow's, ewe's or goat's milk, or often blends. Ubiquitous *féta* cheese tops every Greek salad or appears alone garnished with olive oil and oregano. *Graviéra* is a common, variably-sharp hard cheese; milder (semi-)soft cheeses such as *manoúri*, *myzithra* or *anthótyro* are served plain or used for stuffing.

Dessert

Most tavernas bring you a *kérazma* or sweet on the house together with the bill. This might be a plate of fresh seasonal fruit, semolina halva *(simigdalísios halvás)* or chocolate loaf *(kormós)*.

Postprandial fruit platters feature watermelon or Persian melon in summer, grapes or pears in autumn, sliced apple in winter and citrus, kiwi slices or maybe strawberries in spring.

Elsewhere, *zaharoplastía* (sticky-cake shops) dish out incredibly decadent sweets, legacies of the Ottomans: *baklavás*, layers of honey-soaked flaky pastry with walnuts; *kataïfi*, shredded wheat filled with chopped almonds and honey; *galaktoboúreko*, custard pie; or *ravaní*, honey-soaked sponge cake.

For dairy desserts, try *ryzógalo*, cold rice pudding, or *kréma* (custard) at a *galaktopolío* (dairy shop). A quality ice-cream *(pagotó)* cult is well established in the Dodecanese; the best outlets on Kos are *Paradosi*, in Plátani village (branch on Avérof) and *Special*, Vassiléos Georgíou 7, Kos Town (plus 3 branches). On Léros, *Elliniko* in Agía Marína is tops, while

NON-ALCOHOLIC DRINKS

Hot coffee *(kafés)* is served *ellinikós* or 'Greek-style', freshly brewed in copper pots and served in small cups. It will probably arrive *glykós* (sweet) or even *varý glykós* (cloyingly sweet) unless you specify *métrios* (medium) or *skétos* (without sugar). Don't drink right to the bottom – the grounds settle there. Instant coffee (called 'Nes' irrespective of brand) has made big inroads in Greece; more appetising is *frappé*, cold instant coffee whipped up in a blender with or without milk *(gála)*, refreshing on a summer's day. If you prefer proper cappuccino (hot or cold), or espresso, numerous Italian-style coffee bars will oblige.

Soft drinks come in all the international varieties, carton fruit juice is generally good, and freshly-squeezed orange juice widely available. Bottled *(enfialoméno)* still mineral water is typically from Crete or the Greek mainland mountains.

on Pátmos, *DeSantis/ Marechiaro*, on a Skála backstreet, is the place.

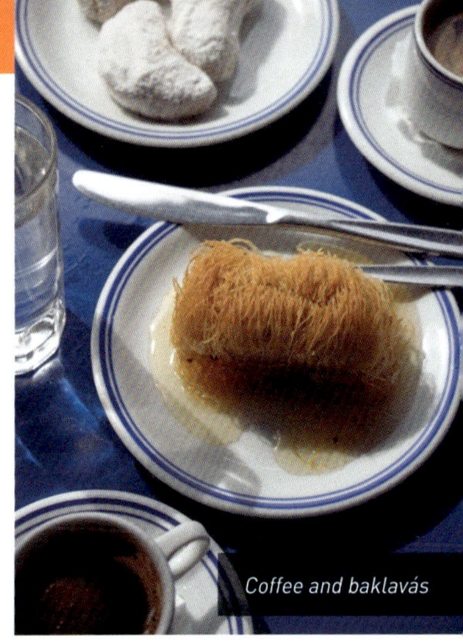
Coffee and baklavás

WHAT TO DRINK

Greek winemaking dates back four millennia; quality, especially at certain mainland vintners, has risen dramatically in recent decades. Kos wine is more than respectable, and featured at most tavernas. The cheapest wine is *hýma* or *varelísio* (in bulk), usually from the mainland. Red, white or rosé are given in full, half- or quarter-litre measures, in lightweight metal cups or glass flagons.

Retsína has been around since ancient times, when Greeks discovered the preservative properties of pine resin for storing wine. It can be an acquired taste and should be served well chilled. Purists state that no true *retsína* exists beyond the mainland; the best bottled brand is Georgiadi from Thessaloníki. Avoid CAIR (Rhodes) *retsína*.

Oúzo is taken as an aperitif with ice and water; the anethole (anise camphor) in it turns the mixture cloudy. On Kos and its neighbours, the most popular brands come from the islands of Lésvos or Sámos. Similar distillates are tsikoudiá (anise-free) and tsípouro. Turkish rakı is popular on Kos and Léros.

A dozen mass-market beers are produced in Greece, as well as imports from Britain, Germany, Belgium, Mexico and Ireland. Foreign brands are Amstel, Kaiser, Heineken and

Fischer. Popular Greek labels include Alfa, Mythos, Mamos, Eza, Fix and Vergina. Brinks (Crete), Corfu Beer or any beer from Santoríni are also reliably good.

USEFUL EXPRESSIONS

Could we order, please? **Na parangiloúme, parakaló?**
I'm a vegetarian **Íme hortofágos**
I'm a vegan **Íme vegan**
I'm gluten intolerant **Den honévo gluténi**
Cheers! **Giámas!**
Bon appetit! **Kalí órexi!**
Ice, please **págos, parakaló**

MENU READER

aláti salt
arní lamb
býra beer
eliés olives
fasolákia runner beans
garídes small shrimp
gemistá stuffed
hirinó pork
hórta wild greens
katsíki goat
keftedákia meatballs
(o)khtapódi octopus
kotópoulo chicken
krasí wine
maheropírouna cutlery
mávro pipéri black pepper
moskhári, vodinó beef
(pagoméno) neró (chilled) water
patátes potatoes
piáto plate
potíri glass
psári fish
psitó roasted
psomí bread
revýthia chickpeas
rýzi, piláfi rice
saláta salad
soupiá cuttlefish
sta kárvouna grilled
sto foúrno baked
thrápsalo deep-water squid
tiganiá meat, sautéed
tiganitó fried
vlíta amaranth greens
xifías swordfish
yaprákia stuffed vine leaves

PLACES TO EAT

Price categories reflect the cost of a meal per person with modest drink intake. Except where suggested, reservations are not necessary (or even possible) – one waits, or an extra table is fitted in. Unless otherwise stated, tavernas are open daily for lunch and dinner, early May–late Oct. All establishments take cards (often not AmEx or Diners) unless 'cash only' is indicated.

€€€€	over 40 euros
€€€	29–40 euros
€€	20–29 euros
€	below 20 euros

KOS TOWN AND SUBURBS

Ambavris € *Makrygiánni 17, tel: 22420 25656.* This well-loved farmhouse-courtyard taverna lost its home in the 2017 tremor and relocated to town. Choose a 10-platter *mezédes* medley which might include lamb meatballs in *oúzo* sauce, husked beans with garlic, snails, *pinigoúri*, *pikhtí* (cool months only), spicy *loukánika*, ambelofásola (runner beans) and stuffed *anthí or courgettes*. Affordably-priced bottled or bulk *oúzo* and *tsípouro*. Open lunch/dinner all year

Antonas €€ *Grigoríou tou Pémptou 7, tel 6946 864857.* Garishly-lit 1980s time capsule, a locals' backstreet hangout, whose limited menu includes garlic-fiery melitzanosaláta, mountainous portions of lamb chops with medallion chips, bottled tsípouro and bulk wine. Cash only.

Barbouni €€€€ *Georgíou Avérof 26, tel: 22420 20170.* Classier-than-normal waterside seafood spot gazing across to Turkey, and the evening ferry heading north. All usual fishy suspects plus novelties like sushi or sashimi, risotto with cuttlefish and its ink, shellfish linguini (sic) in white dill sauce, spinach salad with pine nuts and *krasotýri*, plus a good Greek wine list. Limited choice of desserts (try the chocolate soufflé with mastic ice cream). Thanks to Turkish clientele, some *rakı* (pick Tekirdağ).

Degli Amici (Lendi's) €€€ *Vasiléos Georgíou 22, tel: 22420 26568.* Albanian-run Italian trattoria with sea views (across a road), doing pasta, mussel and meat dishes, plus pizzas. Italian desserts (panna cotta, tiramisu) to order, grappa or limoncello as kérazma; good if pricy bulk rosé.

Pote tin Kyriaki € *Pisándrou 9, Old Town, tel: 22420 48460 or 6930 352099.* This *mezedopolío's* signature platters include *marathópita* (fennel pie), stuffed *anthí*, mushroom sautéed with veggies, *kavourdistí* (pork fry up) and assorted seafood at decent prices, complemented by proprietress Stamatia's strong *tsikoudiá* or good red *hýma*, and a soundtrack of Greek music (live Sat). Book after 9pm. Open dinner only late May–Oct Mon–Sat, Nov–mid-May Fri–Sat.

Votsalakia € *Georgíou Avérof 10, tel: 22420 26555.* The locals' favourite seafood taverna, thanks to fair fish prices, cheery seating indoors or out according to weather, non-cheesy soundtrack and friendly staff. Grilled cuttlefish is ace. Open daily lunch and dinner except mid-Dec–mid-Jan.

AROUND THE ISLAND

Ambeli € *2.5km east of Tingáki beachfront crossroads, towards Lámbi, tel: 22420 69682.* Rural taverna serving strictly small mezédes platters like *pikhtí*, *yaprákia*, *bekrí mezé* and crispy medallion-cut chips, washed down with draught beer or wine made from the surrounding vineyard (*ambéli*). May–Oct daily; Nov–April weekends.

Anemos €€ *Seafront, far northeast end, Kardámena tel: 22420 91606.* Favourite sea-view, seafood spot with fair per-kilo or per-portion prices, plus superior mezédes like *nistísimo* (mayonnaise-free), chunky *melitzanosaláta* studded with tomato, onion and pepper – no bread needed. Two octopus tentacles appeared on garnish. Bottled or bulk wine to drink. Open all year, weekends only in winter.

Gin's Place €–€€ *corner Kerámou & Attálou, Platáni, tel: 22420 25166.* The most casserole-orientated of three Kos-Turk tavernas here, with chickpeas, *bámies* (okra), *yaprákia*, stewed pork, and *glóssa* (sole) *plakí* amongst offerings. Fare can be a bit salty; good bulk rosé wine from Crete, the land of proprietor Rasim's ancestors. Lunch and dinner, all year.

Magic Beach €–€€ *tel: 22420 71894 or 6944782789.* The most accomplished and friendly of the snack bars/tavernas above the southwesterly beaches. The terrace, allowing sweeping views across to Nísyros and Tílos islands, is lapped by junipers at the top of the sand dunes. Prices reflect the remoteness and local monopoly. Starters include well-done *kolokythokeftédes* and *khtapódi xydáto*.

Makis €€ *One lane inland, Mastihari, tel: 22420 59061.* Whilst unpromising looking, this has always been one of Kos's best seafood tavernas. Outermost tables catch the breeze and permit oblique sea views, but fresh-off-the-boat (if starkly presented) fish and seafood remain the chief attraction, with token salads and dips to accompany. Open all day, all year.

Neromylos/Watermill € *Platía Karydiás, Ziá, tel: 6972 292109.* Dusk is the time to sit under *Neromylos'* giant walnut tree and savour the house lemonade, or cake with ice cream. Also crêpes, fruit salad, sandwiches and short cocktail list. This is the last intact watermill on Kos, which ground grain until the 1960s. Open 10am–evening Apr–Nov.

Oromedon €€ *Ziá access road. tel: 22420 69983,* http://oromedon.com. Come here after climbing Hristós to watch the famous sunset, while savouring *hortópita* (greens pie), *yaprákia*, *keftedákia* and good bread; there are roast-goat or -pork mains for bigger appetites, and grilled veggies or mushrooms in balsamic vinegar for veggie/vegan palates. Lunch and dinner until midnight, late Apr–late Oct.

Old Pyli €€ *Paleó Pylí access road, Amanioú village, tel: 22420 41659.* Giorgos, originally a Mastihári fisherman, keeps this taverna below ruined medieval Pylí, serving his son's daily catch, plus vegetarian starters, wood-oven-baked bread and local wine (a bit heavy). Unbeatable terrace views.

Palia Pigi € *Pigí district, Pylí village, tel: 22420 41510.* Basic but honest fare (*loukánika*, caper salad, *biftékia*, marinated octopus, *pikhtí*, *anthí*, *bakaliáros*, beets) at this taverna tucked away under a giant ficus, beside a lion-headed cistern fountain, amidst a bird-filled oasis. Lunch and dinner, late March–Nov.

Plori €€ *100m/yards west of shore plaza along beach promenade, Tingáki, tel: 22420 69686.* A good selection of *mezédes* like spicy aubergine purée with féta, or *okhtapódi krasáto*; also standard mains for bigger appetites. Good beer and wine selection, sparse *oúzo* list. Both Greeks and foreigners attend. Lunch and dinner all year (weekends only in winter); free sunbeds just across the lawn with a minimum spend.

Şerif €€ *Central junction, Platáni village. tel: 22420 23784.* One of three surviving Platáni tavernas, now reckoned the best, serving creditable Adana kebab and starters like *mantı* (Anatolian ravioli) or *börek* (stuffed with cheese, spinach or pastırma), vegetable casseroles and a full drinks list, including good bulk red from Crete and bottled Kos labels. Open warmer months only.

Teos €€ *Seafront, Kardámena, tel: 22420 92034 or 6988 145692.* Kardámena's go-to seafood place; their own trawler brings in the daily catch, with keen per-kilo prices and the fish appears with a good side-salad and chips. Good Cretan bulk wine. By Kardámena standards, it's ancient (founded 1984), and tellingly one of only two local tavernas open in winter. Lunch and dinner all year (may shut weekdays in winter).

NÍSYROS

Apo Loli Kori €€ *Mandráki, Dimarhíou Street, tel 22420 31024.* Installed below street level in a former wine-press is this creative-cuisine option, with generous portions and well-trained, jolly wait staff. Dinner might be aubergine with yogurt-chimichurri sauce, then orange-glazed pork. Pricy *hýma* wine is organic; the red from northern Greece. Tables – reservations advised – occupy a patio under shady vines. Dinner only, warmer months.

Balkoni tou Emboriou € *Emboriós central plaza, tel: 22420 31607.* A two-level terrace is always packed for the sake of *keftédes*, beets with greens, capers, *lahanodolmádes*, baked swordfish with vegetables, *pittiá* (vegetable risolles) plus grills – and for the amazing view over the volcanic zone.

Gevsea €€ *Lekandió seafront Mandráki, tel: 22420 3106.* The name is a clever pun: *gévsi* is Greek for 'taste', and this is the place for seafood here, with two French-trained Athenians at the helm. Fair prices for by-kilo fish, or perhaps cuttlefish strips on a bed of carrot, spinach and dill. There is a brief wine list and *karafákis* of *oúzo* or *tsípouro*; limited dessert options. With just 40 seats, booking is advisable; staff are friendly enough but service can lag. Lunch and dinner.

Issikas € *Shore lane east of windmill, Mandráki tel: 22420 31792.* The daily offering at this little waterside spot is chalked on a board outside; it might be *mavromátika* (black-eyed peas) and a fry-up of tiny fish, chased by Neméa bulk wine. Open most of the year; cash only.

Loutra €–€€ *Ground-floor corner of the old baths building; no phone.* Summer-only annexe of Issikas, this bohemian *mezedopolío*, its gaily painted interior sporting arched windows looking towards Kos and reverberating to the sound of the sea, has a brief menu of snacks such as *taboúli* salad, *pittiá* with a dollop of hummus, and smoked or marinated fish titbits. Daily-special mains might be baked goat, mussel-rice or shrimp *giouvétsi*.

KÁLYMNOS AND TÉLENDOS

Kafenes € *Platía Hristoú, Póthia, tel: 22430 28727.* Since 1950, this hole-in-the-wall purveys generous platters like crunchy *maridáki*, exceptionally tender *khtapodokeftédes* (octopus rissoles), local cheese or mountainous salads fit for two; try the 'green' with purslane, rocket, sun-dried tomato and lots of parmesan. Expect to wait for a table after dark. Lunch and dinner year round.

Plaka € *East shore promenade, 200m/yards north of jetty, Télendos, tel: 22430 47921.* The only shoreline taverna here that doesn't tout; they don't have to, with very fair prices for tasty fresh tuna, swordfish, wild sea-bass, some meat dishes and the usual salads or starters. Beer, *oúzo* or bulk wine to drink.

Psarokatastasi €€ *Melitsáhas beach approach, tel 6944 982205.* Ask for whole-grain bread to scoop up superior *tyrokafterí*, preceding herbed grilled fish served with *ladolémono* (lemon juice and oil), chips and mini-salad. Beers arrive in iced steins. Superb views north from main terrace, or choose the more secluded patio.

Stoukas €–€€ *Yacht marina, Póthia, tel: 6970 802346 or 6957 406977.* A good all-rounder with big portions, pleasant service, and traffic-free waterside tables. Pork *kopsídia* (round-bone chops), a starter and a beer falls in the first price category; ordering seafood pushes bills up a notch. Lunch and dinner, all year.

LÉROS

Artemis €–€€ *Blefoútis beach, tel: 22470 24253.* No-brainer choice for lunch here after a swim: fare might be *soupiórizo* (cuttlefish rice) with its ink, fried peppers and decent *hýma* rosé. Dearer main dishes push bills up a notch. Open daily Easter–Oct, weekends only winter.

Dimitris O Karaflas €–€€ *Spiliá district, off the Pandéli-Vromólithos road, tel: 22470 25626 or 6977 080599.* Some of the heartiest food on Léros, and knockout views over Vromólithos. Standouts include *kremmydópita* (onion pie), smoked mackerel, roast pork *kotsí* (shank) and heaped salads. Open all year, lunch and dinner.

El Greco €€ *Tables on sand opposite fishing dock, Pandéli, tel 22470 25066.* Fabric table-cloths and springtime bird-song in the trees set the tone here; beet, yogurt and walnut salad precede fresh hake presented artfully on a bed of rocket leaves with tomato. Small (100ml) measures of *tsípouro* for the designated driver.

Pyrofani €€ *Pandéli waterfront, opposite jetty end tel: 6936 748122.* Savour Greek standards with a twist: perfectly grilled *xifías* or *tónnos* paired to almýra, a wild seaside *hórta*; aubergine and courgette *bastounákia* (fries) with yogurt-mint dip; other dishes are fragrant with a sprinkling of ginger and lemon grass.

PÁTMOS

Ktima Petra €–€€ *Pétra beach, south of Gríkou, tel: 22470 33207.* Chunky *melitzanosaláta*, with fresh brown bread to scoop it up, lush rocket salad, *yaprákia*, and pork *giouvétsi* are typical lunchtime offerings, with grills on offer too after dark; most ingredients are from their own *ktíma* (farm). Some patrons take a dip off the pebble beach while waiting for orders. Lunch and dinner Apr–late Sept, lunch only early Oct. Summer reservations advisable.

Lambi €–€€ *Lámbi beach, north end of island, tel: 22470 31490.* Another reliable beach taverna, running since 1958; the food is presented simply but the ingredients are top-notch. Try the faultlessly grilled fresh squid served with delicious chips. Some tables are set out on the famous pebbles of Lámbi beach. Open noon until sunset, Easter Weds–Oct.

Meloi € *Melói beach, tel 22470 31888.* The oldest (since the 1970s) beach taverna on Pátmos, and still among the best for *magireftá* liked baked *anginýres* (artichokes), *pastítsio* or *papoutsáki*. Sip Cretan *hýma* under vines on the sea-view patio.

Pantheon (aka tou Giangou) € *Monastery approach, Hóra, tel: 22470 31226.* Octopus curing on a line in front of the tiny patio mark this friendly spot; the medieval interior sports stone window arches. Fare is equally traditional – boiled courgettes, *pansétta*, small *gópa* fish, *yaprákia*. Booking advised; dinner only, Apr–Nov.

Votris €€€€ *Opposite yacht port, Skála, tel 6988 807376.* The class act amongst Pátmos tavernas. '*Votris*' is old Greek for 'bunch of grapes', so the wine list is a highlight. *Ospriáda* (legume salad) feeds two. Plenty of seafood, but the roast lamb with basmati rice goes down a treat. Service can be leisurely, but you don't come here to wolf food down. Open lunch and dinner (not Mon pm) mid-Apr–mid-Nov.

A–Z TRAVEL TIPS

A SUMMARY OF PRACTICAL INFORMATION

A Accommodation 115
Airports 116
B Bicycle and scooter hire 116
Budgeting for your trip 117
C Car rental 118
Climate 118
Clothing 119
Crime and safety 119
D Driving 120
E Electricity 122
Embassies and consulates 123
Emergencies 123
G Getting there 123
Guides and tours 124
H Health and medical care 125
L Language 126
LGBTQ travellers 128
M Maps 128
Media 128
Money 128
O Opening times 129
P Police 130
Post offices 130
Public holidays 131
R Religion 131
T Telephones 131
Time zones 132
Tipping 132
Toilets 133
Tourist information 133
Transport 133
V Visas and entry requirements 134
W Websites and internet access 135

A

ACCOMMODATION

Hotels. Hotels are classified from five stars down to zero. Ratings are dictated primarily by the common facilities at the hotel, not room quality, so a particular three-star room may be just as comfortable as a nearby five-star room, but the hotel itself may lack an events hall, swimming pool, spa or multiple restaurants on the premises.

Many hotels on Kos have contracts with European tour operators. This means that in peak season it may be difficult to find desirable accommodation. If you intend to arrive between late June and early September, advance booking is essential. At the beginning and end of the season (April–mid-June and October) it is easier to get a good deal direct or through a booking site. Most hotels away from Kos Town, on Nísyros, and on Pátmos close from November to March. Interestingly, Léros has two comfortable hotels working year round, and some hotels on Kálymnos stay open during winter for rock-climbers. In peak season there may be a surcharge if you stay less than four days, or an absolute minimum stay.

One thing to beware of is the proliferation on Kos of mandatorily all-inclusive resorts. While notionally attractive to families, they seldom offer great value or great taste. We do not list any exclusively all-inclusive accommodation; however some of our listings do offer this as an option, something obvious on their websites.

***Domátia* and apartments.** *Enikiazómena domátia* (rented rooms) or full-sized apartments *(diamerísmata)* exist, especially behind the better beaches. Both licensed rooms and apartments are rated by the tourism authorities at from one to three 'keys' based on facilities. Arrivals by ferry or catamaran at Kos Harbour or Skála on Pátmos may be besieged by placard-waving accommodation touts; it is unwise to follow them, as only proprietors of substandard or unlicensed lodgings resort to this tactic, and you will probably choose to move the next morning.

AIRPORTS

Kos' international airport (IATA code KGS, tel: 22420 56000) lies towards the southwest tip of the island, 24km (15 miles) from Kos Town. Its website (www.kgs-airport.gr/en) furnishes real-time arrival and departure information. One of the older and more cramped Greek-island airports, it has been acquired by the Fraport consortium, which is currently enlarging and improving the premises – works should be complete by 2022. If your flight is delayed, there's a pleasant snack bar just outside the airport grounds at the edge of Andimáhia village, plainly visible across the car park.

From June–Sept, there are 11 bus services daily Mon–Sat (6.30am–7.50pm) and five on Sun (8am–7.15pm) (€3.20) into Kos Town, via Mastihári and Kardámena. Over the rest of the year, frequencies halve. A taxi to Kos Town or Psalídi will cost €35–40 depending on time of day, number of bags and exact destination.

Kálymnos and Léros also have airports (taxi access only), currently receiving flights solely from Athens and nearby islands on Sky Express and Olympic Air.

B

BICYCLE AND SCOOTER HIRE

Kos is one of the few Greek municipalities which actively caters to cylists. Psalídi is linked with Lámbi by a popular bike lane, though going through Kos Town itself there are hazardous discontinuities around the inner harbour. Beyond Lámbi or the edge of Kos Town, smart cyclists use the back-roads to get to Tingáki and Marmári, not the lethal main island trunk-road. There are so many agencies renting pedal-bikes on Kos that you practically trip over them. Rates range from €5 per day for the most basic, five-gear bone-shaker to €20 for a top-end, multi-speed mountain bike.

Hiring a small motorbike is popular for cruising the resorts and immediate environs; rates are €15–18 per day for a 50cc machine, lower for three days or more. However, they're not really suitable for covering long distances on Kos, and every year sees serious injuries and fatalities involving riders.

It is illegal in Greece to drive any scooter – even a 50cc one – without a driving license which includes categories AM (two-wheelers with speed 25–45km/hr) or A (scooters up to 125cc displacement). British license categories p and q for scooters of up to 50cc are not recognised, and most agencies now observe this law. If you hire a two-wheeler without the appropriate licence, any travel insurance you have will be void if you are injured or involved in an accident. Agencies may offer you a quad bike as an alternative, at somewhere between the rental cost of a scooter or a car. They are slow and actually less safe than a two-wheeler – thus helmets are issued; the Greek slang for them (*gouroúnia*, or 'swine') is indicative of their low status.

All riders must wear helmets (stiff fines for non-compliance; agencies offer wonky ones) and should proceed with caution, particularly where sand or gravel make road surfaces slippery.

BUDGETING FOR YOUR TRIP

Kos and neighbouring islands are moderately expensive destinations by European standards.

Flight Athens–Kos: €70–160 (one-way by season).

Boat ticket Athens–Kos: €57 (one-way, deck class) to €83 (one-way, cheapest cabin).

Day trip to Nísyros: €24 from Kardámena, €30 from Kos Town

Mid-range hotel: €55–100 (one night for two).

Mid-range restaurant: €22–35 (full meal for one).

Luxury hotel: €100–250 (one night for two)

Admission charges: €3–8 (museums and archaeological sites).

Car rental: €30 per day on Kos, €190 per week (small car in peak season, walk-in rate).

Litre of fuel, diesel/normal/super: €1.45/1.60/1.90

Bus fare: ticket prices range from €2.10–4.80 on Kos, less on Nísyros, Pátmos or Kálymnos.

C

CAR RENTAL (see also Driving)

Advance booking online typically results in savings of up to half off of walk-in rates. Recommended aggregator sites include www.comparecarrentals.co.uk, www.rentalcargroup.com and www.cardelmar.com.

Reputable local agencies give reasonable service and keener pricing than major international chains. Two recommended ones in Kos Town are Safari, corner Harmýlou and Karaiskáki, tel: 22420 21023, www.safari-rentacar.gr, and Autoway, Vassiléos Georgíou 18, tel: 22420 25326, www.autowaykos.gr; on Kálymnos, Auto Market in Póthia (tel: 22430 24202, www.kalymnoscars.gr) or Kipreos (http://kipreosrentals.gr). On Nísyros, Manos K (tel: 22420 31029, https://nisyros-rentacar.gr).

A national driving licence, held for at least one year, driver age over 21, is accepted for EU/EEA nationals. Other nationals must carry an International Driving Permit in addition to their home licence. If the UK exits the EU without a deal, British license-holders will also need an IDP (valid 3 years), obtainable on the spot at any major post office for one photo and a small fee. You will also need a credit card to avoid paying a large cash deposit.

Quoted rates should include VAT and CDW (Collision Damage Waiver). However, all agencies have a waiver excess of between €400 and €800 – the amount you are responsible for if you smash a vehicle, even with CDW coverage. It is strongly suggested you purchase extra cover (often called Waiver Excess Insurance) to nullify this risk. Daily rates offered by agencies themselves are expensive; it's far more advantageous to get a waiver excess policy in advance – by the year or by the day – through specialists like http://www.voyagertravelinsurance.co.uk/hire-car-excess/ or www.carhireexcess.com.

CLIMATE

Global climate change makes generalising about Aegean weather unwise – 2018 and 2019 saw freak storms until July – but you still stand an excellent chance of blue, rain-free skies between late May and mid-

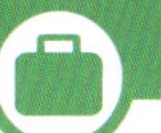

October. Midday temperatures may reach a sweltering 38°C (101°F) during summer, with warm nights, although evenings are cooler early and late in the season when daily highs are about 30° C (86° F).

The northerly *meltémi* wind buffets the northwest coast of Kos, cooling it significantly all season. Kálymnos, Léros and Pátmos can also be very breezy, though Pátmos' east coast (where most beaches are) is relatively calm.

The first autumn storm usually hits late September or early October, but serious rain does not commence until December, falling intermittently until May. Winter outdoors can be very pleasant but the sea is too cold for most bathers until late April.

CLOTHING

In summer you require little clothing. Cotton shorts or lightweight trousers and T-shirts or lightweight dresses are fine for sightseeing. Bring comfortable shoes for archaeological sites, plus a hat and sunglasses. If you have forgotten anything, boutiques in Kos Town and Póthia are well stocked (if not especially cheap outside sale periods).

When visiting churches or monasteries, both men and women should cover their shoulders; men should wear long trousers, and women a skirt that covers their knees.

Very few tavernas have a dress code, although some of the smarter hotels require long trousers and closed-toe shoes for men at dinner. A light wrap or jacket is useful for evenings in early or late season, while a wind-cheater is good for the decks of excursion boats or catamarans.

CRIME AND SAFETY

Kos and neighbours rate relatively well both in terms of personal safety and the security of belongings. But it is still prudent to lock valuables in your room safe, and not to leave phones, tablets, etc. unsupervised on the beach or even in a locked rental car – break-ins are increasing. Don't accept rides from strangers when returning late from clubbing, and always use official taxis.

If you do fall victim to crime, contact the ordinary local police – insurance claim forms will not be valid without their report.

All obvious recreational drugs are illegal in Greece (though medical CBD oil or lotion is now allowed), and those arrested on narcotics charges can spend up to 18 months on remand before charges are filed. If you take any prescription medication, carry your supply in the original pharmacy container.

D

DRIVING

Road conditions. Kos main roads are mostly paved but still dangerous, especially the main trunk road between Kos Town and Kéfalos, too narrow for its traffic load and venue for many accidents. Local driving habits leave much to be desired; favourite tricks to watch for include barging out of side roads without looking, overtaking on one's right, and oncoming vehicles driving in the centre of the pavement. Most of Kos can be visited by normal rental car, though a few remote beaches are best approached by jeep. Adjacent islands present no special road problems.

Signage, and advance notice for turnings, is acceptable at best. Since many place-names have been transliterated idiosyncratically into Roman lettering and signposted at different times, you may find the same village name or attraction written different ways, only one

Are we on the right road for...? **Páma kalá giá...?**
Full tank, please **Óso pári, parakaló**
Super/lead-free/diesel **soúper/amólyvdis/dízel**
Check the oil/tires/battery **Na elénxete ta ládia/ta lástiha/ ti bataría**
My car has broken down **To amáxi mou éhi páthi vlávi**
There's been an accident **Égine éna atýhima**

rendition agreeing with your map. Similarly, distances may yo-yo up and down as signs do not keep pace with road-straightening works.

Brown signs with yellow lettering indicate an archaeological site or other monument – not all of them are must-sees.

Rules and regulations. Traffic drives on the right and passes on the left, yielding to vehicles from the right except at roundabouts where one supposedly yields to the left (often countermanded by confusing stop-or-yield-sign schemes). Speed limits on open roads are 90km/h (55mph) and in towns 50km/h (30mph) unless otherwise stated, although most locals ignore these. Speed-limit and distance signs are in kilometres.

Seat-belt use is compulsory (€350 fine for non-use), as are helmets when riding any two-wheeler (identical fine for non-compliance). Drink-driving laws are strict – expect fines of €400–700 and licence loss if caught – and breathalyser checkpoints proliferate on weekend nights. All cars must carry a reflective warning triangle, a fire extinguisher and a first-aid kit; some rental companies skimp on these. Fines must be paid within ten calendar days at a post office, with proof of payment taken to the designated police station, where your licence may be held to ransom meanwhile.

Kos Town and Póthia are full of one-way systems, which many scooter-riders (and some car-drivers) disregard. Many – especially young conscripts driving army trucks – are inexperienced and may not be properly insured. Give them a wide berth. Pedestrians often step out into the roadway without looking.

Parking space is tightly controlled and hard to find in the business districts of both Kos Town and Póthia. Rather than try to decipher posted rules or find tickets, just park free in the residential districts and walk into the centre. Parking along Kos harbour quay is banned except along one wall of the castle. In Skála Pátmos, it is prudent to use the free public car park behind Theológos beach.

Breakdowns and accidents. If you have an accident or breakdown, put a red warning triangle some distance behind you to warn on-

coming traffic, then ring your rental office. They will probably come out to you themselves rather than summoning one of the emergency roadside services.

If an accident involves another vehicle, do not admit fault or move either car until the police come out and prepare a report; a copy will be given to you to present to the rental agency. It is an offence to leave the scene of an accident, or move either vehicle before this has been done.

Road signs. Most road signs are the standard pictographs used throughout Europe but you may also see some of these written signs:

Detour **ΠΑΡΑΚΑΜΨΗ/Parákampsi**
Parking **ΠΑΡΚΙΓΚ/Párking**
Forbidden **ΑΠΑΓΟΡΕΥΕΤΑΙ/apagorévete**
Be careful **ΠΡΟΣΟΧΗ/Prosohí**
Stop **ΣΤΑΜΑΤΑ/Stamáta**
For pedestrians **ΓΙΑ ΠΕΖΟΥΣ/Gia pezoús**
Danger **ΚΙΝΔΥΝΟΣ/Kíndynos**
No entry **ΑΠΑΓΟΡΕΥΕΤΑΙ Η ΕΙΣΟΔΟΣ/Apagorévete i éxodos**

E

ELECTRICITY

Electrical current is 220–240 volts/50 cycles. Plugs and outlets are of Continental two-prong type C (narrow pins) or F (fat pins). Adaptor plugs are available, but try to buy one before you leave home. UK-to-Continental are slightly harder to find in Greece than North-American-to-Continental.

An adapter **énas prosarmostís**

EMBASSIES AND CONSULATES

There are no consulates of any English-speaking country on the islands in this guide. All national embassies are located in Athens.

Australian Embassy & Consulate: Hatzigiánni Méxi 5, Level 2, 115 28 Ambelókipi; tel: 21087 04000, https://greece.embassy.gov.au

British Embassy & Consulate: Ploutárhou 1, 106 75 Athens; tel: 21072 72600, www.gov.uk/world/organisations/british-embassy-athens

Canadian Embassy: Ethnikís Andistáseos 48, 152 31 Halándri; tel: 21072 73400, www.international.gc.ca/world-monde/greece-grece/

Irish Embassy: Vassiléos Konstandínou 7, 106 74 Athens; tel: 21072 32771, www.dfa.ie/irish-embassy/greece/.

South African Embassy & Consulate: Kifissías 60, 151 25 Maroússi; tel 21061 06645.

US Embassy & Consulate: Vassilísis Sofías 91, 115 21 Athens; tel: 21072 12951, https://gr.usembassy.gov

EMERGENCIES

The following emergency numbers are valid on the islands.

Police: 100

Ambulance: 166

Fire: 199

Coast guard: 108

Forest fire reporting: 191

G

GETTING THERE

By air. Direct scheduled services from Britain, between March and October, include easyJet (www.easyjet.com) from Gatwick and Glasgow, and Jet2 (www.jet2.com) from Birmingham, East Midlands, Edinburgh, Glasgow, Leeds/Bradford, London Stansted and Manchester. British Airways (www.britishairways.com) arrives from Heathrow 2–3 days weekly from early May to late September.

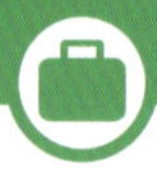

From North America, you must reach Athens first and then continue for another 50min on either Olympic (www.olympicair.com) or Sky Express (www.skyexpress.gr). Flights fill quickly in summer – even business class sells out – and must be booked well in advance. If you land in Thessaloníki, Astra (www.astra-airlines.gr) provides a very good service to Kos.

From the UK, Aegean (https://en.aegeanair.com) and BA provide scheduled full-service flights to Athens. Direct flights from North America to Athens are provided only by Delta Airlines (www.delta.com) from JFK, Emirates (www.emirates.com) or United (www.united.com) from Newark, and seasonally from Chicago and Philadelphia by American Airlines.

From Australia and New Zealand there are only indirect flights; the most reliable providers are Etihad Airways (www.etihadairways.com), Qatar Airways (www.qatarairways.com) and Emirates (www.emirates.com).

By boat. Kos is connected to Piraeus, Athens' main port, by three to six weekly car and passenger ferries; frequency is highest during summer. Boats can be crowded at peak times – buy tickets for cars or a cabin as far in advance as possible. A good online resource for checking schedules is www.gtp.gr.

Currently just one company, Blue Star (www.bluestarferries.gr), serves this route. Journey time varies: 9.5 hours with four intervening stops, 12 hours with five stops. There are also links with many other Dodecanese on the catamarans *Dodekanisos Pride* and *Dodekanisos Express* (www.12ne.gr/el/). Kálymnos and the westerly Kos port of Mastihári are linked two or three times daily by ro-ro ferry.

GUIDES AND TOURS

On nearby Rhodes, Triton Holidays (Plastíra 9, Rhodes Town; tel: 22410 21690; www.tritondmc.gr) can arrange discounted quality accommodation on Nísyros, Kálymnos, Léros and Pátmos, plus all necessary transfers between islands.

H

HEALTH AND MEDICAL CARE

Emergency treatment is given free at state hospital casualty wards (ask for the *tmíma epigóndon peristatikón*) to EU residents, who must carry a European Health Insurance Card, obtainable until Brexit in the UK online at www.ehic.org.uk. They routinely treat 'road rash' from scooter accidents and set broken bones.

Kos' state hospital is in town on Venizélou, just south of the ancient agora. But public health provision is in free-fall across Greece, with dire shortages of appointment slots, medicines and material, so if you are privately insured, go instead directly opposite to Kos Medicare at no. 5 (tel: 22420 23330, www.kosmedicare.gr), with their own ambulance which can be summoned 24hr. There are also state hospitals on Kálymnos and Léros, but only rural clinics on Nísyros and Pátmos.

If you have a minor problem, look for a pharmacy *(farmakío)*, identified by a green cross; most pharmacists speak some English. Pharmacies open Mon–Fri 8am–2pm; outside of these hours only duty pharmacies operate. A roster of the day's after-hours pharmacies should be posted on the door of each pharmacy.

Mosquitoes and gnats are a nuisance all season. Topical repellent is useful from dusk onwards; accommodation proprietors often provide insecticide tablets vaporised by a plug-in device. Infected bites, not an uncommon event, need medical attention. Spiny sea urchins on submerged rocks can injure inattentive swimmers. Avoidance is the best tactic, but failing that, dig out the spine tips with a sterilised sewing needle and olive oil.

The Greek sun is strong; limit your exposure time, apply sunblock (SPF 30+) regularly and use a hat. Children's skin should be especially well protected.

Kos tap water is safe to drink, and the central mountain has two popular, potable springs; Póthia (Kálymnos) has street-corner, purified-water machines to fill bottles, some free, some coin-op; there is

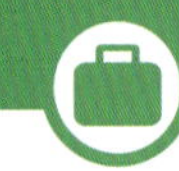

also a popular, free fountain on the road near Horió in Potamí district. Otherwise, bottled water is universally available. Always carry water to the beach or when sightseeing to prevent dehydration.

L

LANGUAGE

The sounds of the Greek language do not always correspond to exact equivalents in English, and some letters of the Greek alphabet do not have a precise match in the Roman alphabet. This explains inconsistent spellings on road signs – for example, *ágios* may be spelled *ághios* and *áyios* in the Roman alphabet, although it is always pronounced the same. Accentuation is also essential when pronouncing Greek. Throughout this book we have accented vowels within each word to show which syllable to stress, except for one-syllable words.

People working anywhere near the tourist industry will have a basic English vocabulary, and many speak English very well.

The table below lists the 24 letters of the Greek alphabet in their upper- and lower-case forms, followed by the closest individual or combined letters to which they correspond in English.

LGBTQ TRAVELLERS

Greece has historically been a very conservative country where tradi-

A	**a**	a	as in ***fa****ther*
B	**ß**	v	as in veto
Γ	**γ**	g	as in ***go*** (except before *i* and *e* sounds, when it's like the *y* in ***yes***)
D	**d**	d	sounds like *th* in ***th****en*
E	**e**	e	as in ***get***

Ζ	ζ	z	same as in English
Η	η	i	as in *ski*
Φ	θ	th	as in ***th**in*
Ι	ι	i	as in *ski*
Κ	κ	k	same as in English
Λ	λ	l	same as in English
Μ	μ	m	same as in English
Ν	ν	n	same as in English
Ξ	ξ	x	as in *bo**x***
Ο	ο	o	as in *road*
Π	π	p	same as in English
Ρ	ρ	r	same as in English
Σ	σ,ς	s	as in *ki**ss***, except like *z* before *m* or *g* sounds
Τ	τ	t	same as in English
Υ	υ	y	as in *countr**y***
Φ	φ	f	same as in English
Χ	χ	h	rough, as in Scottish *lo**ch***
Ψ	ψ	ps	as in *tipsy*
Ω	ω	o	as in *long*
ΑΙ	αι	e	as in *hay*
ΑΥ	αυ	av	as in *avant-garde*
ΕΙ	ει	i	as in *ski*
ΕΥ	ευ	ev	as in *ever*
ΟΙ	οι	i	as in *ski*
ΟΥ	ου	ou	as in *soup*
ΓΓ	γγ	ng	as in *longer*
ΓΚ	γκ	g	as in *gone*
ΓΞ	γξ	nx	as in *anxious*
ΜΠ	μπ	b or mb	as in *beg* or *compass*
MS	ντ	d or nd	as in *dog* or *under*

tional family relationships are a core value. However, the wide variety of international tourists arriving on Kos means that LGBTQ visitors are taken in stride. That said, there are no exclusively, or predominantly, gay clubs or beaches (unlike on islands like Mykonos).

M

MAPS

You'll find free advertiser maps at hotels, Kos airport and car-rental offices, adequate for Kos Town only. The sole maps of Kos and the surrounding islands worth buying are produced by Terrain (www.terrainmaps.gr; all islands in this guide at scales 1:20,000–1:45,000) or Anavasi (www.anavasi.gr; Kos 1:65,000 and Pátmos 1:20,000). They are only sporadically available on the islands concerned, so ideally obtain them in advance.

MEDIA

Newspapers and Magazines. You will be able to buy all major European newspapers at resort newsagents. Greece Is prints an excellent free magazine, with a theoretically annual Kos/Nisyros special issue – snag copies wherever you see them.

Television. Most hotels of three stars and above have a range of satellite channels, including CNN and BBC World. The Greek state channel ET1 often has foreign films in the original language after 10pm.

MONEY

Currency. Greece uses the euro (abbreviated €), with notes of 5, 10, 20, 50, 100, and 200 euros; each euro comprises 100 cents (leptá) and coins have denominations of 1, 2, 5, 10, 20 and 50 cents, plus 1 and 2 euros. Avoid accepting 100- or 200-euro notes as nobody will have change.

Currency exchange. Banks exchange foreign notes, but commissions are comparable to ATMs (see below) and queues long, so preferably obtain cash from an ATM. Exchange rates, the same everywhere, are usually posted on a digital noticeboard inside the bank or in the window.

Exchange controls in force between 2015 and 2019 mean that few if any travel agents still change foreign notes.

Travellers cheques. Not recommended – expect severe delays or outright refusals in banks.

ATMs. All resort areas, and larger inland settlements, have at least one ATM, accepting most debit or credit cards. Despite commissions levied by your home bank, this is the quickest, most convenient way to get cash. If given a choice, always take euros at your own bank's exchange rate – do not let the machine do this, you will lose about 3 percent more.

Credit/debit cards. Card use is now heavily encouraged by the authorities in order to cut down the black economy. Quite unlikely-looking establishments have card apparati, but when phone links go down (not unknown) you will still have to stump up the cash. Bank charges to merchants are high, so don't annoy by carding a €5 purchase!

I want to change some pounds/dollars **Thélo na alláxo merikés líres/meriká dollária**
How much commission do you charge? **Póso promýthia hreónete?**
Do you have a card machine? **Éhete mihánima POS (Point of Sale)?**

O

OPENING TIMES

Opening hours differ for official bodies and private businesses. They also vary significantly between high and low season. To be sure of service or admission, appear between 9am and 1pm, Tues–Fri.

State museums work Wed–Mon, with Tue shut or short hours; private or municipal ones vary. Most archaeological sites are open continuously until 8pm during summer but close much earlier in winter.

Last admissions are 20–30 minutes before the official closing time; we cite the latter in this guide.

Banks operate Mon–Fri 8am–2pm. Smaller shops work Mon–Sat 9am–2.30pm, plus Tue, Thu and Fri 5.30pm–8.30pm (6–9pm in midsummer); supermarkets are open year-round 8am–9pm Mon–Fri, 8am–8pm Sat. A bare few also open 11am–4pm on Sunday. In peak season tourist-orientated shops stay open daily until late. Filling stations work daily 8am–9pm in summer (closing 8pm otherwise); many close altogether on Sunday.

P

POLICE

Ordinary police, including traffic police *(trohéa)*, wear a two-tone blue uniform. The tourist police is a special branch dealing with tourist problems and complaints. They speak English and wear dark grey uniforms.

Emergency: tel: 100

Non-emergency (Kos Town): tel: 22420 22222

Tourist police: Aktí Miaoúli 2, Kos Town, tel: 22420 26666

Where's the nearest police station? **Pou íne to kondinótero astynomikó tmíma?**

POST OFFICES

Post offices (Mon–Fri 7.30am–2pm) are indicated by a yellow-and-blue stylised Hermes head and the initials ELTA (ΕΛΤΑ in Greek). The Kos Town and Póthia (Kálymnos) post offices are marked on our maps. Allow 4–7 days delivery time for postcards to Europe, 9–14 days for the rest of the world.

PUBLIC HOLIDAYS

Official holidays, when everything will be shut, are as follows:

1 January New Year's Day *(Protohroniá)*

6 January Epiphany *(Ta Agía Theofánia)*

25 March Greek Independence Day/Annunciation *(Evangelismós)*

1 May May Day *(Protomagiá)*

15 August Dormition of the Panagía *(Kímisis tis Theotókou)*

28 October 'No' or *'Ohi'* Day

25 December Christmas Day *(Hristoúgenna)*

26 December *Sýnaxis tis Panagías* (Gathering of the Virgin's Entourage)

Movable official holidays include the first day of Lent (Clean Monday; 48 days before Easter Sunday), Good Friday, Easter Monday and Pentecost (Whit Monday, *tou Agíou Pnévmatos*; 50 days after Easter Sunday).

R

RELIGION

Most islanders belong to the Greek Orthodox Church, though there is a significant Muslim minority on Kos, with two of the five mosques used regularly. Mass schedules are posted outside the one Roman Catholic church, Ámnós tou Theoú, southwest of Kos Town. Congregations of evangelicals and Jehovah's Witnesses exist.

T

TELEPHONES

The international code for Greece is 30. Land-line numbers have 10 digits; the first five digits, beginning with 2, tell you which island or town the phone is in. Greek mobile numbers begin with 69 and also have 10 digits.

Card-operated telephone booths are noisy and almost extinct. Rather than use OTE (the Greek telecoms entity) calling cards, most people buy prepaid discount calling cards with free access numbers prefixed 807 (reachable from any call box or private phone) and a 12-digit PIN.

Rates are similar to using Skype to a land line. Hotels levy ruinous surcharges for ordinary direct-dial calls; usually, switchboard circuitry permits use of discount cards from room phones.

Mobile users can roam on any of three local networks, and with recent abolition of roaming charges within the EU, both making and receiving calls, or texting, is reckoned under the terms of your home plan. If the UK Brexits without a deal, this may cease to be true. Do not let non-EU Turkish mobile networks across the narrow straits 'grab' your number; you will have an unpleasant surprise come the next bill. Only if holidaying for more than a week might you consider buying a Greek SIM. It (and the phone) must be registered at purchase, but the number remains valid for some time after your outgoing credit expires – probably until your next trip to Greece.

TIME ZONES

Greece is two hours ahead of Greenwich Mean Time and, until its proposed 2021 abolition, also observes European Daylight Saving Time – moving the clocks one hour forward at 3am on the last Sunday in March, one hour back at 3am on the last Sunday in October.

New York	London	Jo'burg	**Kos**	Sydney	Auckland
5am	10am	11am	**noon**	7pm	9pm

TIPPING

Service is included in restaurant and bar bills, but it is customary to leave 10 percent of the bill on the table for wait-staff.

Taxi drivers are not tipped per se except at Easter week, but collect €0.43 extra per bag in the boot, plus surcharges for entering Kos airport (€2.83) or any harbour (€1.18).

Hotel chambermaids should be tipped around €1 per day. Bellhops get up to €2, depending on quantity and weight of luggage.

TOILETS

Public toilets are scarce. All museums and cafés have decent facilities, but some establishments post signs restricting access to customers. Older waste pipes in Greece are narrow and easily clogged. Never put toilet paper or sanitary products into the bowl – always use the bin provided.

TOURIST INFORMATION

Kos Town's tourist office (theoretically 9am–2pm Mon–Fri, no phone) is indicated on our map but is pretty useless – don't waste your time. The Kálymnos municipal tourist office is shown on the Póthia map (Mon–Fri 8am–3pm; tel: 22430 50596 or 22430 29299).

For tourist information before you travel to Greece, contact one of the following overseas offices of the Greek National Tourism Organisation (www.visitgreece.gr):

UK and Ireland: Portland House, 5th Floor East, 4 Great Portland Street, London W1W 8QJ tel: (020) 7495 9300.

US: 800 3rd Avenue, Street, New York, NY 10022; tel: (212) 421 5777.

TRANSPORT

Bus. Kos buses are divided into two networks: KTEL, for long-distance services (schedules at www.ktel-kos.gr, station tel: 22420 22292) to Ziá, Tingáki, Marmári, Pylí, Mastihári, Kardámena and Kéfalos, and DEAS urban buses (tel: 22420 26276) running various routes out to Psalídi, Bros Thermá, Plátáni and the ancient Asklipion. Both the KTEL station and urban-bus terminal are marked on our town map.

Kálymnos has a reasonable bus service based in Póthia, while Pátmos has a decent one with a hub in Skála. Nísyros has a basic network.

Taxis. Kos is well equipped with grey taxis. Prices to all destinations are regulated and posted outside the arrivals terminal at the airport. Minimum fare is €3.72; the basic charge structure also appears on a laminated sheet mounted on the dashboard. Meters must be set (to €1.29) at the start of each journey; '1' indicates regular fare, '2' indicates double tariff between midnight and 5am, and/or outside urban

areas. Summoning a taxi by phone incurs an extra appointment charge. At Póthia, the main taxi rank is inland at Platía Kýprou (though they meet arriving seacraft). On Léros they meet arriving craft at Lakkí and Agía Marína ports; count on €13 for a transit from Lakkí to Krithóni.

Ferries and catamarans. Large ferries tend to dock at Kos between dusk and dawn headed either direction. Scarcely more expensive, and with far more user-friendly schedules, are the local catamarans *Dodekanisos Express* and *Dodekanisos Pride*, which serve all the islands in this book during daylight hours. On most islands ferries and catamarans share the same port, though on Léros ferries anchor only at Lákki, whilst catamarans call at Agía Marína except when adverse weather diverts them to Lakkí.

Caiques/*kaïkia*/water taxis. On a few routes, passenger-only speedboats or traditional caiques offer regular services: Mastihári–Póthia, Mastihári–Psérimos, Kardámena–Nísyros, Myrtiés (Kálymnos)–Pandéli (Léros), Pátmos to surrounding islets. They can be fun, but definitely not on days with heavy seas.

V

VISAS AND ENTRY REQUIREMENTS

European Union (EU) citizens may enter Greece for an unlimited length of time with a valid passport or national identity card. Nationals of the US, Canada, Australia and New Zealand can stay for 90 cumulative days within any 180-day period upon production of a valid passport; no advance visas are needed. South Africans require a Schengen Visa, applied for in advance at a Greek embassy or consulate. Arrangements for British nationals in the event of a 'hard' Brexit are uncertain at time of writing; visas and enforcement of Schengen rules as above are both mooted.

Foreigners can import or export up to €10,000 or equivalent, provided that large sums of cash are declared upon arrival.

There are no limits on duty-paid goods imported from other EU states. Arriving from a non-EU country (eg Turkey), allowances for importing duty-free goods are 200 cigarettes or 50 cigars or 250g of tobacco; 1 litre of spirits, 2 litres fortified wine or 4 litres of wine; 250ml of cologne or 50ml of perfume.

W

WEBSITES AND INTERNET ACCESS

Here are a few genuinely useful websites pertaining to Kos and neighbouring islands:

www.greece-is.com Sophisticated feature magazine; click on the Dodecanese sub-page.

www.kos.gr Official municipal website; has a calendar of events.

www.kalymnos-isl.gr Excellent municipal site, with good pages on diving and climbing.

www.leros.gr Fairly useful municipal site with reasonably literate English version.

www.nisyros.gr Decent municipal website, with an events calendar kept current.

www.patmosweb.gr, www.patmos-island.com Two competing websites for this island, though neither have been updated for some years now.

http://odysseus.culture.gr Official website of the Greek Ministry of Culture, covering all state-run museums, castles, and archaeological sites.

www.meteo.gr Semi-official weather website, with six-hourly reports from all islands in this guide.

www.windguru.cz Aimed at windsurfers, with reporting stations at Marmári, Psalídi, Kálymnos, Léros and Pátmos.

www.capnbarefoot.info/start Guide to the naturist beaches of the Greek islands, which often happen to be the best ones.

All hotels have Wi-fi zones (usually free in common areas, often charged for in rooms). Most bars, tavernas or cafés advertise free Wi-fi access (code protected) for patrons.

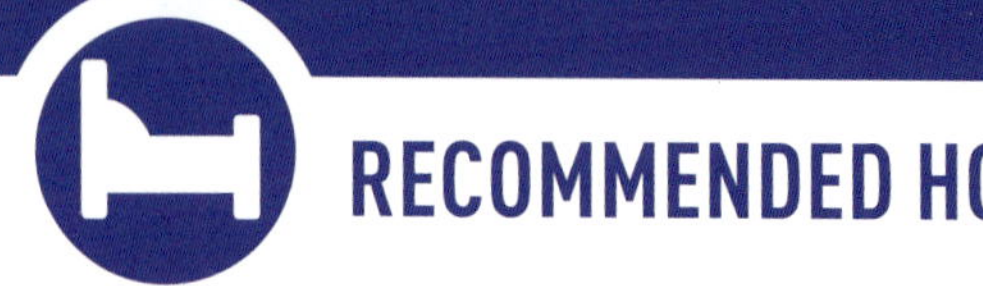

RECOMMENDED HOTELS

The following recommendations for all budgets cover Kos itself and all the excursion-island destinations. Most resort hotels have at least half-a-dozen room and suite categories to choose from. Air conditioning and LCD TVs are ubiquitous, free Wi-fi nearly so.

Unless stated otherwise, establishments operate April/May–October. Quoted rates include taxes and service, bed-and-breakfast basis unless half board. Minimum stays often apply in high season.

The following price categories are for a double room or suite per night in high season. Low season rates can be half these.

€€€€€	**over 350 euros**
€€€€	**200–350 euros**
€€€	**130–200 euros**
€€	**80–130 euros**
€	**under 80 euros**

KOS TOWN

Afendoulis € *Evrypýlou 1, tel: 22420 25321,* www.afendoulishotel.com. Family-run travellers' hotel with cheerful terracotta-tiled rooms, mostly balconied, with big closets, fridges and updated bathrooms. The best rooms face west, with oblique views of sea and pines. The proprietors can organise port transfers and breakfasts (extra), served out front, are worth ordering. Popular so booking advisable. Open late Mar–early Nov.

Albergo Gelsomino €€€€–€€€€€ *Vasiléos Georgíou 1, tel: 22420 20200,* www.gelsominohotel.com. Rescued from dilapidation in 2018, this iconic Italian-built hotel now lives again. Four grades of suites (total 9, mostly junior) over two floors evoke their 1928 origins without being fusty or skimping on creature comforts. The popular executive loft suite has two separate spaces and a balcony off of the bathroom with its slipper bath-tub, two sinks and a rain shower. Won't stay? Stop in for a drink, or a midday snack (until 6pm, budget €30 for two courses and beer) and even

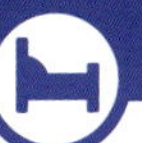

a swim from the stretch of amenitied beach. Allow €45 for a three-course evening meal at the classiest hotel restaurant in town. Open all year.

Kos Aktis Art €€€ *Vasiléos Georgíou 7, tel: 22420 47200,* www.kosaktis.gr. This listed Bauhaus hotel got a designer makeover in 2005, and now always requires booking. Standard doubles and suites have unimpeded sea views and ample balconies, but are showing their age and need another update. Bathrooms are large and bright with shower-baths. Common areas comprise a sunny gym, small beach with decking, and popular waterside restaurant/bar *H2O*, also the venue for good breakfasts. Open all year.

Kos Hotel €€€ *Harmýlou 2, corner Vasiléos Georgíou, tel: 22420 47100,* www.koshotel.gr. Kos Aktis Art's sister property has an apartment (two-room) format, good for families, with well-equipped kitchens. Sea-facing rooms are traffic-noisy from 7am onwards; unlike the inward-facing units. Common facilities include a big pool, competitively-priced spa and huge gym. Open all year.

Sonia Hotel €€ *Irodótou 9, entrance corner of Omírou, tel: 22420 28798,* www.hotelsonia.gr. Former backpacker pension renovated in 2018–19 to modern boutique-hotel standard. Room sizes (including family quads), and balcony views, vary considerably. Only 14 units, so booking advised. Buffet breakfast served indoors or in the rear patio. Sonia's son Afendoulis speaks English. Open early Mar–20 Nov.

AROUND THE ISLAND

Aqua Blu €€€€€ *Near lighthouse, Lámbi, tel: 22420 22440,* www.aquabluhotel.gr. This stunning adults-only hotel is the only Kos member of Small Luxury Hotels. A 'loft' suite with brown-and-green palette, parquet flooring and combo rain shower-Jacuzzi enjoys views to Turkey and Psérimos. The irregularly shaped main pool laps decking and day-beds, or there's a patch of beach with sunbeds. Spa treatments are keenly priced, with couples' treatment rooms; naturally lit gym. In-house gourmet restaurant Cuvée (not Mon pm) offers tasting menus, Mediterranean à la carte and creative dessert choices. Closed for renovations at the time of writing, scheduled to reopen in April 2020.

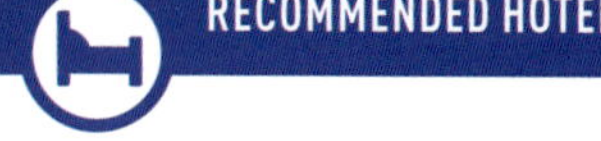

Astir Odysseus €€€€–€€€€€ *Coast road 3km east of central plaza, Tingáki, tel: 22420 49900,* www.astirodysseuskos.gr. Family-friendly spa resort; try for units near the beach as otherwise it's a long way down to the narrow strip of sand. Over 300 rooms and suites mostly look onto gardens. There are five freshwater adult pools, two kids' pools and two tennis courts. Rooms range from standard doubles to 'Presidential Maisonettes' with private pool.

Diamond Deluxe €€€€–€€€€€ *Néa Alikarnasós coast road, end of bike path, Lámbi; tel: 22420 48835,* www.diamondhotel.gr. Stylish, adults-only 'wellness and business' hotel, with two pools, water features, and bar. 'Swim up' doubles open directly onto the bigger pool, while seven suites have private ones. Superior doubles sport round beds, smart devices for room service orders, and free international calls. Marble-clad bathrooms have rain showers and baths. Basement spa, gym, and small but deep indoor pool.

Esperia €€–€€€ *Main access road, Marmári, tel: 22420 42010,* www.hotelesperiakos.gr. One of the few non-all-inclusive Marmári hotels. Low-rise bungalows ring a large, wind-protected pool and tennis court, with family quads in the rear wing. Medium-sized doubles are brightly-furnished and have large balconies overlooking the gardens and pool.

Fenareti € *Mastihári, tel: 22420 59002, or 6948 882644;* http://fenareti.kosweb.com. Hillside hotel in a relaxed coastal area overlooking the beach. There are mosaic-floored studio-units with private bathrooms, outdoor seating areas, and kitchenettes. Deals usually offered.

Grecotel Kos Imperial Thalasso €€€€–€€€€€ *Psalídi, tel: 22420 58000,* www.kosimperial.com. Well-designed luxury spread where electric carts shuttle guests and luggage through lush vegetation to the more remote bungalows (standard rooms in the main wing). All units are pleasantly old-fashioned. Grecotel's beach is poor, but there are three adult pools (all salt-water, all unheated) and one has a 'lazy river' and 'tropical waterfall'. In-house food is good and varied; choose either half board or Premium Plus à la carte option. The Elixir Spa has thalassotherapy and a fresh-water pool.

Irina Beach €–€€ *2km (1.2 miles) east of shore junction, Tingáki, tel: 22420 69850,* www.irinabeachhotel.com. Various well-kept options, from

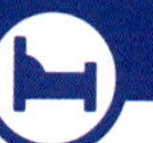

studios to family apartments. Upstairs double suites have a sofa to sleep a third, ample closet space, sea-views, and bathrooms with rain showers. The large, garden pool is ideal and there is a good beach (better than the hotel beach, no facilities) 200m/yards east.

Michelangelo Resort & Spa €€€€–€€€€€ *Ágios Fokás, tel: 22420 45810,* www.michelangelo.gr. Common areas have the 'wow' factor, though the grounds (with token landscaping) are a little stark. The signature spa has all usual treatments and goodies, but feels dark. Several categories of rooms or suites in tiered hillside wings – all scheduled for a 2020 refit – are airy, most with at least partial views across to Turkey's Knidos Peninsula. Two full-service restaurants provide enough variety over a long stay; half-board is a popular option. An infinity pool with swim-up bar is not clichéd in its setting, and long enough (set to get longer in 2020) for serious swimming; there's a sand-and-shingle beach below.

Olympia Mare €€–€€€ *1km (0.6 miles) southwest of town, beach side of road, Kardámena, tel: 22420 91711,* www.olympiamare.com. There are posher, all-inclusive establishments nearby, but none with Olympia Mare's position: twenty steps across the lawn to the sea. 1980s-built apartments –though both bathrooms and living areas have been updated – sleep a family of four; most have sea-view verandas.

Palazzo del Mare €€€€€ *Marmári, tel: 22420 54565,* www.palazzodelmare.gr. Sumptuous, adults-only resort, where the main pool extends 400m/yards towards the beach. All ground-floor rooms have direct access to the main pool and executive and presidential suites private pools. Three bars, two restaurants and plentiful sports facilities, including tennis courts, a football field and beach volleyball. Normally booked as a TUI Sensimar package, or on the number above. The hotel is hard to find – leave the main highway at Limnára turning, then keep left at every junction.

NÍSYROS

Porfyris € *Mandráki centre, tel: 22420 31376,* www.porfyrishotel.gr. The most comfortable conventional hotel here. Balconies overlook either Kámbos and the sea, hillside or the large pool. A small shad-

ed terrace fits 12 for yoga practice; can get booked up by conventions, so book early.

Romantzo € *Mandráki port, tel: 22420 31340,* www.nisyros-romantzo.gr. The best budget choice here: updated basalt-clad rooms and studios, some with bay views – though there's a huge communal terrace on the top floor. Surprisingly good breakfast. Minimal road noise; ample parking.

Ta Liotridia €€€ *shore lane near the windmill, Mandráki, tel: 22420 31580,* www.nisyros-taliotridia.com. Two suites in a restored olive mill – one of the few such projects here – for up to four people; worth the price for the terraces and volcanic-stone-and-wood decor. Lively bar downstairs.

KÁLYMNOS

Acroyali € *Myrtiés, below lower road,* tel: 6938 *913210 or 22430 47521,* www.acroyali.gr. Six exceptionally tasteful, quiet sea-view apartments, with colour splashes against marble flooring, each sleeping four; you're five steps from the best bit of Myrtiés beach. Advance booking mandatory.

Masouri Blu €€–€€€ *bottom of steps down from main plaza, Masoúri, tel 22430 47451,* www.masouriblu.gr. 'Step into the Blue' is the motto of this friendly boutique hotel. Pastel-hued room furnishings and tiling in bathrooms, some with rain showers. Sea-side units have knockout views; some family rooms. Breakfast by the water; sunbeds on the best patch of local beach. Popular with wedding parties, given its ample common areas. Open late Apr–early Nov.

Villa Melina €–€€ *Evangelístria district, Póthia, tel: 22430 22682,* www.villa-melina.com. Póthia's top choice: either rooms in a late 19th-century sponge magnate's mansion, or modern studios done up in pale green and ochre and family apartments around the fresh-water pool and gardens. Good buffet breakfasts served on the patio; a warm welcome from owners Andonis and Themelina. Open all year.

TÉLENDOS

Porto Potha €–€ *north edge of settlement, tel: 22430 47321,* www.telendoshotel.gr. This modern hotel offers great views to Kálymnos, standard doubles, plus studios in a separate wing, including two 'deluxe' suites for four people. There's a large pool, a good patch of tamarisk-shaded beach and friendly managing family.

PSÉRIMOS

Psérimos Village €€€–€€€€ *Avlákia tel: 22430 53017,* http://halikoshotels.com/hhotelpserimosvillas. Beautifully-designed hotel with 18 'cottages' ranging from single-space studios to open-plan mezzanine bedrooms, and large multi-room houses with fully-equipped kitchens accommodating up to six people. All have shaded front patios; the best sea views are from two upstairs studios. On-site pool, and the beach is just 100m away, with umbrellas and sunbeds provided.

LÉROS

Archontiko Angelou €€–€€€ *signposted well inland, Álinda, tel: 22470 22749,* www.hotel-angelou-leros.com. Atmospheric converted 1895 mansion amidst orchards, akin to a French country hotel. The eight rooms (not all a/c), two of which are suites, have balconies, mini bars, and antique furnishings, but no TVs. The garden bar has tables under jacarandas lining the original carriage loop-drive. Vegan/gluten-free breakfasts are charged separately. Open June–Sept guaranteed, by request otherwise.

Crithoni's Paradise €€–€€€ *Krithóni, inland, tel: 22470 25120,* www.crithonisparadisehotel.gr. Léros's only mega-resort, a low-rise hillside complex of four wings with a smallish pool, disabled access and large, well-appointed rooms – though subject (like everywhere locally) to mosquito invasion. Decent buffet breakfast; affordable poolside drinks; handy on-site car/scooter rental. Open all year.

Nefeli Hotel €–€€€ *Krithóni, tel: 22470 24611,* www.nefelihotels-leros.com. Set amidst bougainvillea, lantana, rosemary, fig trees and patches

of lawn stand bungalow studios, apartments and suites, many with sea view. All units feature stone flooring and light-blue and white soft furnishings. A quality breakfast features cake-of-the-day; the in-house bar has snacks and good music. There's no pool, but nearby is Krithóni cove, fine for a quick swim. Open all year; winter rentals by the month.

Tony's Beach € *Vromólithos beach, tel: 6940 873532,* www.tonysbeach.com. Spacious two-room units designed for four people, with big terraces overlooking a small pool or the sea. Designer bathrooms and rudimentary kitchenettes. Breakfast is €8 extra. Disabled access and ample parking; free beach sunbeds.

PÁTMOS

Blue Bay €€ *Last building in town going east, Konsoláto district, Skála, tel: 22470 31165,* www.bluebaypatmos.gr. Blue Bay hasn't the midnight ferry and 4am fishing-boat noise that blights most Konsoláto hotels. Rooms (and two suites), attractively-furnished, have fridges and balconies (most with bay-and-islet view), if basic bathrooms. Decent breakfasts, and an appealing bar. Open Easter to early Nov.

Eirini Luxury Hotel Villas €€€€–€€€€€ *5km (3 miles) southeast of Skála, just above Loukákia cove tel: 22470 33034,* www.eirinivillas.gr. Stunning new-build, family-friendly complex with seven two-storey villas, with one or two bedrooms. Kitchens with proper ovens are designed for serious cooking; larger villas have two bathrooms and either a Jacuzzi or private swimming pool. The sitting rooms have entertainment centres and open fireplaces. A large communal pool laps the fine-dining Pleiades Restaurant, where breakfast (included) is also served.

Studios Mathios €–€€€ *Sápsila Cove, tel: 22470 32583,* www.mathiosapartments.gr. With a vehicle, these bucolically-set superior studios (with renovated bathrooms) and apartments make an idyllic base for exploring Patmos, with their creative furnishing, extensive gardens and welcoming hosts Theologos and Giakoumina. New since 2019 is an ancestral two-bedroom stone cottage, whose beams were salvaged from wartime shipwrecks; the kitchen preserves an original bread-oven.

DICTIONARY

ENGLISH–GREEK

adj adjective **adv** adverb **BE** British English **n** noun **prep** preposition **v** verb

A

access *n* πρόσβαση *prohz•vah•see*
accessory αξεσουάρ *ah•kseh•soo•ahr*
accident ατύχημα *ah•tee•khee•mah*
accompany συνοδεύω *see•noh•THeh•voh*
account *n* λογαριασμός *loh•ghahr•yahz•mohs*
adaptor προσαρμοστής *proh•sahr•moh•stees*
address *n* διεύθυνση *THee•ehf•theen•see*
admission είσοδος *ee•soh•Thohs*
adult ενήλικας *eh•nee•lee•kahs*
advance προκαταβολή *proh•kah•tah•voh•lee*
after μετά *meh•tah*
afternoon απόγευμα *ah•poh•yehv•mah*
after-sun lotion λοσιόν μετά την ηλιοθεραπεία *loh•siohn meh•tah teen ee•lioh•theh•rah•pee•ah*
age *n* ηλικία *ee•lee•kee•ah*
agree συμφωνώ *seem•foh•noh*
air conditioning κλιματισμός *klee•mah•teez•mohs*
air pump *n* αντλία αέρος *ahn•dlee•ah ah•eh•rohs*
airline αεροπορική εταιρία *ah•eh•roh•poh•ree•kee eh•the•ree•ah*
airmail αεροπορικώς *ah•eh•roh•poh•ree•kohs*
airport αεροδρόμιο *ah•eh•roh•THroh•mee•oh*
aisle seat διάδρομος *THee•ah•Throh•mohs*
allergic αλλεργικός *ahl•ehr•yee•kohs*
allergy αλλεργία *ah•lehr•yee•ah*
alone μόνος *moh•nohs*
aluminum foil αλουμινόχαρτο *ah•loo•mee•noh•khah•rtoh*
amazing καταπληκτικός *kah•tahp•leek•tee•kohs*
ambassador πρεσβευτής *prehz•vehf•tees*
amber κεχριμπάρι *kehkh•reem•bah•ree*
ambulance ασθενοφόρο *ahs•theh•noh•foh•roh*
American *adj* αμερικάνικος *ah•meh•ree•kah•nee•kohs;* *(nationality)* Αμερικανός *ah•meh•ree•kah•nohs*
amount *n* ποσό *poh•soh*
amusement park πάρκο ψυχαγωγίας *pahr•koh psee•khah•ghoh•yee•ahs*
animal ζώο *zoh•oh*
another άλλος *ah•lohs*
antibiotic αντιβιοτικό *ahn•dee•vee•oh•tee•koh*
antiques store κατάστημα με αντίκες *kah•tah•stee•mah meh ahn•tee•kehs*
antiseptic cream αντισηπτική κρέμα *ahn•dee•seep•tee•kee kreh•mah*
anything οτιδήποτε *oh•tee•THee•poh•teh*
apartment διαμέρισμα *THee•ah•meh•reez•mah*
apologize ζητώ συγγνώμη *zee•toh seegh•noh•mee*
appendix σκωληκοειδίτιδα *skoh•lee•koh•ee•THee•tee•THah*
appointment ραντεβού *rahn•deh•voo*
architecture αρχιτεκτονική *ahr•khee•teh•ktoh•nee•kee*
area code κωδικός περιοχής *koh•THee•kohs peh•ree•oh•khees*
arm *n* χέρι *kheh•ree*
arrange κανονίζω *kah•noh•nee•zoh*
arrest *v* συλλαμβάνω *see•lahm•vah•noh*
arrive φτάνω *ftah•noh*
art τέχνη *tekh•nee*
art gallery γκαλερί τέχνης *gah•leh•ree tekh•nees*
ashtray σταχτοδοχείο *stakh•toh•THoh•khee•oh*
ask ζητώ *zee•toh*
aspirin ασπιρίνη *ahs•pee•ree•nee*
asthmatic ασθματικός *ahsth•mah•tee•kohs*
ATM ATM *ehee•tee•ehm*
attack *n* επίθεση *eh•pee•theh•see;* *v* επιτίθεμαι *eh•pee•tee•theh•meh*
attractive ελκυστικός *ehl•kees•tee•kohs*

authenticity αυθεντικότητα *ahf•thehn•dee•koh•tee•tah*

B

baby μωρό *moh•roh*
baby food βρεφική τροφή *vreh•fee•kee troh•fee*
baby seat καρέκλα μωρού *kah•reh•klah moh•roo*
babysitter μπέιμπι σίτερ *beh•ee•bee see•tehr*
back *n* πλάτη *plah•tee*
back ache πόνος στην πλάτη *poh•nohs steen plah•tee*
backgammon τάβλι *tah•vlee*
bad κακός *kah•kohs*
baggage αποσκευές *ah•pohs•keh•vehs*
baggage check φύλαξη αποσκευών *fee•lah•ksee ah•poh•skeh•vohn*
baggage reclaim παραλαβή αποσκευών *pah•rah•lah•vee ah•poh•skeh•vohn*
bakery αρτοποιείο *ah•rtoh•pee•ee•oh*
balcony μπαλκόνι *bahl•koh•nee*
ballet μπαλέτο *bah•leh•toh*
bandage γάζα *ghah•zah*
bank τράπεζα *trah•peh•zah*
bank account λογαριασμός τραπέζης *loh•ghahr•yahz•mohs trah•peh•zees*
bank loan τραπεζικό δάνειο *trah•peh•zee•koh THah•nee•oh*
bar μπαρ *bahr*
barber κουρείο *koo•ree•oh*
basket καλάθι *kah•lah•THee*
basketball μπάσκετ *bah•skeht*
bathing suit μαγιό *mah•yoh*
bathroom μπάνιο *bah•nioh*
battery μπαταρία *bah•tah•ree•ah*
beach παραλία *pah•rah•lee•ah*
beautiful όμορφος *oh•mohr•fohs*
bed κρεβάτι *kreh•vah•tee*
bed and breakfast διαμονή με πρωινό *THiah•moh•nee meh proh•ee•noh*
bedding σεντόνια *sehn•doh•niah*
bedroom υπνοδωμάτιο *eep•noh•THoh•mah•tee•oh*
before πριν *preen*
beginner αρχάριος *ahr•khah•ree•ohs*
belong ανήκω *ah•nee•koh*
belt ζώνη *zoh•nee*
bicycle ποδήλατο *poh•THee•lah•toh*
big μεγάλος *meh•ghah•lohs*
bikini μπικίνι *bee•kee•nee*
bird πουλί *poo•lee*
bite *n (insect)* τσίμπημα *tsee•bee•mah*
bladder ουροδόχος κύστη *oo•roh•THoh•khohs kee•stee*
blanket κουβέρτα *koo•veh•rtah*
bleed *n* αιμορραγία *eh•moh•rah•yee•ah; v* αιμορραγώ *eh•moh•rah•yoh*
blinds περσίδες *peh•rsee•THehs*
blister φουσκάλα *foo•skah•lah*
blood αίμα *eh•mah*
blood group ομάδα αίματος *oh•mah•THah eh•mah•tohs*
blood pressure πίεση *pee•eh•see*
blouse μπλούζα *bloo•zah*
boarding card κάρτα επιβίβασης *kah•rtah eh•pee•vee•vah•sees*
boat βάρκα *vahr•kah*
boat trip ταξίδι με πλοίο *tah•ksee•THee meh plee•oh*
body σώμα *soh•mah*
bone οστό *oh•stoh*
book *n* βιβλίο *veev•lee•oh; v* κάνω κράτηση *kah•noh krah•tee•see*
bookstore βιβλιοπωλείο *veev•lee•oh•poh•lee•oh*
boot μπότα *boh•tah*
border *(country)* σύνορο *see•noh•roh*
boring βαρετός *vah•reh•tohs*
borrow δανείζομαι *THah•nee•zoh•meh*
botanical garden βοτανικός κήπος *voh•tah•nee•kohs kee•pohs*
bottle μπουκάλι *boo•kah•lee*
bottle opener τιρμπουσόν *teer•boo•sohn*
bowel έντερο *ehn•deh•roh*
box office ταχυδρομική θυρίδα *tah•khee•THroh•mee•kee THee•ree•THah*
boxing *n* μποξ *bohks*
boy αγόρι *ah•ghoh•ree*
boyfriend φίλος *fee•lohs*
bra σουτιέν *soo•tiehn*
break *n* διάλειμμα *THee•ah•lee•mah; v* σπάω *spah•oh*
breakdown *n (car)* βλάβη *vlah•vee*
breakfast πρωινό *proh•ee•noh*
break-in *n* διάρρηξη *THee•ah•ree•ksee*
breast στήθος *stee•THohs*
breathe αναπνέω *ah•nahp•neh•oh*
breathtaking φαντασμαγορικός *fahn•dahz•mah•ghoh•ree•kohs*
bridge *n (over water)* γέφυρα *yeh•fee•rah; (card game)* μπριτζ *breetz*
briefcase χαρτοφύλακας *khah•rtoh•fee•lah•kahs*
briefs (men's, women's) σλιπ *sleep (women's);* κυλοτάκι *kee•loh•tah•kee*
bring φέρνω *fehr•noh*
Britain Βρετανία *vreh•tah•nee•ah*
British *adj* βρετανικός *vreh•tah•nee•kohs; (nationality)* Βρετανός *vreh•tah•nohs*
brochure φυλλάδιο *fee•lah•THee•oh*

broken σπασμένος *spahz•meh•nohs*
broom *n* σκούπα *skoo•pah*
browse ξεφυλλίζω *kseh•fee•lee•zoh*
bruise *n* μελανιά *meh•lah•niah*
brush *n* βούρτσα *voor•tsah*; *v* βουρτσίζω *voor•tsee•zoh*
build κτίζω *ktee•zoh*
building κτίριο *ktee•ree•oh*
burn *n* έγκαυμα *eh•gahv•mah*
bus λεωφορείο *leh•oh•foh•ree•oh*
bus route διαδρομή λεωφορείων *THee•ah•THroh•mee leh•oh•foh•ree•ohn*
bus station σταθμός λεωφορείων *stahTH•mohs leh•oh•foh•ree•ohn*
bus stop στάση λεωφορείου *stah•see leh•oh•foh•ree•oo*
business class μπίζνες θέση *bee•znehs theh•see*
business trip επαγγελματικό ταξίδι *eh•pah•gehl•mah•tee•koh tah•ksee•THee*
busy (occupied) απασχολημένος *ah•pahs•khoh•lee•meh•nohs*
but αλλά *ah•lah*
butane gas υγραέριο *eegh•rah•eh•ree•oh*
butcher shop κρεοπωλείο *kreh•oh•poh•lee•oh*
button κουμπί *koo•bee*
buy αγοράζω *ah•ghoh•rah•zoh*

C

cabaret καμπαρέ *kah•bah•reh*
cabin καμπίνα *kah•bee•nah*
cable car τελεφερίκ *teh•leh•feh•reek*
cafe καφετέρια *kah•feh•teh•ree•ah*
calendar ημερολόγιο *ee•meh•roh•loh•yee•oh*
call collect με χρέωση του καλούμενου *meh khreh•oh•see too kah•loo•meh•noo*
call *n* κλήση *klee•see*; *v* καλώ *kah•loh*
camcorder φορητή βιντεοκάμερα *foh•ree•tee vee•deh•oh•kah•meh•rah*
camera φωτογραφική μηχανή *foh•tohgh•rah•fee•kee mee•khah•nee*
camera case θήκη μηχανής *thee•kee mee•khah•nees*
camera store κατάστημα με φωτογραφικά είδη *kah•tah•stee•mah meh foh•tohgh•rah•fee•kah ee•THee*
camp bed κρεβάτι εκστρατείας *kreh•vah•tee ehk•strah•tee•ahs*
camping κάμπινγκ *kah•mpeeng*
camping equipment εξοπλισμός κάμπιγκ *eh•ksohp•leez•mohs kah•mpeeng*
campsite χώρος κάμπινγκ *khoh•rohs kah•mpeeng*
can opener ανοιχτήρι *ah•neekh•tee•ree*
Canada Καναδάς *kah•nah•THahs*
canal κανάλι *kah•nah•lee*
cancel *v* ακυρώνω *ah•kee•roh•noh*
cancer (disease) καρκίνος *kahr•kee•nohs*
candle κερί *keh•ree*
canoe κανό *kah•noh*
car αυτοκίνητο *ahf•toh•kee•nee•toh*
car park [BE] χώρος στάθμευσης *khoh•rohs stahth•mehf•sees*
car rental ενοικίαση αυτοκινήτων *eh•nee•kee•ah•see ahf•toh•kee•nee•tohn*
car wash πλύσιμο αυτοκινήτου *plee•see•moh ahf•toh•kee•nee•too*
carafe καράφα *kah•rah•fah*
caravan τροχόσπιτο *troh•khohs•pee•toh*
cards χαρτιά *khahr•tiah*
carpet (fitted) μοκέτα *moh•keh•tah*
carton κουτί *koo•tee*
cash desk [BE] ταμείο *tah•mee•oh*
cash *n* μετρητά *meht•ree•tah*; *v* εξαργυρώνω *eh•ksahr•ghee•roh•noh*
casino καζίνο *kah•see•noh*
castle κάστρο *kahs•troh*
catch *v (bus)* παίρνω *pehr•noh*
cathedral καθεδρικός ναός *kah•theh•THree•kohs nah•ohs*
cave *n* σπήλαιο *spee•leh•oh*
CD σι ντι *see dee*
cell phone κινητό *kee•nee•toh*
change *n* αλλαγή *ah•lah•yee*; *v* αλλάζω *ah•lah•zoh*
cheap φτηνός *ftee•nohs*
check *n (bank)* επιταγή *eh•pee•tah•yee*; *(bill)* λογαριασμός *loh•ghahr•yahz•mohs*
choose διαλέγω *THiah•leh•ghoh*
clean καθαρός *kah•thah•rohs*
cling film [BE] διαφανή μεμβράνη *THee•ah•fah•nee mehm•vrah•nee*
clothing store κατάστημα ρούχων *kah•tahs•tee•mah roo•khohn*
cold *adj (temperature)* κρύος *kree•ohs*; *n (chill)* κρυολόγημα *kree•oh•loh•yee•mah*
collapse *v* καταρρέω *kah•tah•reh•oh*
collect *v* παίρνω *peh•rnoh*
color *n* χρώμα *khroh•mah*
comb *n* χτένα *khteh•nah*; *v* χτενίζω *khteh•nee•zoh*
come έρχομαι *ehr•khoh•meh*
come back *v (return)* επιστρέφω *eh•pees•treh•foh*

commission *n (agent fee)* προμήθεια *proh•mee•thee•ah*
company *n (business)* εταιρία *eh•teh•ree•ah; (companionship)* παρέα *pah•reh•ah*
complain παραπονιέμαι *pah•rah•poh•nieh•meh*
computer υπολογιστής *ee•poh•loh•yee•stees*
concert συναυλία *see•nahv•lee•ah*
concert hall αίθουσα συναυλιών *eh•thoo•sah see•nahv•lee•ohn*
conditioner (hair) γαλάκτωμα για τα μαλλιά *ghah•lah•ktoh•mah yah tah mah•liah*
condom προφυλακτικό *proh•fee•lah•ktee•koh*
conference συνέδριο *see•neh•THree•oh*
confirm επιβεβαιώνω *eh•pee•veh•veh•oh•noh*
constipation δυσκοιλιότητα *thees•kee•lee•oh•tee•tah*
Consulate Προξενείο *proh•kseh•nee•oh*
consult *v* συμβουλεύομαι *seem•voo•leh•voh•meh*
contact *v* επικοινωνώ *eh•pee•kee•noh•noh*
contact fluid υγρό για φακούς επαφής *eegh•roh yah fah•koos eh•pah•fees*
contact lens φακός επαφής *fah•kohs eh•pah•fees*
contagious μεταδοτικός *meh•tah•THoh•tee•kohs*
contain περιέχω *peh•ree•eh•khoh*
contraceptive pill αντισυλληπτικό χάπι *ahn•dee•see•leep•tee•koh khah•pee*
cook *n (chef)* μάγειρας *mah•yee•rahs; v* μαγειρεύω *mah•yee•reh•voh*
copper χαλκός *khahl•kohs*
corkscrew τιρμπουσόν *teer•boo•sohn*
corner γωνία *ghoh•nee•ah*
correct *v* διορθώνω *THee•ohr•thoh•noh*
cosmetics καλλυντικά *kah•leen•dee•kah*
cot [BE] παιδικό κρεβάτι *peh•THee•koh kreh•vah•tee*
cotton βαμβάκι *vahm•vah•kee*
cough *n* βήχας *vee•khahs; v* βήχω *vee•khoh*
counter ταμείο *tah•mee•oh*
country (nation) χώρα *khoh•rah*
countryside εξοχή *eh•ksoh•khee*
couple *n (pair)* ζευγάρι *zehv•ghah•ree*
courier *n (messenger)* κούριερ *koo•ree•ehr*
court house δικαστήριο *THee•kahs•tee•ree•oh*
cramp *n* κράμπα *krahm•bah*
credit card πιστωτική κάρτα *pees•toh•tee•kee kahr•tah*
crib [cot BE] παιδικό κρεβάτι *peh•THee•koh kreh•vah•tee*
crown *n (dental, royal)* κορώνα *koh•roh•nah*
cruise *n* κρουαζιέρα *kroo•ahz•yeh•rah*
crutch *n (walking support)* δεκανίκι *THeh•kah•nee•kee*
crystal *n* κρύσταλλο *kree•stah•loh*
cup φλυτζάνι *flee•jah•nee*
cupboard ντουλάπα *doo•lah•pah*
currency νόμισμα *noh•meez•mah*
currency exchange office γραφείο ανταλλαγής συναλλάγματος *ghrah•fee•oh ahn•dah•lah•yees see•nah•lahgh•mah•tohs*
customs (tolls) τελωνείο *teh•loh•nee•oh*
customs declaration (tolls) τελωνειακή δήλωση *teh•loh•nee•ah•kee THee•loh•see*
cut *n (wound)* κόψιμο *koh•psee•moh*
cut glass *n* σκαλιστό γυαλί *skah•lees•toh yah•lee*
cycle helmet κράνος ποδηλάτη *krah•nohs poh•THee•lah•tee*
cyclist ποδηλάτης *poh•THee•lah•tees*
Cypriot *adj* κυπριακός *keep•ree•ah•kohs; (nationality)* Κύπριος *kee•pree•ohs*
Cyprus Κύπρος *kee•prohs*

D

damage *n* ζημιά *zee•miah; v* καταστρέφω *kah•tah•streh•foh*
dance *v* χορεύω *khoh•reh•voh*
dangerous επικίνδυνος *eh•pee•keen•THee•nohs*
dark *adj (color)* σκούρος *skoo•rohs*
dawn *n* ξημερώματα *ksee•meh•roh•mah•tah*
day trip ημερήσια εκδρομή *ee•meh•ree•see•ah ehk•THroh•mee*
deaf κουφός *koo•fohs*
decide αποφασίζω *ah•poh•fah•see•zoh*
deck *n* κατάστρωμα *kah•tah•stroh•mah*
deck chair σεζ-λονγκ *sehz lohng*
declare δηλώνω *THee•loh•noh*
deduct *(money)* αφαιρώ *ah•feh•roh*
defrost ξεπαγώνω *kseh•pah•ghoh•noh*
degrees (temperature) βαθμοί *vahth•mee*
delay *n* καθυστέρηση *kah•thee•steh•ree•see; v* καθυστερώ *kah•thee•steh•roh*

delicious νόστιμος *nohs•tee•mohs*
deliver παραδίδω *pah•rah•THee•THoh*
dental floss οδοντικό νήμα *oh•THohn•dee•koh nee•mah*
dentist οδοντίατρος *oh•THohn•dee•ah•trohs*
deodorant αποσμητικό *ah•pohz•mee•tee•koh*
department store πολυκατάστημα *poh•lee•kah•tahs•tee•mah*
departure (travel) αναχώρηση *ah•nah•khoh•ree•see*
departure lounge αίθουσα αναχωρήσεων *eh•thoo•sah ah•nah•khoh•ree•seh•ohn*
depend εξαρτώμαι *eh•ksahr•toh•meh*
deposit *n (down payment)* προκαταβολή *proh•kah•tah•voh•lee*
describe περιγράφω *peh•reegh•rah•foh*
designer σχεδιαστής *skheh•THee•ahs•tees*
detergent απορρυπαντικό *ah•poh•ree•pahn•dee•koh*
develop (photos) εμφανίζω *ehm•fah•nee•zoh*
diabetes διαβήτης *THee•ah•vee•tees*
diabetic διαβητικός *THee•ah•vee•tee•kohs*
diagnosis διάγνωση *THee•ahgh•noh•see*
dialing code κωδικός *koh•THee•kohs*
diamond *n* διαμάντι *THiah•mahn•dee*
diaper πάνα μωρού *pah•nah moh•roo*
diarrhea διάρροια *THee•ah•ree•ah*
dice *n* ζάρια *zah•riah*
dictionary λεξικό *leh•ksee•koh*
diesel ντήζελ *dee•zehl*
diet *n* δίαιτα *THee•eh•tah*
difficult δύσκολος *THee•skoh•lohs*
dining room τραπεζαρία *trah•peh•zah•ree•ah*
dinner βραδινό *vrah•THee•noh*
direct *v* κατευθύνω *kah•tehf•thee•noh*
direction *n (instruction)* οδηγία *oh•THee•yee•ah*
dirty *adj* βρώμικος *vroh•mee•kohs*
disabled άτομο με ειδικές ανάγκες *ah•toh•moh meh ee• •nahn THee•kehs ah •gehs*
discounted ticket μειωμένο εισιτήριο *mee•oh•meh•noh ee•see•tee•ree•oh*
dishwashing liquid λίγο υγρό πιάτων *lee•ghoh ee•ghroh piah•tohn*
district περιφέρεια *peh•ree•feh•ree•ah*
disturb ενοχλώ *eh•noh•khloh*
diving equipment καταδυτικός εξοπλισμός *kah•tah•THee•tee•kohs eh•ksoh•pleez•mohs*
divorced διαζευγμένος *THee•ah•zehv•ghmeh•nohs*
dock προκυμαία *proh•kee•meh•ah*
doctor γιατρός *yah•trohs*
doll κούκλα *kook•lah*
dollar δολάριο *THoh•lah•ree•oh*
door πόρτα *pohr•tah*
dosage δοσολογία *THoh•soh•loh•yee•ah*
double *adj* διπλός *THeep•lohs*
double bed διπλό κρεβάτι *THeep•loh kreh•vah•tee*
double room δίκλινο δωμάτιο *THeek•lee•noh THoh•mah•tee•oh*
downtown area κέντρο της πόλης *kehn•droh tees poh•lees*
dozen ντουζίνα *doo•zee•nah*
dress *n* φόρεμα *foh•reh•mah*
drink *n* ποτό *poh•toh*; *v* πίνω *pee•noh*
drive *v* οδηγώ *oh•THee•ghoh*
drugstore φαρμακείο *fahr•mah•kee•oh*
dry cleaner καθαριστήριο *kah•thah•rees•tee•ree•oh*
dubbed μεταγλωττισμένος *meh•tahgh•loh•teez•meh•nohs*
dusty σκονισμένος *skoh•neez•meh•nohs*
duty (customs) φόρος *foh•rohs*; *(obligation)* καθήκον *kah•thee•kohn*
duty-free goods αφορολόγητα είδη *ah•foh•roh•loh•yee•tah ee•THee*
duty-free shop κατάστημα αφορολόγητων *kah•tahs•tee•mah ah•foh•roh•loh•yee•tohn*

E

each κάθε ένα *kah•theh eh•nah*
ear αυτί *ahf•tee*
earache πόνος στο αυτί *poh•nohs stoh ahf•tee*
early νωρίς *noh•rees*
east ανατολικά *ah•nah•toh•lee•kah*
easy *adj* εύκολος *ehf•koh•lohs*
eat τρώω *troh•oh*
economical οικονομικός *ee•koh•noh•mee•kohs*
economy class τουριστική θέση *too•ree•stee•kee theh•see*
elastic ελαστικός *eh•lahs•tee•kohs*
electrical outlet πρίζα *pree•zah*
e-mail ηλεκτρονικό ταχυδρομείο *(e-mail) ee•lehk•troh•nee•koh tah•hee•dro•mee•oh (ee•meh•eel)*

embassy πρεσβεία *prehz•vee•ah*
emerald σμαράγδι *zmah•rahgh•THee*
emergency έκτακτη ανάγκη *ehk•tahk•tee ah•nah•gee*
emergency exit έξοδος κινδύνου *eh•ksoh•THohs keen•THee•noo*
empty *adj* άδειος *ahTH•yohs*
end *n* τέλος *teh•lohs; v* τελειώνω *teh•lee•oh•noh*
engine μηχανή *mee•khah•nee*
England Αγγλία *ahng•lee•ah*
English *adj* αγγλικός *ahng•lee•kohs;* **(nationality)** Άγγλος *ahng•lohs;* **(language)** αγγλικά *ahng•lee•kah*
enjoy ευχαριστιέμαι *ehf•khah•rees•tieh•meh*
enough αρκετά *ahr•keh•tah*
entertainment guide οδηγός ψυχαγωγίας *oh•THee•ghohs psee•khah•ghoh•yee•ahs*
entrance fee τιμή εισόδου *tee•mee ee•soh•THoo*
epileptic επιληπτικός *eh•pee•leep•tee•kohs*
error λάθος *lah•thohs*
escalator κυλιόμενες σκάλες *kee•lee•oh•meh•nehs skah•lehs*
essential απαραίτητος *ah•pah•reh•tee•tohs*
e-ticket ηλεκτρονικό εισιτήριο *ee•leh•ktroh•nee•koh ee•see•tee•ree•oh*
European Union Ευρωπαϊκή Ένωση *ehv•roh•pah•ee•kee eh•noh•see*
euro ευρώ *ehv•roh*
evening βράδυ *vrah•THee*
examination (medical) ιατρική εξέταση *ee•ah•tree•kee eh•kseh•tah•see*
example παράδειγμα *pah•rah•THeegh•mah*
excess baggage υπέρβαρο *ee•pehr•vah•roh*
exchange *v (money)* αλλάζω *ah•lah•zoh*
exchange rate τιμή συναλλάγματος *tee•mee see•nah•lahgh•mah•tohs*
excursion εκδρομή *ehk•THroh•mee*
exhibition έκθεση *ehk•theh•see*
exit *n* έξοδος *eh•ksoh•THohs*
expensive ακριβός *ahk•ree•vohs*
expiration date ημερομηνία λήξεως *ee•meh•roh•mee•nee•ah lee•kseh•ohs*
exposure (photos) στάση *stah•see*
express (mail) εξπρές *ehk•sprehs*
extension (number) εσωτερική γραμμή *eh•soh•teh•ree•kee ghrah•mee*
extra (additional) άλλο ένα *ah•loh eh•nah*
eye *n* μάτι *mah•tee*

F

fabric (cloth) ύφασμα *ee•fahs•mah*
face *n* πρόσωπο *proh•soh•poh*
facial καθαρισμός προσώπου *kah•thah•reez•mohs proh•soh•poo*
facility εξυπηρέτηση *eh•ksee•pee•reh•tee•see*
faint λιποθυμώ *lee•poh•thee•moh*
fall *v* πέφτω *pehf•toh*
family οικογένεια *ee•koh•yeh•nee•ah*
famous διάσημος *THee•ah•see•mohs*
fan *n (air)* ανεμιστήρας *ah•neh•mees•tee•rahs*
far *adv* μακριά *mahk•ree•ah*
fare εισιτήριο *ee•see•tee•ree•oh*
farm *n* φάρμα *fahr•mah*
fast *adv* γρήγορα *ghree•ghoh•rah*
fat *adj (person)* παχύς *pah•khees*
faucet βρύση *vree•see*
fault λάθος *lah•thohs*
favorite αγαπημένος *ah•ghah•pee•meh•nohs*
fax facility υπηρεσία φαξ *ee•pee•reh•see•ah fahks*
feed *v* ταΐζω *tah•ee•zoh*
female θηλυκός *thee•lee•kohs*
fence *n* φράχτης *frahkh•tees*
ferry φέρυ-μπωτ *feh•ree•boht*
festival φεστιβάλ *fehs•tee•vahl*
fever πυρετός *pee•reh•tohs*
fiancé αρραβωνιαστικός *ah•rah•voh•niahs•tee•kohs*
fiancée αρραβωνιαστικιά *ah•rah•voh•niahs•tee•kiah*
filling (dental) σφράγισμα *sfrah•yeez•mah*
film *n (camera)* φιλμ *feelm*
filter *n* φίλτρο *feel•troh*
fine *adv* καλά *kah•lah; n* πρόστιμο *prohs•tee•moh*
finger *n* δάχτυλο *THakh•tee•loh*
fire *n* φωτιά *foh•tiah*
fire brigade [BE] πυροσβεστική *pee•rohz•vehs•tee•kee*
fire escape έξοδος κινδύνου *eh•ksoh•THohs keen•THee•noo*
fire extinguisher πυροσβεστήρας *pee•rohz•vehs•tee•rahs*
first class πρώτη θέση *proh•tee theh•see*
first-aid kit κουτί πρώτων βοηθειών *koo•tee proh•tohn voh•ee•thee•ohn*
fishing ψάρεμα *psah•reh•mah*
flag *n* σημαία *see•meh•ah*
flashlight φακός *fah•kohs*
flat *adj* επίπεδος *eh•pee•peh•Thohs; n* διαμέρισμα *THee•ah•mehr•ees•mah*
flea ψύλλος *psee•lohs*
flight πτήση *ptee•see*

flight number αριθμός πτήσεως *ah•reeth•mohs ptee•seh•ohs*
flip-flops σαγιονάρες *sah•yoh•nah•rehs*
flood *n* πλημμύρα *plee•mee•rah*
florist ανθοπωλείο *ahn•thoh•poh•lee•oh*
flower *n* λουλούδι *loo•loo•THee*
flu γρίππη *ghree•pee*
flush τραβώ το καζανάκι *trah•voh toh kah•zah•nah•kee*
fly *n* μύγα *mee•ghah*; *v* πετάω *peh•tah•oh*
follow *v* ακολουθώ *ah•koh•loo•thoh*
foot πόδι *poh•THee*
football [BE] ποδόσφαιρο *poh•THohs•feh•roh*
footpath μονοπάτι *moh•noh•pah•tee*
forecast *n* πρόβλεψη *prohv•leh•psee*
foreign ξένος *kseh•nohs*
foreign currency ξένο συνάλλαγμα *kseh•noh see•nah•lahgh•mah*
forest *n* δάσος *THah•sohs*
forget ξεχνώ *ksehkh•noh*
form *n* έντυπο *ehn•dee•poh*
fortunately ευτυχώς *ehf•tee•khohs*
forward προωθώ *proh•oh•thoh*
fountain συντριβάνι *seen•dree•vah•nee*
free *adj (available)* ελεύθερος *eh•lehf•theh•rohs*
freezer κατάψυξη *kah•tah•psee•ksee*
frequent *adj* συχνός *seekh•nohs*
fresh *adj* φρέσκος *frehs•kohs*
friend *n* φίλος *fee•lohs*
frightened φοβισμένος *foh•veez•meh•nohs*
from από *ah•poh*
front *n* προκυμαία *proh•kee•meh•ah*
full *adj* γεμάτος *yeh•mah•tohs*
furniture έπιπλα *eh•peep•lah*
fuse *n* ασφάλεια *ahs•fah•lee•ah*

G

gambling τζόγος *joh•ghohs*
game (toy) παιχνίδι *pehkh•nee•THee*
garage γκαράζ *gah•rahz*
garden *n* κήπος *kee•pohs*
gas βενζίνη *vehn•zee•nee*
gas station βενζινάδικο *vehn•zee•nah•THee•koh*
gastritis γαστρίτιδα *ghahs•tree•tee•THah*
gate (airport) έξοδος *eh•ksoh•THohs*
genuine αυθεντικός *ahf•thehn•dee•kohs*
get off (transport) κατεβαίνω *kah•teh•veh•noh*
get out (of vehicle) βγαίνω *vyeh•noh*
gift δώρο *THoh•roh*
gift store κατάστημα με είδη δώρων *kah•tahs•tee•mah meh ee•THee THoh•rohn*
girl κορίτσι *koh•ree•tsee*
girlfriend φίλη *fee•lee*
give δίνω *THee•noh*
glass (container) ποτήρι *poh•tee•ree*
glasses (optical) γυαλιά *yah•liah*
glove *n* γάντι *ghahn•dee*
go πηγαίνω *pee•yeh•noh*
gold *n* χρυσός *khree•sohs*
golf γκόλφ *gohlf*
golf course γήπεδο γκολφ *yee•peh•THoh gohlf*
good καλός *kah•lohs*
grass γρασίδι *ghrah•see•THee*
gratuity φιλοδώρημα *fee•loh•THoh•ree•mah*
greasy (hair, skin) λιπαρός *lee•pah•rohs*
Greece Ελλάδα *eh•lah•THah*
Greek *adj* ελληνικός *eh•lee•nee•kohs*; **(nationality)** Έλληνας *eh•lee•nahs*
greengrocer [BE] οπωροπωλείο *oh•poh•roh•poh•lee•oh*
ground (earth) έδαφος *eh•THah•fohs*
group *n* γκρουπ *groop*
guarantee *n* εγγύηση *eh•gee•ee•see*; *v* εγγυώμαι *eh•gee•oh•meh*
guide book τουριστικός οδηγός *too•ree•stee•kohs oh•THee•ghohs*
guided tour ξενάγηση *kseh•nah•yee•see*
guitar κιθάρα *kee•thah•rah*
gynecologist γυναικολόγος *yee•neh•koh•loh•ghohs*

H

hair μαλλιά *mah•liah*
hairbrush βούρτσα *voor•tsah*
hair dresser κομμωτήριο *koh•moh•tee•ree•oh*
hair dryer σεσουάρ *seh•soo•ahr*
half μισός *mee•sohs*
hammer σφυρί *sfee•ree*
hand *n* χέρι *kheh•ree*
hand luggage αποσκευές χειρός *ah•pohs•keh•vehs khee•rohs*
handbag τσάντα *tsahn•dah*
handicraft λαϊκή τέχνη *lah•ee•kee tehkh•nee*
handicapped-accessible toilet προσβάσιμη τουαλέτα για ανάπηρους *prohs•vah•see•mee too•ah•leh•tah yah ah•nah•pee•roos*
handkerchief χαρτομάντηλο *khah•rtoh•mahn•dee•loh*
handle *n* πόμολο *poh•moh•loh*
hanger κρεμάστρα *kreh•mahs•trah*

harbor *n* λιμάνι *lee•mah•nee*
hat καπέλο *kah•peh•loh*
have *(possession)* έχω *eh•khoh*
have to (obligation) οφείλω *oh•fee•loh*
head *n* κεφάλι *keh•fah•lee*
headache πονοκέφαλος *poh•noh•keh•fah•lohs*
health food store κατάστημα με υγιεινές τροφές *kah•tahs•tee•mah meh ee•yee•ee•nehs troh•fehs*
health insurance ασφάλεια υγείας *ahs•fah•lee•ah ee•yee•ahs*
hearing aid ακουστικό βαρυκοΐας *ah•koo•stee•koh vah•ree•koh•ee•ahs*
heart *v* καρδιά *kahr•THee•ah*
heart attack καρδιακό έμφραγμα *kahr•THee•ah•koh ehm•frahgh•mah*
heat wave καύσωνας *kahf•soh•nahs*
heater (water) θερμοσίφωνας *thehr•moh•see•foh•nahs*
heating θέρμανση *thehr•mahn•see*
heavy βαρύς *vah•rees*
height ύψος *ee•psohs*
helicopter ελικόπτερο *eh•lee•kohp•teh•roh*
help *n* βοήθεια *voh•ee•thee•ah; v* βοηθώ *voh•ee•thoh*
here εδώ *eh•THoh*
highway εθνική οδός *ehth•nee•kee oh•THohs*
hike *v* κάνω πεζοπορία *kah•noh peh•zoh•poh•ree•ah*
hill λόφος *loh•fohs*
hire [BE] *v* νοικιάζω *nee•kiah•zoh*
history ιστορία *ee•stoh•ree•ah*
hitchhiking οτοστόπ *oh•toh•stohp*
hobby (pastime) χόμπυ *khoh•bee*
hold on περιμένω *peh•ree•meh•noh*
hole (in clothes) τρύπα *tree•pah*
holiday [BE] διακοπές *THee•ah•koh•pehs*
honeymoon μήνας του μέλιτος *mee•nahs too meh•lee•tohs*
horse track ιπποδρόμιο *ee•poh•THroh•mee•oh*
hospital νοσοκομείο *noh•soh•koh•mee•oh*
hot (weather) ζεστός *zehs•tohs*
hot spring θερμή πηγή *thehr•mee pee•yee*
hotel ξενοδοχείο *kseh•noh•THoh•khee•oh*
household articles είδη οικιακής χρήσεως *ee•THee ee•kee•ah•kees khree•seh•ohs*
husband σύζυγος *see•zee•ghohs*

I

ice *n* πάγος *pah•ghohs*
identification ταυτότητα *tahf•toh•tee•tah*
illegal παράνομος *pah•rah•noh•mohs*
illness αρρώστεια *ahr•ohs•tee•ah*
imitation απομίμηση *ah•poh•mee•mee•see*
immediately αμέσως *ah•meh•sohs*
impressive εντυπωσιακός *ehn•dee•poh•see•ah•kohs*
included συμπεριλαμβάνεται *seem•beh•ree•lahm•vah•neh•teh*
indigestion δυσπεψία *THehs•peh•psee•ah*
indoor εσωτερικός *eh•soh•teh•ree•kohs*
indoor pool εσωτερική πισίνα *eh•soh•teh•ree•kee pee•see•nah*
inexpensive φτηνός *ftee•nohs*
infected μολυσμένος *moh•leez•meh•nohs*
inflammation φλεγμονή *flegh•moh•nee*
information πληροφορίες *plee•roh•foh•ree•ehs*
information office γραφείο πληροφοριών *ghrah•fee•oh plee•roh•foh•ree•ohn*
injection ένεση *eh•neh•see*
injured τραυματισμένος *trahv•mah•teez•meh•nohs*
innocent αθώος *ah•thoh•ohs*
insect bite τσίμπημα από έντομο *tseem•bee•mah ah•poh ehn•doh•moh*
insect repellent εντομοαπωθητικό *ehn•doh•moh•ah•poh•thee•tee•koh*
inside μέσα *meh•sah*
insist επιμένω *eh•pee•meh•noh*
insomnia αϋπνία *ah•eep•nee•ah*
instruction οδηγία *oh•THee•yee•ah*
insulin ινσουλίνη *een•soo•lee•nee*
insurance ασφάλεια *ahs•fah•lee•ah*
insurance certificate πιστοποιητικό ασφάλειας *pees•toh•pee•ee•tee•koh ahs•fah•lee•ahs*
insurance claim ασφάλεια αποζημίωσης *ahs•fah•lee•ah ah•poh•zee•mee•oh•sees*
insurance company ασφαλιστική εταιρία *ahs•fah•lees•tee•kee eh•teh•ree•ah*
interest rate επιτόκιο *eh•pee•toh•kee•oh*
interesting ενδιαφέρων *ehn•THee•ah•feh•rohn*
international διεθνής *THee•eth•nees*

International Student Card διεθνής φοιτητική κάρτα *THee•ehth•nees fee•tee•tee•kee kahr•tah*
internet ίντερνετ *ee•nteh•rnet*
internet cafe ίντερνετ καφέ *ee•nteh•rnet kah•feh*
interpreter διερμηνέας *THee•ehr•mee•neh•ahs*
interval διάλειμμα *THee•ah•lee•mah*
introduce συστήνω *see•stee•noh*
introductions συστάσεις *see•stah•sees*
invitation πρόσκληση *prohs•klee•see*
invite *v* προσκαλώ *prohs•kah•loh*
iodine ιώδειο *ee•oh•THee•oh*
iron *n* σίδερο *see•THeh•roh; v* σιδερώνω *see•THeh•roh•noh*
itemized bill αναλυτικός λογαριασμός *ah•nah•lee•tee•kohs loh•ghahr•yahz•mohs*

J

jacket σακάκι *sah•kah•kee*
jammed σφηνωμένος *sfee•noh•meh•nohs*
jar *n* βάζο *vah•zoh*
jaw σαγόνι *sah•ghoh•nee*
jeans μπλου-τζην *bloo•jeen*
jellyfish μέδουσα *meh•THoo•sah*
jet-ski τζετ-σκι *jeht•skee*
jeweler κοσμηματοπωλείο *kohz•mee•mah•toh•poh•lee•oh*
job δουλειά *THoo•liah*
jogging τζόγκιγκ *joh•geeng*
joke *n* ανέκδοτο *ah•nehk•THoh•toh*
journey ταξίδι *tah•ksee•THee*
junction *(intersection)* κόμβος *kohm•vohs*

K

keep *v* κρατώ *krah•toh*
key *n* κλειδί *klee•THee*
key card κάρτα-κλειδί *kahr•tah•klee•dee*
key ring μπρελόκ *breh•lohk*
kidney νεφρό *nehf•roh*
kind είδος *ee•THohs*
king βασιλιάς *vah•see•liahs*
kiosk περίπτερο *peh•ree•pteh•roh*
kiss *n* φιλί *fee•lee; v* φιλώ *fee•loh*
kitchen χαρτί κουζίνας *khah•rtee koo•zee•nahs*
knapsack σάκκος *sah•kohs*
knee γόνατο *ghoh•nah•toh*
knife μαχαίρι *mah•kheh•ree*
know γνωρίζω *ghnoh•ree•zoh*

L

label *n* ετικέτα *eh•tee•keh•tah*
ladder σκάλα *skah•lah*
lake λίμνη *leem•nee*
lamp λάμπα *lahm•bah*
land *n* γη *ghee; v* προσγειώνομαι *prohz•yee•oh•noh•meh*
language course μάθημα ξένης γλώσσας *mah•thee•mah kseh•nees ghloh•sahs*
large *adj* μεγάλος *meh•ghah•lohs*
last τελευταίος *teh•lehf•teh•ohs*
late *adv* αργά *ahr•ghah*
laugh *v* γελώ *yeh•loh*
laundry facility πλυντήριο *pleen•dee•ree•oh*
lavatory μπάνιο *bah•nioh*
lawyer δικηγόρος *THee•kee•ghoh•rohs*
laxative καθαρτικό *kah•thahr•tee•koh*
learn μαθαίνω *mah•theh•noh*
leave *v (depart)* φεύγω *fehv•ghoh; (let go)* αφήνω *ah•fee•noh*
left *adj* αριστερός *ah•rees•teh•rohs; adv* αριστερά *ah•rees•teh•rah*
leg πόδι *poh•THee*
legal νόμιμος *noh•mee•mohs*
lend δανείζω *THah•nee•zoh*
length μήκος *mee•kohs*
lens φακός *fah•kohs*
lens cap κάλυμμα φακού *kah•lee•mah fah•koo*
less λιγότερο *lee•ghoh•teh•roh*
letter γράμμα *ghrah•mah*
level (even) επίπεδο *eh•pee•peh•THoh*
library βιβλιοθήκη *veev•lee•oh•thee•kee*
lie down ξαπλώνω *ksah•ploh•noh*
life boat ναυαγοσωστική λέμβος *nah•vah•ghoh•sohs•tee•kee lehm•vohs*
lifeguard ναυαγοσώστης *nah•vah•ghoh•sohs•tees*
life jacket σωσίβιο *soh•see•vee•oh*
lift [BE] *n (elevator)* ασανσέρ *ah•sahn•sehr*
lift pass άδεια σκι *ah•THee•ah skee*
light *adj (color)* ανοιχτός *ah•neekh•tohs; n (electric)* φως *fohs*
light bulb λάμπα *lahm•bah*
lighter *adj* ανοιχτότερος *ah•neekh•toh•teh•rohs; n* αναπτήρας *ah•nahp•tee•rahs*
lighthouse φάρος *fah•rohs*
lights (car) φώτα *foh•tah*
line *n (subway)* γραμμή *ghrah•mee*
lips χείλη *khee•lee*
lipstick κραγιόν *krah•yohn*
liter λίτρο *lee•troh*
little μικρός *meek•rohs*
liver συκώτι *see•koh•tee*
living room σαλόνι *sah•loh•nee*
local τοπικός *toh•pee•kohs*
location (space) θέση *theh•see*
lock *n (door)* κλειδαριά *klee•THahr•yah; (river, canal)* φράγμα *frahgh•mah; v* κλειδώνω *klee•THoh•noh*

long *adj* μακρύς *mak•rees*
long-distance bus υπεραστικό λεωφορείο *ee•peh•rahs•tee•koh leh•oh•foh•ree•oh*
long-distance call υπεραστικό τηλεφώνημα *ee•pehr•ahs•tee•koh tee•leh•foh•nee•mah*
long-sighted [BE] πρεσβύωπας *prehz•vee•oh•pahs*
look *v* κοιτάω *kee•tah•oh*
look for ψάχνω *psahkh•noh*
loose (fitting) φαρδύς *fahr•THees*
loss *n* απώλεια *ah•poh•lee•ah*
lotion λοσιόν *loh•siohn*
loud *adj* δυνατός *THee•nah•tohs*
love *v* αγαπώ *ah•ghah•poh*
lower *adj (berth)* κάτω *kah•toh*
lubricant λιπαντικό *lee•pahn•dee•koh*
luck τύχη *tee•khee*
luggage αποσκευές *ah•pohs•keh•vehs*
luggage cart καροτσάκι αποσκευών *kah•roh•tsah•kee ah•pohs•keh•vohn*
luggage locker θυρίδα *thee•ree•THah*
lukewarm χλιαρός *khlee•ah•rohs*
lump *n* σβώλος *svoh•lohs*; *(medical)* εξόγκωμα *eh•ksoh•goh•mah*
lunch *n* μεσημεριανό *meh•see•mehr•yah•noh*
lung πνεύμονας *pnehv•moh•nahs*
luxury πολυτέλεια *poh•lee•teh•lee•ah*

M

magazine περιοδικό *peh•ree•oh•THee•koh*
magnificent μεγαλοπρεπής *meh•ghah•lohp•reh•pees*
mailbox ταχυδρομικό κουτί *tah•kheeTH•roh•mee•koh koo•tee*
mail *n* αλληλογραφία *ah•lee•lohgh•rah•fee•ah*
main κύριος *kee•ree•ohs*
make-up μακιγιάζ *mah•kee•yahz*
man (male) άνδρας *ahn•THrahs*
manager διευθυντής *THee•ehf•theen•dees*
manicure μανικιούρ *mah•nee•kioor*
manual (car) χειροκίνητος *khee•roh•kee•nee•tohs*
map *n* χάρτης *khahr•tees*
market *n* αγορά *ah•ghoh•rah*
married παντρεμένος *pahn•dreh•meh•nohs*
mask *n (diving)* μάσκα *mahs•kah*
mass *n (church)* λειτουργία *lee•toor•yee•ah*
massage *n* μασάζ *mah•sahz*
match *n (sport)* αγώνας *ah•ghoh•nahs*; *(fire starter)* σπίρτο *speer•toh*
maybe ίσως *ee•sohs*
meal γεύμα *yehv•mah*
mean *v* σημαίνω *see•meh•noh*
measure *v* μετρώ *meht•roh*
measurement μέτρηση *meh•tree•see*
medication φάρμακα *fahr•mah•kah*
meet συναντώ *see•nahn•doh*
memorial μνημείο *mnee•mee•oh*
mend διορθώνω *THee•ohr•thoh•noh*
menstrual cramp πόνος περιόδου *poh•nohs peh•ree•oh•THoo*
mention αναφέρω *ah•nah•feh•roh*
message *n* μήνυμα *mee•nee•mah*
metal *n* μέταλλο *meh•tah•loh*
microwave (oven) φούρνος μικροκυμάτων *foor•nohs mee•kroh•kee•mah•tohn*
migraine ημικρανία *ee•mee•krah•nee•ah*
mileage χιλιόμετρα *khee•lioh•meh•trah*
mini-bar μινι-μπαρ *mee•nee•bahr*
minimart παντοπωλείο *pahn•doh•poh•lee•oh*
minimum ελάχιστος *eh•lah•khees•tohs*
minute *n (time)* λεπτό *lehp•toh*
mirror *n* καθρέφτης *kah•threhf•tees*
mistake λάθος *lah•thohs*
misunderstanding παρεξήγηση *pah•reh•ksee•yee•see*
mobile phone [BE] κινητό *kee•nee•toh*
modern μοντέρνος *moh•deh•rnohs*
moisturizer *(cream)* ενυδατική κρέμα *eh•nee•THah•tee•kee kreh•mah*
money χρήματα *khree•mah•tah*
money order ταχυδρομική επιταγή *tah•kheeTH•roh•mee•kee eh•pee•tah•yee*
money-belt ζώνη για χρήματα *zoh•nee yah khree•mah•tah*
monument μνημείο *mnee•mee•oh*
moped μοτοποδήλατο *moh•toh•poh•THee•lah•toh*
more παραπάνω *pah•rah•pah•noh*
morning πρωί *proh•ee*
mosquito κουνούπι *koo•noo•pee*
mosquito bite τσίμπημα κουνουπιού *tseem•bee•mah koo•noo•piooh*
motorboat εξωλέμβιο *eh•ksoh•lehm•vee•oh*
motorway [BE] εθνική οδός *ehth•nee•kee oh•THohs*
mountain βουνό *voo•noh*

moustache μουστάκι *moos•tah•kee*
mouth *n* στόμα *stoh•mah*
move *v (room)* μετακομίζω *meh•tah•koh•mee•zoh*
movie ταινία *teh•nee•ah*
movie theater κινηματογράφος *kee•nee•mah•tohgh•rah•fohs*
much πολύ *poh•lee*
muscle *n* μυς *mees*
museum μουσείο *moo•see•oh*
music μουσική *moo•see•kee*
musician μουσικός *moo•see•kohs*
must *v* πρέπει *preh•pee*

N

nail salon σαλόνι νυχιών *sah•loh•nee nee•khiohn*
name *n* όνομα *oh•noh•mah*
napkin πετσέτα *peh•tseh•tah*
nappy [BE] πάνα μωρού *pah•nah moh•roo*
narrow στενός *steh•nohs*
national εθνικός *eth•nee•kohs*
nationality υπηκοότητα *ee•pee•koh•oh•tee•tah*
nature φύση *fee•see*
nature reserve εθνικός δρυμός *eth•nee•kohs THree•mohs*
nature trail μονοπάτι *moh•noh•pah•tee*
nausea ναυτία *nahf•tee•ah*
near *adv* κοντά *kohn•dah*
nearby εδώ κοντά *eh•THoh kohn•dah*
necessary απαραίτητος *ah•pah•reh•tee•tohs*
necklace κολλιέ *koh•lieh*
need *v* χρειάζομαι *khree•ah•zoh•meh*
neighbor *n* γείτονας *yee•toh•nahs*
nerve νεύρο *nehv•roh*
never ποτέ *poh•teh*
new καινούργιος *keh•noor•yohs*
newspaper εφημερίδα *eh•fee•meh•ree•THah*
newsstand περίπτερο *peh•ree•pteh•roh*
next επόμενος *eh•poh•meh•nohs*
next to δίπλα *THeep•lah*
night νύχτα *neekh•tah*
night club νυχτερινό κέντρο *neekh•teh•ree•noh kehn•droh*
noisy θορυβώδης *thoh•ree•voh•THees*
none *adj* κανένας *kah•neh•nahs*
non-smoking μη καπνίζοντες *mee kap•nee•zohn•dehs*
north βόρεια *voh•ree•ah*
nose *n* μύτη *mee•tee*
nudist beach παραλία γυμνιστών *pah•rah•lee•ah yeem•nees•tohn*
nurse *n* νοσοκόμα *noh•soh•koh•mah*

O

occupied κατειλημένος *kah•tee•lee•meh•nohs*
office γραφείο *ghrah•fee•oh*
old *adj (thing)* παλιός *pah•liohs; (person)* γέρικος *yeh•ree•kohs*
old town παλιά πόλη *pah•liah poh•lee*
old-fashioned ντεμοντέ *deh•mohn•deh*
once μια φορά *miah foh•rah*
one-way ticket απλό εισιτήριο *ahp•loh ee•see•tee•ree•oh*
open *adj* ανοιχτός *ah•neekh•tohs; v* ανοίγω *ah•nee•ghoh*
opening hours ώρες λειτουργίας *oh•rehs lee•toor•yee•ahs*
opera όπερα *oh•peh•rah*
opposite απέναντι *ah•peh•nahn•dee*
optician οφθαλμίατρος *ohf•thahl•mee•aht•rohs*
orchestra ορχήστρα *ohr•khees•trah*
order *v* παραγγέλνω *pah•rah•gehl•noh*
organized οργανωμένος *ohr•ghah•noh•meh•nohs*
others άλλα *ah•lah*
out *adv* έξω *eh•ksoh*
outdoor εξωτερικός *eh•ksoh•teh•ree•kohs*
outside *adj* έξω *eh•ksoh*
oval οβάλ *oh•vahl*
oven φούρνος *foor•nohs*
over there εκεί *eh•kee*
overnight (package) ένα βράδυ *eh•nah vrah•THee*
owe χρωστώ *khroh•stoh*
owner κάτοχος *kah•toh•khohs*

P

pacifier πιπίλα *pee•pee•lah*
pack *v (baggage)* φτιάχνω τις βαλίτσες *ftee•ahkh•noh tees vah•lee•tsehs*
paddling pool [BE] ρηχή πισίνα *ree•khee pee•see•nah*
padlock λουκέτο *loo•keh•toh*
pain *n* πόνος *poh•nohs*
painkiller παυσίπονο *pahf•see•poh•noh*
paint *v* ζωγραφίζω *zohgh•rah•fee•zoh*
pair ζευγάρι *zehv•ghah•ree*
pajamas πυτζάμες *pee•jah•mehs*
palace ανάκτορα *ah•nahk•toh•rah*
panorama πανόραμα *pah•noh•rah•mah*
pants παντελόνι *pahn•deh•loh•nee*
paper χαρτί *khar•tee*
paralysis παραλυσία *pah•rah•lee•see•ah*
parcel πακέτο *pah•keh•toh*
parents γονείς *ghoh•nees*
park *n* πάρκο *pahr•koh*
parking lot χώρος στάθμευσης *khoh•rohs stahth•mehf•sees*

parking meter παρκόμετρο *pahr•koh•meht•roh*
party *n (social gathering)* πάρτυ *pah•rtee*
pass *v* περνώ *pehr•noh*
passenger επιβάτης *eh•pee•vah•tees*
passport διαβατήριο *THiah•vah•tee•ree•oh*
pastry store ζαχαροπλαστείο *zah•khah•rohp•lahs•tee•oh*
path μονοπάτι *moh•noh•pah•tee*
pay *v* πληρώνω *plee•roh•noh*
payment πληρωμή *plee•roh•mee*
peak *n* κορυφή *koh•ree•fee*
pearl μαργαριτάρι *mahr•ghah•ree•tah•ree*
pebbly (beach) με χαλίκια *meh khah•lee•kiah*
pedestrian crossing διάβαση πεζών *THee•ah•vah•see peh•zohn*
pedestrian zone πεζόδρομος *peh•zohTH•roh•mohs*
pen *n* στυλό *stee•loh*
per την *teen*
perhaps ίσως *ee•sohs*
period (menstrual) περίοδος *peh•ree•oh•THohs*; **(time)** χρονική περίοδος *khroh•nee•kee peh•ree•oh•Thohs*
permit *n* άδεια *ah•THee•ah*
petrol [BE] βενζίνη *vehn•zee•nee*
pewter κασσίτερος *kah•see•teh•rohs*
phone *n* τηλέφωνο *tee•leh•foh•noh*
phone call τηλεφώνημα *tee•leh•foh•nee•mah*
phone card τηλεκάρτα *tee•leh•kahr•tah*
photo *v* φωτογραφία *foh•tohgh•rah•fee•ah*
photocopier φωτοτυπικό *foh•toh•tee•pee•koh*
phrase *n* φράση *frah•see*
pick up παίρνω *pehr•noh*
picnic area περιοχή για πικνίκ *peh•ree•oh•khee yah peek•neek*
piece τεμάχιο *teh•mah•khee•oh*
pillow μαξιλάρι *mah•ksee•lah•ree*
pillow case μαξιλαροθήκη *mah•ksee•lah•roh•thee•kee*
pipe (smoking) πίπα *pee•pah*
piste [BE] μονοπάτι *moh•noh•pah•tee*
pizzeria πιτσαρία *pee•tsah•ree•ah*
plan *n* σχέδιο *skheh•THee•oh*
plane *n* αεροπλάνο *ah•eh•rohp•lah•noh*
plant *n* φυτό *fee•toh*
plastic wrap διαφανή μεμβράνη *THee•ah•fah•nee mehm•vrah•nee*
platform αποβάθρα *ah•poh•vahth•rah*
platinum πλατίνα *plah•tee•nah*
play *v* **(games)** παίζω *peh•zoh*; *(music)* παίζω *peh•zoh*
playground παιδική χαρά *peh•THee•kee khah•rah*
pleasant ευχάριστος *ehf•khah•rees•tohs*
plug *n* πρίζα *pree•zah*
point *n* σημείο *see•mee•oh*; *v* δείχνω *THeekh•noh*
poison *n* δηλητήριο *THee•lee•tee•ree•oh*
poisonous δηλητηριώδης *THee•lee•tee•ree•oh•THees*
police *n* αστυνομία *ah•stee•noh•mee•ah*
police station αστυνομικό τμήμα *ah•stee•noh•mee•koh tmee•mah*
pond *n* λιμνούλα *leem•noo•lah*
popular δημοφιλής *THee•moh•fee•lees*
porter αχθοφόρος *ahkh•thoh•foh•rohs*
portion *n* μερίδα *meh•ree•THah*
possible πιθανός *pee•thah•nohs*
postbox [BE] ταχυδρομικό κουτί *tah•kheeTH•roh•mee•koh koo•tee*
post card καρτποστάλ *kahrt•poh•stahl*
post office ταχυδρομείο *tah•kheeTH•roh•mee•oh*
pottery αγγειοπλαστική *ahn•gee•ohp•lahs•tee•kee*
pound (sterling) λίρα *lee•rah*
pregnant έγκυος *eh•gee•ohs*
prescribe συνταγογραφώ *seen•dah•ghoh•ghrah•foh*
prescription συνταγή γιατρού *seen•dah•yee yaht•roo*
present δώρο *THoh•roh*
press *v* σιδερώνω *see•THeh•roh•noh*
pretty *adj* όμορφος *oh•mohr•fohs*
prison *n* φυλακή *fee•lah•kee*
private bathroom ιδιωτικό μπάνιο *ee•THee•oh•tee•koh bah•nioh*
problem πρόβλημα *prohv•lee•mah*
program *n* πρόγραμμα *prohgh•rah•mah*
program of events πρόγραμμα θεαμάτων *proh•ghrah•mah theh•ah•mah•tohn*
prohibited απαγορευμένος *ah•pah•ghoh•rehv•meh•nohs*
pronounce προφέρω *proh•feh•roh*
public δημόσιος *THee•moh•see•ohs*
public holiday αργία *ahr•yee•ah*
pump *n* τρόμπα *troh•mbah*
purpose σκοπός *skoh•pohs*
put *v* βάζω *vah•zoh*

Q

quality ποιότητα *pee•oh•tee•tah*
quantity ποσότητα *poh•soh•tee•tah*
quarantine *n* καραντίνα *kah•rahn•dee•nah*
quarter (quantity) ένα τέταρτο *eh•nah teh•tah•rtoh*
quay αποβάθρα *ah•poh•vath•rah*
question *n* ερώτηση *eh•roh•tee•see*
queue [BE] *v* περιμένω στην ουρά *peh•ree•meh•noh steen oo•rah*
quick γρήγορος *ghree•ghoh•rohs*
quiet *adj* ήσυχος *ee•see•khohs*

R

racket (tennis, squash) ρακέτα *rah•keh•tah*
radio *n* ραδιόφωνο *rah•THee•oh•foh•noh*
railway station [BE] σιδηροδρομικός σταθμός *see•THee•rohTH•roh•mee•kohs stahth•mohs*
rain *n* βροχή *vroh•khee; v* βρέχει *vreh•khee*
raincoat αδιάβροχο *ah•THee•ahv•roh•khoh*
rapids ρεύμα ποταμού *rehv•mah poh•tah•moo*
rare (unusual) σπάνιος *spah•nee•ohs*
rash *n* εξάνθημα *eh•ksahn•thee•mah*
ravine ρεματιά *reh•mah•tiah*
razor ξυραφάκι *ksee•rah•fah•kee*
razor blade ξυραφάκι *ksee•rah•fah•kee*
ready *adj* έτοιμος *eh•tee•mohs*
real (genuine) γνήσιος *ghee•see•ohs;* **(true)** αληθινός *ah•lee•thee•nohs*
receipt απόδειξη *ah•poh•THee•ksee*
reception (hotel) ρεσεψιόν *reh•seh•psiohn*
recommend συστήνω *sees•tee•noh*
reduction έκπτωση *ehk•ptoh•see*
refund *n* επιστροφή χρημάτων *eh•pees•troh•fee khree•mah•tohn*
region περιοχή *peh•ree•oh•khee*
registration number αριθμός κυκλοφορίας *ah•reeth•mohs kee•kloh•foh•ree•ahs*
religion θρησκεία *three•skee•ah*
remember θυμάμαι *thee•mah•meh*
rent *v* νοικιάζω *nee•kiah•zoh*
repair *n* επισκευή *eh•pee•skeh•vee; v* επισκευάζω *eh•pee•skeh•vah•zoh*
repeat *v* επαναλαμβάνω *eh•pah•nah•lahm•vah•noh*
replacement part ανταλλακτικό *ahn•dah•lahk•tee•koh*
report *v* αναφέρω *ah•nah•feh•roh*
restaurant εστιατόριο *ehs•tee•ah•toh•ree•oh*
restroom τουαλέτα *too•ah•leh•tah*
retired συνταξιούχος *seen•dah•ksee•oo•khohs*
return ticket [BE] εισιτήριο με επιστροφή *ee•see•tee•ree•oh meh eh•pee•stroh•fee*
reverse the charges με χρέωση του καλούμενου *meh khreh•oh•see too kah•loo•meh•noo*
revolting αηδιαστικός *ah•ee•THee•ah•stee•kohs*
rib πλευρό *plehv•roh*
right *adj* **(correct)** σωστός *soh•stohs;* **(side)** δεξιός *THeh•ksee•ohs*
river ποταμός *poh•tah•mohs*
road δρόμος *THroh•mohs*
road assistance οδική βοήθεια *oh•THee•kee voh•ee•thee•ah*
road sign πινακίδα *pee•nah•kee•Thah*
robbery ληστεία *lees•tee•ah*
rock *n* βράχος *vrah•khohs*
rock climbing αναρρίχηση *ah•nah•ree•khee•see*
romantic ρομαντικός *roh•mahn•dee•kohs*
roof *n* στέγη *steh•yee*
room *n* δωμάτιο *THoh•mah•tee•oh*
room service υπηρεσία δωματίου *ee•pee•reh•see•ah THoh•mah•tee•oo*
rope *n* σχοινί *skhee•nee*
round *adj* στρογγυλός *strohn•gkee•lohs; n (of golf)* παιχνίδι *pehkh•nee•THee*
round-trip ticket εισιτήριο με επιστροφή *ee•see•tee•ree•oh meh eh•pee•stroh•fee*
route *n* διαδρομή *THee•ahTH•roh•mee*
rowing κωπηλασία *koh•pee•lah•see•ah*
rubbish [BE] σκουπίδια *skoo•peeTH•yah*
rude αγενής *ah•yeh•nees*
rug χαλί *khah•lee*
run *v* τρέχω *treh•khoh*
rush hour ώρα αιχμής *oh•rah ehkh•mees*

S

safe *adj (not dangerous)* ασφαλής *ahs•fah•lees*
sailing boat ιστιοπλοϊκό *ees•tee•oh•ploh•ee•koh*
sales tax ΦΠΑ *fee•pee•ah*
same ίδιος *ee•THee•ohs*
sand άμμος *ah•mohs*
sandals πέδιλα *peh•THee•lah*
sandy (beach) με άμμο *meh ah•moh*

sanitary napkin σερβιέτα *sehr•vee•eh•tah*
satin σατέν *sah•tehn*
saucepan κατσαρόλα *kah•tsah•roh•lah*
sauna σάουνα *sah•oo•nah*
scarf κασκόλ *kahs•kohl*
scissors ψαλίδι *psah•lee•THee*
scratch γρατζουνιά *ghrah•joo•niah*
screw *n* βίδα *vee•THah*
screwdriver κατσαβίδι *kah•tsah•vee•THee*
sea θάλασσα *thah•lah•sah*
seafront προκυμαία *proh•kee•meh•ah*
seat *n* θέση *theh•see*
second-hand shop κατάστημα μεταχειρισμένων ειδών *kah•tah•stee•mah meh•tah•khee•reez•meh•nohn ee•THohn*
sedative ηρεμιστικό *ee•reh•mee•stee•koh*
see βλέπω *vleh•poh*
send στέλνω *stehl•noh*
senior citizen ηλικιωμένος *ee•lee•kee•oh•meh•nohs*
separately ξεχωριστά *kseh•khoh•ree•stah*
service *n* **(business)** υπηρεσία *ee•pee•reh•see•ah*; **(mass)** λειτουργία *lee•toor•yee•ah*
service charge χρέωση υπηρεσίας *khreh•oh•see ee•pee•reh•see•ahs*
sewer υπόνομος *ee•poh•noh•mohs*
shade (color) απόχρωση *ah•pohkh•roh•see*; **(darkness)** σκιά *skee•ah*
shampoo *n* σαμπουάν *sahm•poo•ahn*
shape *n* σχήμα *skhee•mah*
shaving cream κρέμα ξυρίσματος *kreh•mah ksee•reez•mah•tohs*
shelf *n* ράφι *rah•fee*
ship *n* πλοίο *plee•oh*
shirt πουκάμισο *poo•kah•mee•soh*
shock (electric) ηλεκτροπληξία *ee•leh•ktroh•plee•ksee•ah*
shoe παπούτσι *pah•poo•tsee*
shoe polish βερνίκι παπουτσιών *vehr•nee•kee pah•poo•tsiohn*
shoe repair επισκευή παπουτσιών *eh•pee•skeh•vee pah•poo•tsiohn*
shoe store κατάστημα υποδημάτων *kah•tah•stee•mah ee•poh•THee•mah•tohn*
shop (store) κατάστημα *kah•tah•stee•mah*
shopping mall εμπορικό κέντρο *ehm•boh•ree•koh keh•ntroh*
shore *n* ακτή *ahk•tee*
short *adj* κοντός *kohn•dohs*
shorts *n* σορτς *sohrts*
short-sighted [BE] μύωπας *mee•oh•pahs*
shoulder *n* **(anatomy)** ώμος *oh•mohs*
show δείχνω *THeekh•noh*
shower *n* ντους *dooz*
shower gel αφρόλουτρο για ντους *ahf•roh•loot•roh yah dooz*
shut *adj* κλειστός *klees•tohs*
sick *adj* άρρωστος *ah•rohs•tohs*
side (of road) μεριά *mehr•yah*
sightseeing sight αξιοθέατο *ah•ksee•oh•theh•ah•toh*
sightseeing tour ξενάγηση στα αξιοθέατα *kseh•nah•yee•see stah ah•ksee•oh•theh•ah•tah*
sign (road) σήμα *see•mah*
silk μετάξι *meh•tah•ksee*
silver ασήμι *ah•see•mee*
simple απλός *ahp•lohs*
single (not married) ελεύθερος *eh•lehf•theh•rohs*
single room μονόκλινο δωμάτιο *moh•noh•klee•noh THoh•mah•tee•oh*
single ticket [BE] απλό εισιτήριο *ahp•loh ee•see•tee•ree•oh*
sink (bathroom) νιπτήρας *nee•ptee•rahs*
sit κάθομαι *kah•thoh•meh*
size *n* μέγεθος *meh•yeh•thohs*
skates παγοπέδιλα *pah•ghoh•peh•THee•lah*
skating rink παγοδρόμιο *pah•ghohTH•roh•mee•oh*
ski boots μπότες του σκι *boh•tehs too skee*
ski poles μπαστούνια του σκι *bahs•too•niah too skee*
ski school σχολή σκι *skhoh•lee skee*
skiing σκι *skee*
skin *n* δέρμα *Thehr•mah*
skirt φούστα *foo•stah*
sleep *v* κοιμάμαι *kee•mah•meh*
sleeping bag υπνόσακκος *ee•pnoh•sah•kohs*
sleeping car βαγκόν-λι *vah•gohn•lee*
sleeping pill υπνωτικό χάπι *eep•noh•tee•koh khah•pee*
slippers παντόφλες *pahn•dohf•lehs*
slope (ski) πλαγιά *plah•yah*
slow *adj* αργός *ahr•ghohs*
small μικρός *meek•rohs*
smell *v* μυρίζω *mee•ree•zoh*
smoke *v* καπνίζω *kahp•nee•zoh*
smoking area περιοχή για καπνίζοντες *peh•ree•oh•khee yah kahp•nee•zohn•dehs*
snack bar κυλικείο *kee•lee•kee•oh*
sneakers αθλητικά παπούτσια *ath•lee•tee•kah pah•poo•tsiah*

snorkeling equipment εξοπλισμό για ελέυθερη κατάδυση *eh•ksohp•leez•moh yah eh•lehf•theh•ree kah•tah•THee•see*
snow *v* χιονίζει *khioh•nee•zee*
soap *n* σαπούνι *sah•poo•nee*
soccer ποδόσφαιρο *poh•THohs•feh•roh*
socket πρίζα *pree•zah*
socks κάλτσες *kahl•tsehs*
sofa καναπές *kah•nah•pehs*
sole (shoes) σόλα *soh•lah*
something κάτι *kah•tee*
sometimes μερικές φορές *meh•ree•kehs foh•rehs*
soon σύντομα *seen•doh•mah*
soother [BE] πιπίλα *pee•pee•lah*
sore throat πονόλαιμος *poh•noh•leh•mohs*
sort *n* είδος *ee•THohs; v* διαλέγω *THiah•leh•ghoh*
south *adj* νότιος *noh•tee•ohs*
souvenir σουβενίρ *soo•veh•neer*
souvenir store κατάστημα σουβενίρ *kah•tahs•tee•mah soo•veh•neer*
spa σπα *spah*
space *n* **(area)** χώρος *khoh•rohs*
spare (extra) επιπλέον *eh•peep•leh•ohn*
speak μιλώ *mee•loh*
special requirement ειδική ανάγκη *ee•THee•kee ah•nahn•gkee*
specialist ειδικός *ee•THee•kohs*
specimen δείγμα *THeegh•mah*
speed *v* τρέχω *treh•khoh*
spend ξοδεύω *ksoh•THeh•voh*
spine σπονδυλική στήλη *spohn•THee•lee•kee stee•lee*
spoon *n* κουτάλι *koo•tah•lee*
sport αθλητισμός *ahth•lee•teez•mohs*
sporting goods store κατάστημα αθλητικών ειδών *kah•tahs•tee•mah ath•lee•tee•kohn ee•THohn*
sports massage αθλητικό μασάζ *ahth•lee•tee•koh mah•sahz*
sports stadium αθλητικό στάδιο *ahth•lee•tee•koh stah•THee•oh*
square τετράγωνος *teht•rah•ghoh•nohs*
stadium στάδιο *stah•THee•oh*
stain *n* λεκές *leh•kehs*
stairs σκάλες *skah•lehs*
stale μπαγιάτικος *bah•yah•tee•kohs*
stamp *n* **(postage)** γραμματόσημο *ghrah•mah•toh•see•moh*
start *v* αρχίζω *ahr•khee•zoh*
statement (legal) δήλωση *THee•loh•see*
statue άγαλμα *ah•ghahl•mah*
stay *v* μένω *meh•noh*
sterilizing solution αποστειρωτικό διάλυμα *ah•pohs•tee•roh•tee•koh THee•ah•lee•mah*
sting *n* **(insect)** τσίμπημα *tsee•bee•mah*
stolen κλεμένος *kleh•meh•nohs*
stomach *n* στομάχι *stoh•mah•khee*
stomachache στομαχόπονος *stoh•mah•khoh•poh•nohs*
stop *n* **(bus)** στάση *stah•see; v* σταματώ *stah•mah•toh*
store guide [BE] οδηγός καταστήματος *oh•THee•ghohs kah•tahs•tee•mah•tohs*
stove κουζίνα *koo•zee•nah*
straight ahead ευθεία *ehf•thee•ah*
strange παράξενος *pah•rah•kseh•nohs*
straw (drinking) καλαμάκι *kah•lah•mah•kee*
stream *n* ρυάκι *ree•ah•kee*
street δρόμος *THroh•mohs*
string *n (cord)* σπάγγος *spah•gohs*
student φοιτητής *fee•tee•tees*
study *v* σπουδάζω *spoo•THah•zoh*
style *n* στυλ *steel*
subtitled με υπότιτλους *meh ee•poh•teet•loos*
subway μετρό *meh•troh*
subway station σταθμός μετρό *stahth•mohs meh•troh*
suggest προτείνω *proh•tee•noh*
suit (men's) κουστούμι *koos•too•mee;* **(women's)** ταγιέρ *tah•yehr*
suitable κατάλληλος *kah•tah•lee•lohs*
sunburn *n* έγκαυμα ηλίου *ehn•gahv•mah ee•lee•oo*
sunglasses γυαλιά ηλίου *yah•liah ee•lee•oo*
sunshade [BE] ομπρέλλα *ohm•breh•lah*
sunstroke ηλίαση *ee•lee•ah•see*
sun tan lotion λοσιόν μαυρίσματος *loh•siohn mahv•rees•mah•tohs*
sunscreen αντιηλιακό *ahn•dee•ee•lee•ah•koh*
superb έξοχος *eh•ksoh•khohs*
supermarket σουπερμάρκετ *soo•pehr•mahr•keht*
supervision επίβλεψη *eh•peev•leh•psee*
surname επίθετο *eh•pee•theh•toh*
sweatshirt φούτερ *foo•tehr*
swelling πρήξιμο *pree•ksee•moh*
swimming κολύμβηση *koh•leem•vee•see*
swimming pool πισίνα *pee•see•nah*
swimming trunks μαγιό *mah•yoh*
swimsuit μαγιό *mah•yoh*

switch *n* διακόπτης *THiah•koh•ptees*
swollen πρησμένος *preez•meh•nohs*
symptom σύμπτωμα *seem•ptoh•mah*

T

table τραπέζι *trah•peh•zee*
tablecloth τραπεζομάντηλο *trah•peh•zoh•mahn•dee•loh*
tablet χάπι *khah•pee*
take παίρνω *pehr•noh*
take a photograph βγάζω φωτογραφία *vghah•zoh foh•tohgh•rah•fee•ah*
take away [BE] πακέτο για το σπίτι *pah•keh•toh yah toh spee•tee*
tall ψηλός *psee•lohs*
tampon ταμπόν *tahm•bohn*
tax *n* φόρος *foh•rohs*
taxi ταξί *tah•ksee*
taxi driver ταξιτζής *tah•ksee•jees*
taxi rank [BE] πιάτσα ταξί *piah•tsah tah•ksee*
teaspoon κουταλάκι *koo•tah•lah•kee*
team *n* ομάδα *oh•mah•THah*
teenager έφηβος *eh•fee•vohs*
telephone *n* τηλέφωνο *tee•leh•foh•noh*
telephone booth τηλεφωνικός θάλαμος *tee•leh•foh•nee•kohs thah•lah•mohs*
telephone call κλήση *klee•see*
telephone directory τηλεφωνικός κατάλογος *tee•leh•foh•nee•kohs kah•tah•loh•ghohs*
telephone number αριθμός τηλεφώνου *ah•reeth•mohs tee•leh•foh•noo*
tell λέω *leh•oh*
temperature (body) θερμοκρασία *theh•rmohk•rah•see•ah*
temple ναός *nah•ohs*
temporary προσωρινός *proh•soh•ree•nohs*
tennis τέννις *teh•nees*
tennis court γήπεδο τέννις *yee•peh•THoh teh•nees*
tent σκηνή *skee•nee*
terrible φοβερός *foh•veh•rohs*
theater θέατρο *theh•aht•roh*
theft κλοπή *kloh•pee*
there εκεί *eh•kee*
thermal bath ιαματικό λουτρό *ee•ah•mah•tee•koh loot•roh*
thermos flask θερμός *thehr•mohs*
thick χοντρός *khohn•drohs*
thief κλέφτης *klehf•tees*
thin *adj* λεπτός *lehp•tohs*
think νομίζω *noh•mee•zoh*
thirsty διψάω *THee•psah•oh*
those εκείνα *eh•kee•nah*
throat λαιμός *leh•mohs*
thumb αντίχειρας *ahn•dee•khee•rahs*
ticket εισιτήριο *ee•see•tee•ree•oh*
ticket office γραφείο εισιτήριων *ghrah•fee•oh ee•see•tee•ree•ohn*
tie *n* γραβάτα *ghrah•vah•tah*
tight *adj* στενός *steh•nohs*
tights [BE] *n* καλσόν *kahl•sohn*
timetable [BE] δρομολόγιο *THroh•moh•loh•yee•oh*
tire λάστιχο *lahs•tee•khoh*
tired κουρασμένος *koo•rahz•meh•nohs*
tissue χαρτομάντηλο *khahr•toh•mahn•dee•loh*
toaster τοστιέρα *toh•stieh•rah*
tobacco καπνός *kahp•nohs*
tobacconist καπνοπωλείο *kahp•noh•poh•lee•oh*
toilet [BE] τουαλέτα *too•ah•leh•tah*
toilet paper χαρτί υγείας *khahr•tee ee•yee•ahs*
toiletries καλλυντικά *kah•leen•dee•kah*
tongue γλώσσα *ghloh•sah*
too (extreme) πάρα πολύ *pah•rah poh•lee*
tooth δόντι *THohn•dee*
toothache πονόδοντος *poh•noh•THohn•dohs*
toothbrush οδοντόβουρτσα *oh•THohn•doh•voor•tsah*
toothpaste οδοντόπαστα *oh•THohn•doh•pahs•tah*
top *adj* πάνω *pah•noh*
torn σχισμένος *skheez•meh•nohs*
tour guide ξεναγός *kseh•nah•ghohs*
tourist τουρίστας *too•rees•tahs*
towards προς *prohs*
tower πύργος *peer•ghohs*
town πόλη *poh•lee*
town hall δημαρχείο *THee•mahr•khee•oh*
toy store κατάστημα παιχνιδιών *kah•tahs•tee•mah peh•khnee•THiohn*
traditional παραδοσιακός *pah•rah•THoh•see•ah•kohs*
traffic κίνηση *kee•nee•see*
trail μονοπάτι *moh•noh•pah•tee*
trailer τροχόσπιτο *troh•khohs•pee•toh*
train τρένο *treh•noh*
train station σταθμός των τρένων *stahth•mohs tohn treh•nohn*
tram τραμ *trahm*
transfer μεταφέρω *meh•tah•feh•roh*
transit *n* μεταφορά *meh•tah•foh•rah*
translate μεταφράζω *meh•tah•frah•zoh*
translation μετάφραση *meh•tah•frah•see*
translator μεταφραστής *meh•tah•frah•stees*

trash σκουπίδια *skoo•peeTH•yah*
trash can κάδος απορριμμάτων *kah•THohs ah•poh•ree•mah•tohn*
travel agency ταξιδιωτικό γραφείο *tah•ksee•THyoh•tee•koh ghrah•fee•oh*
travel sickness [BE] ναυτία *nahf•tee•ah*
traveler's check ταξιδιωτική επιταγή *tah•ksee•THee•oh•tee•kee eh•pee•tah•yee*
tray δίσκος *THees•kohs*
tree δέντρο *THehn•droh*
trim *n* διόρθωμα *THee•ohr•thoh•mah*
trolley [BE] (cart) καροτσάκι *kah•roh•tsah•kee*
trolley-bus τρόλλεϋ *troh•leh•ee*
trousers [BE] παντελόνι *pahn•deh•loh•nee*
try on δοκιμάζω *THoh•kee•mah•zoh*
T-shirt μπλουζάκι *bloo•zah•kee*
tunnel τούνελ *too•nehl*
turn *v* γυρίζω *yee•ree•zoh*
turn down *v (volume, heat)* χαμηλώνω *khah•mee•loh•noh*
turn off *v* σβήνω *svee•noh*
turn on *v* ανάβω *ah•nah•voh*
turn up *v (volume, heat)* ανεβάζω *ah•neh•vah•zoh*
TV τηλεόραση *tee•leh•oh•rah•see*
twin bed διπλό κρεβάτι *THeep•loh kreh•vah•tee*
typical τυπικός *tee•pee•kohs*

U

ugly άσχημος *ahs•khee•mohs*
unconscious αναίσθητος *ah•nehs•thee•tohs*
underground [BE] υπόγειος *ee•poh•ghee•ohs*
underpants [BE] κυλοτάκι *kee•loh•tah•kee*
understand καταλαβαίνω *kah•tah•lah•veh•noh*
uneven (ground) ανώμαλος *ah•noh•mah•lohs*
unfortunately δυστυχώς *THees•tee•khohs*
uniform *n* στολή *stoh•lee*
unique μοναδικός *moh•nah•THee•kohs*
unit μονάδα *moh•nah•THah*
United Kingdom Ηνωμένο Βασίλειο *ee•noh•meh•noh vah•see•lee•oh*
United States Ηνωμένες Πολιτείες *ee•noh•meh•nehs poh•lee•tee•ehs*
university Πανεπιστήμιο *pah•neh•pees•tee•mee•oh*
unlimited mileage απεριόριστα χιλιόμετρα *ah•peh•ree•ohr•ees•tah khee•lioh•meht•rah*
unpleasant δυσάρεστος *THee•sah•reh•stohs*
upper (berth) πάνω (κουκέτα) *pah•noh (koo•keh•tah)*
upstairs επάνω *eh•pah•noh*
urgent επείγον *eh•pee•ghohn*
use *v* χρησιμοποιώ *khree•see•moh•pee•oh*
useful χρήσιμος *khree•see•mohs*

V

vacancy ελεύθερο δωμάτιο *eh•lehf•theh•roh THoh•mah•tee•oh*
vacant ελεύθερος *eh•lehf•theh•rohs*
vacation διακοπές *THee•ah•koh•pehs*
vacation resort θέρετρο διακοπών *theh•reh•troh THee•ah•koh•pohn*
vaccination εμβόλιο *ehm•voh•lee•oh*
valid ισχύει *ee•skhee•ee*
valley κοιλάδα *kee•lah•THah*
valuable πολύτιμος *poh•lee•tee•mohs*
value *n* αξία *ah•ksee•ah*
VAT [BE] ΦΠΑ *fee•pee•ah*
vegetarian χορτοφάγος *khohr•toh•fah•ghohs*
vein φλέβα *fleh•vah*
velvet βελούδο *veh•loo•THoh*
very πολύ *poh•lee*
video βιντεοκασέτα *vee•deh•oh•kah•seh•tah*
video game παιχνίδι βίντεο *pehkh•nee•THee vee•deh•oh*
village χωριό *khohr•yoh*
visa βίζα *vee•zah*
visit *n* επίσκεψη *eh•pees•keh•psee*
volleyball βόλεϋ *voh•leh•ee*
vomit *v* κάνω εμετό *kah•noh eh•meh•toh*

W

wait *v* περιμένω *peh•ree•meh•noh*
waiter *n* γκαρσόν *gahr•sohn*
waitress δεσποινίς *THehs•pee•nees*
wake *v* ξυπνώ *kseep•noh*
walk *v* περπατώ *pehr•pah•toh*
walking route διαδρομή περιήγησης *THee•ah•THroh•mee peh•ree•ee•yee•sees*
wall τοίχος *tee•khohs*
wallet πορτοφόλι *pohr•toh•foh•lee*
want θέλω *theh•loh*
warm ζεστός *zehs•tohs*
washing machine πλυντήριο *pleen•deer•ee•oh*
watch *n* ρολόι *roh•loh•ee*
watch strap λουρί ρολογιού *loo•ree roh•loh•yioo*
water *n* νερό *neh•roh*
waterfall καταρράχτης *kah•tah•rahkh•tees*

waterproof αδιάβροχος *ah•THee•ahv•roh•khohs*
wave *n* κύμα *kee•mah*
way δρόμος *THroh•mohs*
wear *v* φορώ *foh•roh*
weather καιρός *keh•rohs*
weather forecast πρόβλεψη καιρού *prohv•leh•psee keh•roo*
wedding γάμος *ghah•mohs*
west δυτικά *THee•tee•kah*
wetsuit στολή δύτη *stoh•lee THee•tee*
wheelchair αναπηρική καρέκλα *ah•nah•pee•ree•kee kah•rehk•lah*
wide φαρδύς *fahr•THees*
wife σύζυγος *see•zee•ghohs*
window παράθυρο *pah•rah•thee•roh*
window seat θέση δίπλα στο παράθυρο *theh•see THeep•lah stoh pah•rah•thee•roh*
winery οινοποιείο *ee•noh•pee•ee•oh*
wireless internet ασύρματο ίντερνετ *ah•see•rmah•toh ee•nteh•rnet*
with με *meh*
withdraw κάνω ανάληψη *kah•noh ah•nah•lee•psee*
without χωρίς *khoh•rees*
witness μάρτυρας *mahr•tee•rahs*
wood (forest) δάσος *THah•sohs*; **(material)** ξύλο *ksee•loh*
work δουλεύω *THoo•leh•voh*
worry ανησυχώ *ah•nee•see•khoh*
worse χειρότερος *khee•roh•teh•rohs*
wound (cut) πληγή *plee•yee*
write (down) γράφω *ghrah•foh*
wrong λάθος *lah•thohs*

X

x-ray ακτινογραφία *ahk•tee•nohgh•rah•fee•ah*

Y

yacht γιωτ *yoht*
yellow κίτρινος *keet•ree•nohs*
young νέος *neh•ohs*
youth hostel ξενώνας νεότητας *kseh•noh•nahs neh•oh•tee•tahs*

Z

zoo ζωολογικός κήπος *zoh•oh•loh•yee•kohs kee•pohs*

GREEK-ENGLISH

A

ATM *ehee•tee•ehm* ATM
άγαλμα *ah•ghahl•mah* statue
αγαπημένος *ah•ghah•pee•meh•nohs* favorite
αγαπώ *ah•ghah•poh* *v* love
αγγειοπλαστική *ahn•gee•ohp•lahs•tee•kee* pottery
Αγγλία *ahng•lee•ah* England
αγγλικά *ahng•lee•kah* English language
αγγλικός *ahng•lee•kohs* *adj* English
Άγγλος *ahng•lohs* English (nationality)
αγενής *ah•yeh•nees* rude
αγορά *ah•ghoh•rah* *n* market
αγοράζω *ah•ghoh•rah•zoh* buy
αγόρι *ah•ghoh•ree* boy
αγώνας *ah•ghoh•nahs* *n* match (sport)
άδεια *ah•THee•ah* *n* permit
άδεια σκι *ah•THee•ah* skee lift pass
άδειος *ahTH•yohs* *adj* empty
αδιάβροχο *ah•THee•ahv•roh•khoh* raincoat
αδιάβροχος *ah•THee•ahv•roh•khohs* waterproof
αδύναμος *ah•THee•nah•mohs* weak
αεροδρόμιο *ah•eh•roh•THroh•mee•oh* airport
αεροπλάνο *ah•eh•rohp•lah•noh* *n* plane
αεροπορική εταιρία *ah•eh•roh•poh•ree•kee eh•teh•ree•ah* airline
αεροπορικώς *ah•eh•roh•poh•ree•kohs* airmail
αηδιαστικός *ah•ee•THee•ah•stee•kohs* revolting
αθλητικά παπούτσια *ath•lee•tee•kah pah•poo•tsiah* sneakers
αθλητικό στάδιο *ahth•lee•tee•koh stah•THee•oh* sports stadium
αθλητικός όμιλος *ahth•lee•tee•kohs oh•mee•lohs* sports club
αθλητισμός *ahth•lee•teez•mohs* sport
αθώος *ah•thoh•ohs* innocent
αιμορραγία *eh•moh•rah•yee•ah* *n* bleed
αιμορραγώ *eh•moh•rah•yoh* *v* bleed
αίθουσα συναυλιών *eh•thoo•sah see•nahv•lee•ohn* concert hall
ακολουθώ *ah•koh•loo•thoh* *v* follow

ακουστικό βαρυκοΐας *ah•koo•stee•koh vah•ree•koh•ee•ahs* hearing aid
ακριβός *ahk•ree•vohs* expensive
ακτή *ahk•tee n* shore
ακτινογραφία *ahk•tee•nohgh•rah•fee•ah* x-ray
ακυρώνω *ah•kee•roh•noh v* cancel
αληθινός *ah•lee•thee•nohs* real (genuine)
αλλά *ah•lah conj* but
άλλα *ah•lah* others
αλλαγή *ah•lah•yee n* change
αλλάζω *ah•lah•zoh v* exchange (money)
αλλεργικός *ahl•ehr•yee•kohs* allergic
αλληλογραφία *ah•lee•lohgh•rah•fee•ah n* mail
άλλο ένα *ah•loh eh•nah* extra (additional)
άλλος *ah•lohs* another
αλουμινόχαρτο *ah•loo•mee•noh•khah•rtoh* aluminum foil
Αμερικανός *ah•meh•ree•kah•nohs n* American
αμέσως *ah•meh•sohs* immediately
άμμος *ah•mohs* sand
ανάβω *ah•nah•voh v* turn on
αναίσθητος *ah•nehs•thee•tohs* unconscious
ανάκτορα *ah•nahk•toh•rah* palace
αναλυτικός λογαριασμός *ah•nah•lee•tee•kohs loh•ghahr•yahz•mohs* itemized bill
αναπηρική καρέκλα *ah•nah•pee•ree•kee kah•rehk•lah* wheelchair
αναπνευστήρας *ah•nahp•nehf•stee•rahs* snorkel
αναπνέω *ah•nahp•neh•oh* breathe
αναπτήρας *ah•nahp•tee•rahs n* lighter (cigarette)
αναρρίχηση *ah•nah•ree•khee•see* rock climbing
ανατολικά *ah•nah•toh•lee•kah* east
αναφέρω *ah•nah•feh•roh* mention (report)
αναχώρηση *ah•nah•khoh•ree•see* departure (travel)
άνδρας *ahn•THrahs n* male (man)
ανεμιστήρας *ah•neh•mees•tee•rahs n* fan (air)
ανεβάζω *ah•neh•vah•zoh v* turn up (volume, heat)
ανέκδοτο *ah•nehk•THoh•toh n* joke
ανησυχώ *ah•nee•see•khoh* worry
ανθοπωλείο *ahn•thoh•poh•lee•oh* florist
ανοίγω *ah•nee•ghoh v* open
ανοιχτήρι *ah•neekh•tee•ree* can opener
ανοιχτός *ah•neekh•tohs adj* light (color), open
ανοιχτότερος *ah•neekh•toh•teh•rohs adj* lighter (color)
ανταλλακτικό *ahn•dah•lahk•tee•koh* replacement part
αντιβιοτικό *ahn•dee•vee•oh•tee•koh* antibiotic
αντιηλιακό *ahn•dee•ee•lee•ah•koh* sunscreen
αντισηπτική κρέμα *ahn•dee•seep•tee•kee kreh•mah* antiseptic cream
αντίχειρας *ahn•dee•khee•rahs* thumb
ανώμαλος *ah•noh•mah•lohs* uneven (ground)
αξεσουάρ *ah•kseh•soo•ahr* accessory
αξία *ah•ksee•ah n* value
αξιοθέατο *ah•ksee•oh•theh•ah•tah* sightseeing sight
απαγορευμένος *ah•pah•ghoh•rehv•meh•nohs* prohibited
απαραίτητος *ah•pah•reh•tee•tohs* essential, necessary
απασχολημένος *ah•pahs•khoh•lee•meh•nohs adj* busy (occupied)
απέναντι *ah•peh•nahn•dee* opposite
απεριόριστα χιλιόμετρα *ah•peh•ree•ohr•ees•tah khee•lioh•meht•rah* unlimited mileage
απλό εισιτήριο *ahp•loh ee•see•tee•ree•oh* one-way [single BE] ticket
απλός *ahp•lohs* simple
από *ah•poh* from
απομίμηση *ah•poh•mee•mee•see* imitation
αποβάθρα *ah•poh•vahth•rah* platform, quay
απόγευμα *ah•poh•yehv•mah* afternoon
απόδειξη *ah•poh•THee•ksee* receipt
απορρυπαντικό *ah•poh•ree•pahn•dee•koh* detergent
αποσμητικό *ah•pohz•mee•tee•koh* deodorant
αποσκευές *ah•pohs•keh•vehs* baggage [BE]
αποσκευές χειρός *ah•pohs•keh•vehs khee•rohs* hand luggage
αποστειρωτικό διάλυμα *ah•pohs•tee•roh•tee•koh THee•ah•lee•mah* sterilizing solution
απόχρωση *ah•pohkh•roh•see* shade (color)
απώλεια *ah•poh•lee•ah n* loss
αργά *ahr•ghah adv* late
αργία *ahr•yee•ah* public holiday
αργός *ahr•ghohs adj* slow
αριθμός κυκλοφορίας *ah•reeth•mohs kee•kloh•foh•ree•ahs* registration number

αριθμός πτήσεως *ah•reeth•mohs ptee•seh•ohs* flight number
αριθμός τηλεφώνου *ah•reeth•mohs tee•leh•foh•noo* telephone number
αριστερός *ah•rees•teh•rohs* left *(adj)*
αριστερά *ah•rees•teh•rah* left *(adv)*
αρκετά *ahr•keh•tah* enough
αρραβωνιαστικιά *ah•rah•voh•niahs•tee•kiah* fiancée
αρραβωνιαστικός *ah•rah•voh•niahs•tee•kohs* fiancé
αρρώστεια *ahr•ohs•tee•ah* illness
άρρωστος *ah•rohs•tohs adj* sick
αρτοποιείο *ah•rtoh•pee•ee•oh* bakery
αρχάριος *ahr•khah•ree•ohs* beginner
αρχίζω *v ahr•khee•zoh* start
ασανσέρ *ah•sahn•sehr n* lift (elevator)
ασήμι *ah•see•mee* silver
ασύρματο ίντερνετ *ah•see•rmah•toh ee•nteh•rnet* wireless internet
ασθενοφόρο *ahs•theh•noh•foh•roh* ambulance
ασθματικός *ahsth•mah•tee•kohs* asthmatic
ασπιρίνη *ahs•pee•ree•nee* aspirin
αστυνομία *ah•stee•noh•mee•ah n* police
αστυνομικό τμήμα *ah•stee•noh•mee•koh tmee•mah* police station
ασφάλεια *ahs•fah•lee•ah n* fuse; insurance
ασφάλεια αποζημίωσης *ahs•fah•lee•ah ah•poh•zee•mee•oh•sees* insurance claim
ασφάλεια υγείας *ahs•fah•lee•ah ee•yee•ahs* health insurance
ασφαλής *ahs•fah•lees adj* safe (not dangerous)
ασφαλιστική εταιρία *ahs•fah•lees•tee•kee eh•teh•ree•ah* insurance company
άσχημος *ahs•khee•mohs* ugly
άτομο με ειδικές ανάγκες *ah•toh•moh meh ee•THee•kehs ah•nahn•gehs* disabled
ατύχημα *ah•tee•khee•mah* accident
αυθεντικός *ahf•thehn•dee•kohs* genuine
αυθεντικότητα *ahf•thehn•dee•koh•tee•tah* authenticity
αϋπνία *ah•eep•nee•ah* insomnia
αυτοκίνητο *ahf•toh•kee•nee•toh* car
αυχένας *ahf•kheh•nahs* neck (part of body)
αφήνω *ah•fee•noh v* leave (let go)
αφορολόγητα είδη *ah•foh•roh•loh•yee•tah ee•THee* duty-free goods
αφρόλουτρο για ντουζ *ahf•roh•loot•roh yah dooz* shower gel
αχθοφόρος *ahkh•thoh•foh•rohs* porter

Β

βαμβάκι *vahm•vah•kee* cotton
βαγκόν-λι *vah•gohn•lee* sleeping car
βάζο *vah•zoh n* jar
βάζω *vah•zoh v* put
βαλές *vah•lehs* jack
βαρετός *vah•reh•tohs* boring
βάρκα *vahr•kah* boat
βαρύς *vah•rees* heavy
βασιλιάς *vah•see•liahs* king
βγαίνω *vyeh•noh* get out (of vehicle)
βελούδο *veh•loo•THoh* velvet
βενζινάδικο *vehn•zee•nah•THee•koh* gas [petrol BE] station
βενζίνη *vehn•zee•nee* gasoline [petrol BE]
βερνίκι παπουτσιών *vehr•nee•kee pah•poo•tsiohn* shoe polish
βήχας *vee•khahs n* cough
βήχω *vee•khoh v* cough
βιβλίο *veev•lee•oh n* book
βιβλιοθήκη *veev•lee•oh•thee•kee* library
βιβλιοπωλείο *veev•lee•oh•poh•lee•oh* bookstore
βίδα *vee•THah n* screw
βίζα *vee•zah* visa
βιντεοκασέτα *vee•deh•oh•kah•seh•tah* video
βλάβη *vlah•vee* breakdown *n* (car)
βλέπω *vleh•poh* see
βοήθεια *voh•ee•thee•ah n* help
βοηθώ *voh•ee•thoh v* help
βόλεϋ *voh•leh•ee* volleyball
βόρεια *voh•ree•ah* north
βοτανικός κήπος *voh•tah•nee•kohs kee•pohs* botanical garden
βουνό *voo•noh* mountain
βουρτσίζω *voor•tsee•zoh v* brush
βραδινό *vrah•THee•noh* dinner
βράδυ *vrah•THee* evening
βράζω *vrah•zoh* boil
βράχος *vrah•khohs n* rock
βρετανικός *vreh•tah•nee•kohs* British *adj*
Βρετανός *vreh•tah•nohs* British (nationality)
βρέχει *vreh•khee v* rain
βροχή *vroh•khee n* rain
βρύση *vree•see* faucet
βρώμικος *vroh•mee•kohs adj* dirty

Γ

γάμος *ghah•mohs* wedding
γάζα *ghah•zah* bandage
γαλάκτωμα για τα μαλλιά *ghah•lah•ktoh•mah yah tah mah•liah* conditioner (hair)
γάντι *ghahn•dee n* glove

γαστρίτιδα *ghahs•tree•tee•THah* gastritis
γεμάτος *yeh•mah•tohs adj* full
γείτονας *yee•toh•nahs n* neighbor
γελώ *yeh•loh v* laugh
γεμιστή *yeh•mees•tee* stuffed olive
γέρικος *yeh•ree•kohs* old (person)
γεύμα *yehv•mah* meal
γέφυρα *yeh•fee•rah n* bridge (over water)
γη *ghee n* land
γήπεδο γκολφ *yee•peh•THoh gohlf* golf course
γήπεδο τέννις *yee•peh•THoh teh•nees* tennis court
γιατρός *yah•trohs* doctor
γιωτ *yoht* yacht
γκαράζ *gah•rahz* garage
γκαρσόν *gahr•sohn* waiter
γκόλφ *gohlf* golf
γκρουπ *groop n* group
γλώσσα *ghloh•sah* tongue
γνωρίζω *ghnoh•ree•zoh* know
γόνατο *ghoh•nah•toh* knee
γονείς *ghoh•nees* parents
γράμμα *ghrah•mah* letter
γραμματόσημο *ghrah•mah•toh•see•moh n* stamp (postage)
γραμμή *ghrah•mee n* line (subway)
γραβάτα *ghrah•vah•tah n* tie
γρασίδι *ghrah•see•THee* grass
γραφείο *ghrah•fee•oh* office
γραφείο ανταλλαγής συναλλάγματος *ghrah•fee•oh ahn•dah•lah•yees see•nah•lahgh•mah•tohs* currency exchange office
γραφείο εισιτήριων *ghrah•fee•oh ee•see•tee•ree•ohn* ticket office
γραφείο πληροφοριών *ghrah•fee•oh plee•roh•foh•ree•ohn* information office
γράφω *ghrah•foh* write (down)
γρήγορα *ghree•ghoh•rah adv* fast
γρήγορος *ghree•ghoh•rohs* quick
γρίππη *ghree•pee* flu
γυαλιά *yah•liah* glasses (optical)
γυαλιά ηλίου *yah•liah ee•lee•oo* sun glasses
γυναικολόγος *yee•neh•koh•loh•ghohs* gynecologist
γυρίζω *yee•ree•zoh v* turn
γωνία *ghoh•nee•ah* corner

Δ

δανείζω *THah•nee•zoh* lend
δάσος *THah•sohs n* forest (wood)
δάχτυλο *THakh•tee•loh n* finger
δείγμα *THeegh•mah* specimen
δείχνω *THeekh•noh v* point (show)
δέντρο *THehn•droh* tree
δεξιός *THeh•ksee•ohs adj* right (not left)
δέρμα *THehr•mah n* skin
δημαρχείο *THee•mahr•khee•oh* town hall
δημοφιλής *THee•moh•fee•lees* popular
δηλητήριο *THee•lee•tee•ree•oh n* poison
δηλητηριώδης *THee•lee•tee•ree•oh•THees* poisonous
δηλώνω *THee•loh•noh* declare
δήλωση *THee•loh•see* statement (legal)
δημόσιος *THee•moh•see•ohs* public
διαμάντι *THiah•mahn•dee n* diamond
διαμέρισμα *THee•ah•meh•reez•mah* apartment
διάβαση πεζών *THee•ah•vah•see peh•zohn* pedestrian crossing
διαβατήριο *THiah•vah•tee•ree•oh* passport
διαβητικός *THee•ah•vee•tee•kohs* diabetic
διαδρομή *THee•ahTH•roh•mee n* route
διάδρομος *THee•ah•THroh•mohs* aisle seat
διαζευγμένος *THee•ah•zehv•ghmeh•nohs* divorced
διακοπές *THee•ah•koh•pehs* vacation [holiday BE]
διακόπτης *THiah•koh•ptees n* switch
διαμέρισμα *THee•ah•mehr•ees•mah n* flat
διάρροια *THee•ah•ree•ah* diarrhea
διάσημος *THee•ah•see•mohs* famous
διεθνής *THee•eth•nees* international
διεθνής φοιτητική κάρτα *THee•ehth•nees fee•tee•tee•kee kahr•tah* International Student Card
διερμηνέας *THee•ehr•mee•neh•ahs* interpreter
διεύθυνση *THee•ehf•theen•see n* address
διευθυντής *THee•ehf•theen•dees* manager
δικηγόρος *THee•kee•ghoh•rohs* lawyer
δίκλινο δωμάτιο *THeek•lee•noh THoh•mah•tee•oh* double room
δίνω *THee•noh* give
διόρθωμα *THee•ohr•thoh•mah n* trim
δίπλα *THeep•lah* next to
διπλό κρεβάτι *THeep•loh kreh•vah•tee* twin bed
δίσκος *THees•kohs* tray
διψάω *THee•psah•oh* thirsty
δοκιμάζω *THoh•kee•mah•zoh*

try on
δολάριο *THoh•lah•ree•oh* dollar
δόντι *THohn•dee* tooth
δοσολογία *THoh•soh•loh•yee•ah* dosage
δουλειά *THoo•liah* job
δουλεύω *THoo•leh•voh* work
δρομολόγιο *THroh•moh•loh•yee•oh* time table
δρόμος *THroh•mohs* road, street, way
δυνατός *THee•nah•tohs adj* loud
δυσάρεστος *THee•sah•reh stohs* unpleasant
δύσκολος *THee•skoh•lohs* difficult
δυσπεψία *THes•peh•psee•ah* indigestion
δυστυχώς *THees•tee•khohs* unfortunately
δυτικά *THee•tee•kah* west
δωμάτιο *THoh•mah•tee•oh* *n* room
δώρο *THoh•roh* gift

Ε

ελιά *eh•liah* olive
εμβόλιο *ehm•voh•lee•oh* vaccination
εμπορικό κέντρο *ehm•boh•ree•koh keh•ntroh* shopping mall [centre BE]
εγγύηση *eh•gee•ee•see n* guarantee
εγγυώμαι *eh•gee•oh•meh v* guarantee
έγκαυμα ηλίου *ehn•gahv•mah ee•lee•oo n* sun burn
έγκυος *eh•gee•ohs* pregnant
έδαφος *eh•THah•fohs* ground (earth)
εδώ *eh•THoh* here
εδώ κοντά *eh•THoh kohn•dah* nearby
εθνική οδός *ehth•nee•kee oh•THohs* highway, motorway
εθνικός *eth•nee•kohs* national
εθνικός δρυμός *eth•nee•kohs THree•mohs* nature reserve
είμαι *ee•meh* be
είμαι κουφός *koo•fohs* deaf
είδη οικιακής χρήσεως *ee•THee ee•kee•ah•kees khree•seh•ohs* household articles
ειδική ανάγκη *ee•THee•kee ah•nahn•gkee* special requirement
ειδικός *ee•THee•kohs* specialist
είδος *ee•THohs* kind (sort)
εισιτήριο *ee•see•tee•ree•oh* fare (ticket)
εισιτήριο με επιστροφή *ee•see•tee•ree•oh meh eh•pee•stroh•fee* roundtrip [return BE] ticket
εκδρομή *ehk•THroh•mee* excursion
εκεί *eh•kee* there, over there
εκείνα *eh•kee•nah* those
έκθεση *ehk•theh•see* exhibition
έκπτωση *ehk•ptoh•see* reduction
έκτακτη ανάγκη *ehk•tahk•tee ah•nah•gee* emergency
ελάχιστος *eh•lah•khees•tohs* minimum
ελεύθερο δωμάτιο *eh•lehf•theh•roh THoh•mah•tee•oh* vacancy
ελεύθερος *eh•lehf•theh•rohs adj* free, single, vacant
ελικόπτερο *eh•lee•kohp•teh•roh* helicopter
Ελλάδα *eh•lah•THah* Greece
Έλληνας *eh•lee•nahs* Greek (nationality)
ελληνικός *eh•lee•nee•kohs adj* Greek
ένα βράδυ *eh•nah vrah•THee* overnight
ένα τέταρτο *eh•nah teh•tah•rtoh* quarter (quantity)
ενδιαφέρων *en•THee•ah•feh•rohn* interesting
ένεση *eh•neh•see* injection
ενήλικας *eh•nee•lee•kahs* adult
ενοχλώ *eh•noh•khloh* disturb
έντομο *ehn•doh•moh* insect
εντομοαπωθητικό *ehn•doh•moh•ah•poh•thee•tee•koh* insect repellent
έντυπο *ehn•dee•poh n* form
εντυπωσιακός *ehn•dee•poh•see•ah•kohs* impressive
ενυδατική κρέμα *eh•nee•THah•tee•kee kreh•mah* moisturizer (cream)
εξάνθημα *eh•ksahn•thee•mah n* rash
εξαργυρώνω *eh•ksahr•ghee•roh•noh v* cash
εξόγκωμα *eh•ksoh•goh•mah n* lump (medical)
έξοδος *eh•ksoh•THohs n* gate (airport); exit
έξοδος κινδύνου *eh•ksoh•THohs keen•THee•noo* emergency, fire exit
εξοχή *eh•ksoh•khee* countryside
έξοχος *eh•ksoh•khohs* superb
εξπρές *ehk•sprehs* express (mail)
εξυπηρέτηση *eh•ksee•pee•reh•tee•see* facility
έξω *eh•ksoh adv* out
έξω *eh•ksoh adj* outside
εξωλέμβιο *eh•ksoh•lehm•vee•oh* motorboat
εξωτερικός *eh•ksoh•teh•ree•kohs* outdoor
επαναλαμβάνω *eh•pah•nah•lahm•vah•noh v* repeat
επάνω *eh•pah•noh* upstairs
επείγον *eh•pee•ghohn* urgent
επιμένω *eh•pee•meh•noh* insist
επιβάτης *eh•pee•vah•tees*

passenger
επιβεβαιώνω *eh•pee•veh•veh•oh•noh* confirm
επίβλεψη *eh•peev•leh•psee* supervision
επίθεση *eh•pee•theh•see n* attack
επίθετο *eh•pee•theh•toh* surname
επικοινωνώ *eh•pee•kee•noh•noh v* contact
επιληπτικός *eh•pee•leep•tee•kohs* epileptic
επίπεδο *eh•pee•peh•THoh* level (even)
επίπεδος *eh•pee•peh•THohs adj* flat
έπιπλα *eh•peep•lah* furniture
επιπλέον *eh•peep•leh•ohn* spare (extra)
επισκευάζω *eh•pee•skeh•vah•zoh v* repair
επισκευή *eh•pee•skeh•vee n* repair
επισκευή παπουτσιών *eh•pee•skeh•vee pah•poo•tsiohn* shoe repair
επίσκεψη *eh•pees•keh•psee n* visit
επιστροφή χρημάτων *eh•pees•troh•fee khree•mah•tohn n* refund
επιταγή *eh•pee•tah•yee n* check [cheque BE] (bank)
επιτίθεμαι *eh•pee•tee•theh•meh v* attack
επιτόκιο *eh•pee•toh•kee•oh* interest rate
επόμενος *eh•poh•meh•nohs* next
έρχομαι *ehr•khoh•meh* come
ερώτηση *eh•roh•tee•see n* question
εστιατόριο *ehs•tee•ah•toh•ree•oh* restaurant
εσωτερική γραμμή *eh•soh•theh•ree•kee ghrah•mee* extension (number)
εσωτερική πισίνα *eh•soh•teh•ree•kee pee•see•nah* indoor pool
εσωτερικός *eh•soh•teh•ree•kohs* indoor
ετικέτα *eh•tee•keh•tah n* label
έτοιμος *eh•tee•mohs adj* ready
ευθεία *ehf•thee•ah* straight ahead
εύκολος *ehf•koh•lohs adj* easy
ευρώ *ehv•roh* euro
Ευρωπαϊκή Ένωση *ehv•roh•pah•ee•kee eh•noh•see* European Union
ευτυχώς *ehf•tee•khohs* fortunately
ευχαριστιέμαι *ehf•khah•rees•tieh•meh* enjoy
ευχάριστος *ehf•khah•rees•tohs* pleasant
εφημερίδα *eh•fee•mehree•THah* newspaper
έφηβος *eh•fee•vohs* teenager
έχω *eh•khoh* have (possession)

Ζ

ζαχαροπλαστείο *zah•khah•rohp•lahs•tee•oh* pastry store
ζεστός *zes•tohs* hot, warm (weather)
ζημιά *zee•miah n* damage
ζητώ *zee•toh* ask
ζωγραφίζω *zohgh•rah•fee•zoh v* paint
ζωγράφος *zohgh•rah•fohs* painter
ζώνη *zoh•nee* belt
ζώνη για χρήματα *zoh•nee yah khree•mah•tah* money-belt

Η

ημερομηνία λήξεως *ee•meh•roh•mee•nee•ah lee•kseh•ohs* expiration date
ημερολόγιο *ee•meh•roh•loh•yee•oh* calendar
ημικρανία *ee•mee•krah•nee•ah* migraine
ηλεκτρικός *ee•lehk•tree•kohs* electric
ηλεκτρονικό εισιτήριο *ee•leh•ktroh•nee•koh ee•see•tee•ree•oh* e-ticket
ηλεκτρονικό ταχυδρομείο *ee•lehk•troh•nee•koh tah•hee•dro•mee•oh (ee•meh•eel)* e-mail
ηλεκτροπληξία *ee•leh•ktroh•plee•ksee•ah* shock (electric)
ηλίαση *ee•lee•ah•see* sun stroke
ηλικιωμένος *ee•lee•kee•oh•meh•nohs* senior citizen
Ηνωμένες Πολιτείες *ee•noh•meh•nehs poh•lee•tee•ehs* United States
Ηνωμένο Βασίλειο *ee•noh•meh•noh vah•see•lee•oh* United Kingdom
ηρεμιστικό *ee•reh•mee•stee•koh* sedative
ήσυχος *ee•see•khohs adj* quiet

Θ

θάλασσα *thah•lah•sah* sea
θέατρο *theh•aht•roh* theater
θέλω *theh•loh* want
θέρμανση *thehr•mahn•see* heating
θερμή πηγή *thehr•mee pee•yee* hot spring
θερμόμετρο *thehr•moh•meht•roh* thermometer
θερμοκρασία *theh•rmohk•rah•see•ah* temperature (body)
θερμός *thehr•mohs* thermos flask
θέρετρο διακοπών *theh•reh•troh THee•ah•koh•pohn* vacation resort
θέση *theh•see n* location (space), seat

θέση δίπλα στο παράθυρο *theh•see THeep•lah stoh pah•rah•thee•roh* window seat
θηλυκός *thee•lee•kohs* female
θορυβώδης *thoh•ree•voh•THees* noisy
θρησκεία *three•skee•ah* religion
θυμάμαι *thee•mah•meh* remember
θυρίδα *thee•ree•THah* luggage locker (lock-up)

I

ιατρική εξέταση *ee•ah•tree•kee eh•kseh•tah•see* examination (medical)
ίδιος *ee•THee•ohs* same
ιδιωτικό μπάνιο *ee•THee•oh•tee•koh bah•nioh* private bathroom
ιερέας *ee•eh•reh•ahs* priest
ινσουλίνη *een•soo•lee•nee* insulin
ίντερνετ *ee•nteh•rnet* internet
ίντερνετ καφέ *ee•nteh•rnet kah•feh* internet cafe
ιπποδρομία *ee•poh•THroh•mee•ah* horse racing
ιστιοπλοϊκό *ees•tee•oh•ploh•ee•koh* sailing boat
ιστορία *ee•stoh•ree•ah* history
ισχύει *ee•skhee•ee* valid
ίσως *ee•sohs* maybe, perhaps
ιώδειο *ee•oh•THee•oh* iodine

K

κάδος απορριμμάτων *kah•THohs ah•poh•ree•mah•tohn* trash can
καθαρισμός προσώπου *kah•thah•reez•mohs proh•soh•poo* facial
καθαρός *kah•thah•rohs* clean
καθαρτικό *kah•thahr•tee•koh* laxative
καθεδρικός ναός *kah•theh•THree•kohs nah•ohs* cathedral
καθήκον *kah•thee•kohn* duty (obligation)
κάθομαι *kah•thoh•meh* sit
καθρέφτης *kah•threhf•tees* *n* mirror
καθυστέρηση *kah•thee•steh•ree•see n* delay
καθυστερώ *kah•thee•steh•roh v* delay
καινούργιος *keh•noor•yohs* new
καιρός *keh•rohs* weather
καλά *kah•lah adv* fine (well)
καλαμάκι *kah•lah•mah•kee* straw (drinking)
καλάθι *kah•lah•THee* basket
καλός *kah•lohs* good
καλσόν *kahl•sohn n* tights
κάλτσες *kahl•tsehs* socks
κάλυμμα φακού *kah•lee•mah fah•koo* lens cap
καλώ *kah•loh v* call
κάμπινγκ *kah•mpeeng* camping
καναπές *kah•nah•pehs* sofa
κανένας *kah•neh•nahs adj* none
κάνω ανάληψη *kah•noh ah•nah•lee•psee* withdraw
κάνω εμετό *kah•noh eh•meh•toh v* vomit
κάνω κράτηση *kah•noh krah•tee•see v* book
κάνω πεζοπορία *kah•noh peh•zoh•poh•ree•ah v* hike
καπέλο *kah•peh•loh* hat
καπνίζω *kahp•nee•zoh v* smoke
καπνοπωλείο *kahp•noh•poh•lee•oh* tobacconist
καπνός *kahp•nohs* tobacco
καραντίνα *kah•rahn•dee•nah n* quarantine
καράφα *kah•rah•fah* carafe
καρδιά *kahr•THee•ah v* heart
καρδιακό έμφραγμα *kahr•THee•ah•koh ehm•frahgh•mah* heart attack
καροτσάκι *kah•roh•tsah•kee* trolley (cart)
καροτσάκια αποσκευών *kah•roh•tsah•kiah ah•pohs•keh•vohn* baggage [BE] carts [trolleys]
κάρτα-κλειδί *kahr•tah klee•dee* key card
καρτποστάλ *kahrt•poh•stahl* post card
κασκόλ *kahs•kohl* scarf
κασσίτερος *kah•see•teh•rohs* pewter
κάστρο *kahs•troh* castle
καταδυτικός εξοπλισμός *kah•tah•THee•tee•kohs eh•ksoh•pleez•mohs* diving equipment
καταλαβαίνω *kah•tah•lah•veh•noh* understand
κατάλληλος *kah•tah•lee•lohs* suitable
καταρράχτης *kah•tah•rahkh•tees* waterfall
κατάστημα *kah•tah•stee•mah* shop (store)
κατάστημα με αντίκες *kah•tah•stee•mah meh ahn•tee•kehs* antiques store
κατάστημα με είδη δώρων *kah•tahs•tee•mah meh ee•THee THoh•rohn* gift store
κατάστημα με υγιεινές τροφές *kah•tahs•tee•mah meh ee•yee•ee•nehs troh•fehs* health food store
κατάστημα μεταχειρισμένων ειδών *kah•tah•stee•mah meh•tah•khee•reez•meh•nohn ee•THohn* second-hand shop
κατάστημα αθλητικών ειδών *kah•tahs•tee•mah ath•lee•tee•kohn ee•THohn* sporting goods store
κατάστημα ρούχων *kah•tahs•tee•mah roo•khohn* clothing store

κατάστημα σουβενίρ *kah•tahs•tee•mah soo•veh•neer* souvenir store
κατάστημα υποδημάτων *kah•tah•stee•mah ee•poh•THee•mah•tohn* shoe store
καταστρέφω *kah•tah•streh•toh v* damage
κατάψυξη *kah•tah•psee•ksee* freezer
κατεβαίνω *kah•teh•veh•noh* get off (transport)
κατειλημένος *kah•tee•lee•meh•nohs* occupied
κάτι *kah•tee* something
κάτοχος *kah•toh•khohs* owner
κατσαβίδι *kah•tsah•vee•THee* screwdriver
κατσαρόλα *kah•tsah•roh•lah* saucepan
κάτω *kah•toh adj* lower (berth)
καύσωνας *kahf•soh•nahs* heat wave
καφετέρια *kah•feh•teh•ree•ah* cafe
κέντρο της πόλης *kehn•droh tees poh•lees* downtown area
κεφάλι *keh•fah•lee n* head
κήπος *kee•pohs n* garden
κιθάρα *kee•thah•rah* guitar
κινηματογράφος *kee•nee•mah•tohgh•rah•fohs* movie theater
κίνηση *kee•nee•see* traffic
κινητό *kee•nee•toh* cell phone [mobile phone BE]
κίτρινος *keet•ree•nohs* yellow
κλειδαριά *klee•THahr•yah n* lock (door)
κλειδί *klee•THee n* key
κλειδώνω *klee•THoh•noh v* lock (door)
κλειστός *klees•tohs adj* shut
κλεμένος *kleh•meh•nos* stolen
κλέφτης *klehf•tees* thief
κλήση *klee•see n* call
κλιματισμός *klee•mah•teez•mohs* air conditioning
κλοπή *kloh•pee* theft
κομμωτήριο *koh•moh•tee•ree•oh* hair dresser
κόμβος *kohm•vohs* junction (intersection)
κοιμάμαι *kee•mah•meh v* sleep
κοιλάδα *kee•lah•THah* valley
κοιτάω *kee•tah•oh v* look
κολύμβηση *koh•leem•vee•see* swimming
κοντά *kohn•dah adv* near
κοντός *kohn•dohs adj* short
κορίτσι *koh•ree•*tsee girl
κορυφή *koh•ree•fee n* peak
κοσμηματοπωλείο *kohz•mee•mah•toh•poh•lee•oh* jeweler
κουβέρτα *koo•veh•rtah* blanket
κουζίνα *koo•zee•nah* stove
κουνούπι *koo•noo•pee* mosquito
κουρασμένος *koo•rahz•meh•nohs* tired
κουστούμι *koos•too•mee* men's suit
κουταλάκι *koo•tah•lah•kee* teaspoon
κουτάλι *koo•tah•lee n* spoon
κουτί *koo•tee* carton
κουτί πρώτων βοηθειών *koo•tee proh•tohn voh•ee•thee•ohn* first-aid kit
κράμπα *krahm•bah n* cramp
κραγιόν *krah•yohn* lipstick
κρατώ *krah•toh v* keep
κρέμα ξυρίσματος *kreh•mah ksee•reez•mah•tohs* shaving cream
κρεμάστρα *kreh•mahs•trah* hanger
κρεβάτι *kreh•vah•tee* bed
κρυολόγημα *kree•oh•loh•yee•mah n* cold (flu)
κρύος *kree•ohs adj* cold (temperature)
κρύσταλλο *kree•stah•loh n* crystal
κύμα *kee•mah n* wave
κυλικείο *kee•lee•kee•oh* snack bar
κυλιόμενες σκάλες *kee•lee•oh•meh•nehs skah•lehs* escalator
Κύπρος *kee•prohs* Cyprus
κύριος *kee•ree•ohs* main
κωδικός περιοχής *koh•THee•kohs peh•ree•oh•khees* area code
κωπηλασία *koh•pee•lah•see•ah* rowing

Λ

λάμπα *lahm•bah* lamp, light bulb
λάθος *lah•thohs* error, wrong
λαιμόκοψη *leh•moh•koh•psee* neck (shirt)
λαιμός *leh•mohs* throat
λάστιχο *lahs•tee•khoh* tire [tyre BE]
λειτουργία *lee•toor•yee•ah n* mass (church)
λεκές *leh•kehs n* stain
λεξικό *leh•ksee•koh* dictionary
λεπτό *lehp•toh n* minute (time)
λεπτός *lehp•tohs adj* thin
λέω *leh•oh* tell
λεωφορείο *leh•oh•foh•ree•oh* bus
ληστεία *lees•tee•ah* robbery
λιμάνι *lee•mah•nee n* harbor
λίμνη *leem•nee* lake
λιμνούλα *leem•noo•lah n* pond
λιγότερο *lee•ghoh•teh•roh* less
λιπαντικό *lee•pahn•dee•koh* lubricant
λιπαρός *lee•pah•rohs* greasy (hair, skin)
λιποθυμώ *lee•poh•thee•moh* faint
λίρα *lee•rah* pound (sterling)
λίτρο *lee•troh* liter

λογαριασμός *loh•ghahr•yahz•mohs* n check (bill), account
λοσιόν *loh•siohn* lotion
λοσιόν μαυρίσματος *loh•siohn mahv•rees•mah•tohs* sun tan lotion
λουκέτο *loo•keh•toh* padlock
λουλούδι *loo•loo•THee* n flower
λουρί ρολογιού *loo•ree roh•loh•yioo* watch strap
λόφος *loh•fohs* hill

M

μαγιό *mah•yoh* swimming trunks, swimsuit
μαθαίνω *mah•theh•noh* learn
μάθημα ξένης γλώσσας *mah•thee mah kseh•nees ghloh•sahs* language course
μακιγιάζ *mah•kee•yahz* make-up
μακριά *mahk•ree•ah* adv far
μακρύς *mak•rees* adj long
μαλλιά *mah•liah* hair
μανικιούρ *mah•nee•kioor* manicure
μαξιλαροθήκη *mah•ksee•lah•roh•thee•kee* pillow case
μαργαριτάρι *mahr•ghah•ree•tah•ree* pearl
μάρτυρας *mahr•tee•rahs* witness
μας *mahs* our
μασάζ *mah•sahz* n massage
μάσκα *mahs•kah* n mask (diving)
μάτι *mah•tee* n eye
μαχαίρι *mah•kheh•ree* knife
με *meh* with
με άμμο *meh ah•moh* sandy (beach)
με υπότιτλους *meh ee•poh•teet•loos* subtitled
με χαλίκια *meh khah•lee•kiah* pebbly (beach)
μεγαλοπρεπής *meh•ghah•lohp•reh•pees* magnificent
μεγάλος *meh•ghah•lohs* adj big, large
μέγεθος *meh•yeh•thohs* n size
μέδουσα *meh•THoo•sah* jellyfish
μένω *meh•noh* v stay
μεριά *mehr•yah* side (of road)
μερίδα *meh•ree•THah* n portion
μερικές φορές *meh•ree•kehs foh•rehs* sometimes
μέσα *meh•sah* inside
μεσημεριανό *meh•see•mehr•yah•noh* n lunch
μετά *meh•tah* after
μετακομίζω *meh•tah•koh•mee•zoh* v move (room)
μέταλλο *meh•tah•loh* n metal
μετάξι *meh•tah•ksee* silk
μεταφέρω *meh•tah•feh•roh* transfer
μεταφορά *meh•tah•foh•rah* n transit
μεταφράζω *meh•tah•frah•zoh* translate
μετάφραση *meh•tah•frah•see* translation
μεταφραστής *meh•tah•frah•stees* translator
μέτρηση *meh•tree•see* measurement
μετρητά *meht•ree•tah* n cash
μετρό *meh•troh* subway
μετρώ *meht•roh* v measure
μη καπνίζοντες *mee kap•nee•zon•des* non-smoking
μήκος *mee•kohs* length
μήνας του μέλιτος *mee•nahs too meh•lee•tohs* honeymoon
μήνυμα *mee•nee•mah* n message
μηχανή *mee•khah•nee* engine
μια φορά *miah foh•rah* once
μικρός *meek•rohs* little, small
μιλώ *mee•loh* speak
μινι-μπαρ *mee•nee bahr* mini-bar
μισός *mee•sohs* half
μνημείο *mnee•mee•oh* memorial, monument
μολυσμένος *moh•leez•meh•nohs* infected
μονάδα *moh•nah•THah* unit
μοναδικός *moh•nah•THee•kohs* unique
μονόκλινο δωμάτιο *moh•noh•klee•noh THoh•mah•tee•oh* single room
μονοπάτι *moh•noh•pah•tee* path, trail
μοντέρνος *moh•deh•rnohs* modern
μοτοποδήλατο *moh•toh•poh•THee•lah•toh* moped
μουσείο *moo•see•oh* museum
μουσική *moo•see•kee* music
μουσικός *moo•see•kohs* musician
μουστάκι *moos•tah•kee* moustache
μπαγιάτικος *bah•yah•tee•kohs* stale
μπάνιο *bah•nioh* bathroom, lavatory
μπαρ *bahr* bar
μπάσκετ *bah•skeht* basketball
μπαστούνια του σκι *bahs•too•niah too skee* ski poles
μπαταρία *bah•tah•ree•ah* battery
μπέιμπι σίτερ *beh•ee•bee see•tehr* babysitter
μπικίνι *bee•kee•nee* bikini
μπλούζα *bloo•zah* blouse
μπλουζάκι *bloo•zah•kee* T-shirt
μπλου-τζην *bloo•jeen* jeans
μποξ *bohks* n boxing
μπότα *boh•tah* boot
μπότες πεζοπορίας *boh•tehs peh•zoh•poh•ree•ahs* walking boots
μπότες του σκι *boh•tehs too skee* ski boots
μπουκάλι *boo•kah•lee* bottle
μπρελόκ *breh•lohk* key ring

μύγα *mee•ghah n* fly (insect)
μυρίζω *mee•ree•zoh v* smell
μυς *mees n* muscle
μύτη *mee•tee n* nose
μύωπας *mee•oh•pahs* short-sighted [BE]
μωρό *moh•roh* baby

N

ναός *nah•ohs* temple
ναυαγοσώστης *nah•vah•ghoh•sohs•tees* lifeguard
ναυαγοσωστική λέμβος *nah•vah•ghoh•sohs•tee•kee lehm•vohs* lifeboat
ναυτία *nahf•tee•ah* nausea, travel sickness
νέος *neh•ohs* young
νερό *neh•roh n* water
νεύρο *nehv•roh* nerve
νεφρό *nehf•roh* kidney
νιπτήρας *nee•ptee•rahs* sink (bathroom)
νόμιμος *noh•mee•mohs* legal
νομίζω *noh•mee•zoh* think
νόμισμα *noh•meez•mah* currency
νοικιάζω *nee•kiah•zoh v* hire, rent
νοσοκόμα *noh•soh•koh•mah n* nurse
νοσοκομείο *noh•soh•koh•mee•oh* hospital
νόστιμος *nohs•tee•mohs* delicious
Νοτιοαφρικανός *noh•tee•oh•ahf•ree•kah•nohs* South African (nationality)
νότιος *noh•tee•ohs adj* south
ντεμοντέ *deh•mohn•deh* old-fashioned
ντήζελ *dee•zehl* diesel
ντουζ *dooz n* shower
ντουζίνα *doo•zee•nah* dozen
νύχι *nee•khee n* nail
νύχτα *neekh•tah* night
νυχτερινό κέντρο *neekh•teh•ree•noh kehn•droh* night club
νωρίς *noh•rees* early

Ξ

ξαπλώνω *ksah•ploh•noh* lie down
ξενάγηση *kseh•nah•yee•see* guided tour
ξενάγηση στα αξιοθέατα *kseh•nah•yee•see stah ah•ksee•oh•theh•ah•tah* sightseeing tour
ξεναγός *kseh•nah•ghohs* tour guide
ξένο συνάλλαγμα *kseh•noh see•nah•lahgh•mah* foreign currency
ξενοδοχείο *kseh•noh•THoh•khee•oh* hotel
ξένος *kseh•nohs* foreign
ξενώνας νεότητας *kseh•noh•nahs neh•oh•tee•tahs* youth hostel
ξεχνώ *ksehkh•noh* forget
ξεχωριστά *kseh•khoh•ree•stah* separately
ξινός *ksee•nohs* sour
ξοδεύω *ksoh•THeh•voh* spend
ξύλο *ksee•loh* wood (material)
ξυπνώ *kseep•noh v* wake
ξυραφάκι *ksee•rah•fah•kee* razor, razor blade

O

ομάδα *oh•mah•THah n* team
όμορφος *oh•mohr•fohs adj* beautiful, pretty
ομπρέλλα *ohm•breh•lah* sun shade
οβάλ *oh•vahl* oval
οδηγία *oh•THee•yee•ah* instruction
οδηγός καταστήματος *oh•THee•ghohs kah•tahs•tee•mah•tohs* store guide
οδηγός ψυχαγωγίας *oh•THee•ghohs psee•khah•ghoh•yee•ahs* entertainment guide
οδηγώ *oh•THee•ghoh v* drive
οδική βοήθεια *oh•THee•kee voh•ee•thee•ah* road assistance
οδοντίατρος *oh•THohn•dee•ah•trohs* dentist
οδοντόβουρτσα *oh•THohn•doh•voor•tsah* tooth brush
οδοντόπαστα *oh•THohn•doh•pahs•tah* tooth paste
οικογένεια *ee•koh•yeh•nee•ah* family
οινοποιείο *ee•noh•pee•ee•oh* winery
όνομα *oh•noh•mah n* name
όπερα *oh•peh•rah* opera
οπωροπωλείο *oh•poh•roh•poh•lee•oh* greengrocer [BE]
οργανωμένος *ohr•ghah•noh•meh•nohs* organized
ορχήστρα *ohr•khees•trah* orchestra
οτιδήποτε *oh•tee•THee•poh•teh* anything
οτοστόπ *oh•toh•stohp* hitchhiking
οφείλω *oh•fee•loh* have to (obligation)
οφθαλμίατρος *ohf•thahl•mee•aht•rohs* optician

Π

παγοπέδιλα *pah•ghoh•peh•THee•lah* skates
πάγος *pah•ghohs n* ice
παιδική χαρά *peh•THee•kee khah•rah* playground
παιδικό κρεβάτι *peh•THee•koh kreh•vah•tee* crib [cot BE]
παίζω *peh•zoh v* play (games, music)
παιχνίδι *pehkh•nee•THee n* game (toy), round

παιχνίδι βίντεο *pehkh•nee•THee vee•deh•oh* video game
πακέτο *pah•keh•toh* parcel
πακέτο για το σπίτι *pah•keh•toh yah toh spee•tee* take away
παλιά πόλη *pah•liah poh•lee* old town
παλιός *pah•liohs* old (thing)
πάνα μωρού *pah•nah moh•roo* diaper
Πανεπιστήμιο *pah•neh•pees•tee•mee•oh* university
πάνες μωρού *pah•nehs moh•roo* nappies
πανόραμα *pah•noh•rah•mah* panorama
παντελόνι *pahn•deh•loh•nee* pants [trousers BE]
παντοπωλείο *pahn•doh•poh•lee•oh* minimart
παντόφλες *pahn•dohf•lehs* slippers
παντρεμένος *pahn•dreh•meh•nohs* married
πάνω *pah•noh adj* top, upper (berth)
παπούτσι *pah•poo•tsee* shoe
πάρα πολύ *pah•rah poh•lee* too (extreme)
παραγγέλνω *pah•rah•gehl•noh v* order
παράδειγμα *pah•rah•THeegh•mah* example
παραδοσιακός *pah•rah•THoh•see•ah•kohs* traditional
παράθυρο *pah•rah•thee•roh* window
παραλαβή αποσκευών *pah•rah•lah•vee ah•poh•skeh•vohn* baggage [BE] claim
παραλία *pah•rah•lee•ah* beach
παραλία γυμνιστών *pah•rah•lee•ah yeem•nees•tohn* nudist beach
παραλυσία *pah•rah•lee•see•ah* paralysis
παράνομος *pah•rah•noh•mohs* illegal
παράξενος *pah•rah•kseh•nohs* strange
παραπάνω *pah•rah•pah•noh* more
παρεξήγηση *pah•reh•ksee•yee•see* misunderstanding
πάρκο *pahr•koh n* park
παρκόμετρο *pahr•koh•meht•roh* parking meter
πάρτυ *pah•rtee n* party (social gathering)
παυσίπονο *pahf•see•poh•noh* painkiller
παχύς *pah•khees adj* fat (person)
πέδιλα *peh•THee•lah* sandals
πεζόδρομος *peh•zohTH•roh•mohs* pedestrian zone
περιμένω *peh•ree•meh•noh v* hold on, wait
περιμένω στην ουρά *peh•ree•meh•noh steen oo•rah v* queue [BE]
περιέχω *peh•ree•eh•khoh* contain
περιοδικό *peh•ree•oh•THee•koh* magazine
περίοδος *peh•ree•oh•THohs* period (menstrual)
περιοχή *peh•ree•oh•khee* region
περιοχή για καπνίζοντες *peh•ree•oh•khee yah kahp•nee•zohn•dehs* smoking area
περιοχή για πικνίκ *peh•ree•oh•khee yah peek neek* picnic area
περίπτερο *peh•ree•pteh•roh* newsstand, kiosk
περνώ *pehr•noh v* pass
περπατώ *pehr•pah•toh v* walk
περσίδες *peh•rsee•THehs* blinds
πετάω *peh•tah•oh v* fly
πετσέτα *peh•tseh•tah* napkin
πέφτω *pehf•toh v* fall
πηγαίνω *pee•yeh•noh* go
πιάτσα ταξί *piah•tsah tah•ksee* taxi rank [BE]
πίεση *pee•eh•see* blood pressure
πιθανός *pee•thah•nohs* possible
πινακίδα *pee•nah•kee•THah* road sign
πίνω *pee•noh v* drink
πίπα *pee•pah* pipe (smoking)
πιπίλα *pee•pee•lah* pacifier [soother BE]
πισίνα *pee•see•nah* swimming pool
πιστοποιητικό ασφάλειας *pees•toh•pee•ee•tee•koh ahs•fah•lee•ahs* insurance certificate
πιστωτική κάρτα *pees•toh•tee•kee kahr•tah* credit card
πιτσαρία *pee•tsah•ree•ah* pizzeria
πλαγιά *plah•yah* slope (ski)
πλαστική σακούλα *plahs•tee•kee sah•koo•lah* plastic bag
πλατίνα *plah•tee•nah* platinum
πλευρό *plehv•roh* rib
πλημμύρα *plee•mee•rah n* flood
πληγή *plee•yee* wound (cut)
πληροφορίες *plee•roh•foh•ree•ehs* information
πληρωμή *plee•roh•mee* payment
πληρώνω *plee•roh•noh v* pay
πλοίο *plee•oh n* ship
πλυντήριο *pleen•deer•ee•oh* washing machine
πνεύμονας *pnehv•moh•nahs* lung
πόμολο *poh•moh•loh n* handle
ποδήλατο *poh•THee•lah•toh* bicycle
πόδι *poh•THee* foot, leg
ποδόσφαιρο *poh•THohs•feh•roh* soccer [football BE]

ποιότητα *pee•oh•tee•tah* quality
πόλη *poh•lee* town
πολυκατάστημα *poh•lee•kah•tahs•tee•mah* department store
πολυτέλεια *poh•lee•teh•lee•ah* luxury
πολύτιμος *poh•lee•tee•mohs* valuable
πονόδοντος *poh•noh•THohn•dohs* toothache
πονοκέφαλος *poh•noh•keh•fah•lohs* headache
πονόλαιμος *poh•noh•leh•mohs* sore throat
πόνος *poh•nohs n* pain
πόνος στο αυτί *poh•nohs stoh ahf•tee* earache
πόρτα *pohr•tah* door
πορτοφόλι *pohr•toh•foh•lee* wallet
ποσό *poh•soh n* amount
ποσότητα *poh•soh•tee•tah* quantity
ποταμός *poh•tah•mohs* river
ποτέ *poh•teh* never
ποτήρι *poh•tee•ree* glass (container)
ποτό *poh•toh n* drink
πουκάμισο *poo•kah•mee•soh* shirt
πράσινος *prah•see•nohs* green
πρέπει *preh•pee v* must
πρεσβεία *prehz•vee•ah* embassy
πρεσβύωπας *prehz•vee•oh•pahs* long-sighted [BE]
πρήξιμο *pree•ksee•moh* swelling
πρησμένος *preez•meh•nohs* swollen
πρίζα *pree•zah n* plug, socket
πριν *preen* before
πρόβλεψη *prohv•leh•psee n* forecast
πρόβλεψη καιρού *prohv•leh•psee keh•roo* weather forecast
πρόβλημα *prohv•lee•mah* problem
πρόγραμμα *prohgh•rah•mah n* program
πρόγραμμα θεαμάτων *proh•ghrah•mah theh•ah•mah•tohn* program of events
προς *prohs* towards
προσαρμοστής *proh•sahr•moh•stees* adaptor
πρόσβαση *prohz•vah•see n* access
προσγειώνομαι *prohz•yee•oh•noh•meh v* land
προσκαλώ *prohs•kah•loh v* invite
πρόσκληση *prohs•klee•see* invitation
πρόστιμο *prohs•tee•moh n* fine (penalty)
πρόσωπο *proh•soh•poh n* face
προσωρινός *proh•soh•ree•nohs* temporary
προτείνω *proh•tee•noh* suggest
προφέρω *proh•feh•roh* pronounce
προφυλακτικό *proh•fee•lah•ktee•koh* condom
προωθώ *proh•oh•thoh* forward
πρωί *proh•ee* morning
πρωινό *proh•ee•noh* breakfast
πρώτη θέση *proh•tee theh•see* first class
πτήση *ptee•see* flight
πυρετός *pee•reh•tohs* fever
πυροσβεστήρας *pee•rohz•vehs•tee•rahs* fire extinguisher
πυροσβεστική *pee•rohz•vehs•tee•kee* fire brigade [BE]
πυτζάμες *pee•jah•mehs* pajamas

Ρ

ραδιόφωνο *rah•THee•oh•foh•noh n* radio
ρακέτα *rah•keh•tah* racket (tennis, squash)
ραντεβού *rahn•deh•voo* appointment
ράφι *rah•fee n* shelf
ρεματιά *reh•mah•tiah* ravine
ρεσεψιόν *reh•seh•psiohn* reception (hotel)
ρεύμα ποταμού *rehv•mah poh•tah•moo* rapids
ρηχή πισίνα *ree•khee pee•see•nah* paddling pool
ρομαντικός *roh•mahn•dee•kohs* romantic
ρολόι *roh•loh•ee n* watch
ρυάκι *ree•ah•kee n* stream

Σ

σμαράγδι *zmah•rahgh•THee* emerald
σαμπουάν *sahm•poo•ahn n* shampoo
σαγιονάρες *sah•yoh•nah•rehs* flip-flops
σαγόνι *sah•ghoh•nee* jaw
σάκκος *sah•kohs* knapsack
σαλόνι *sah•loh•nee* living room
σάουνα *sah•oo•nah* sauna
σαπούνι *sah•poo•nee n* soap
σατέν *sah•tehn* satin
σβήνω *svee•noh v* turn off
σβώλος *svoh•lohs n* lump
σεζ-λονγκ *sehz lohng* deck chair
σενιάν *seh•niahn* rare (steak)
σερβιέτες *sehr•vee•eh•tehs* sanitary towels
σεσουάρ *seh•soo•ahr* hair dryer
σήμα *see•mah* sign (road)
σημαία *see•meh•ah n* flag
σημαίνω *see•meh•noh v* mean
σημείο *see•mee•oh n* point
σίδερο *see•THeh•roh n* iron

σιδερώνω *see•THeh•roh•noh v* iron, press
σιδηροδρομικός σταθμός *see•THee•rohTH•roh•mee•kohs stahth•mohs* rail station
σκάλα *skah•lah* ladder
σκάλες *skah•lehs* stairs
σκηνή *skee•nee* tent
σκι *skee* skiing
σκιά *skee•ah* shade (darkness)
σκοπός *skoh•pohs* purpose
σκούπα *skoo•pah n* broom
σκουπίδια *skoo•peeTH•yah* trash [rubbish BE]
σκούρος *skoo•rohs adj* dark (color)
σλιπ *sleep* briefs
σόλα *soh•lah* sole (shoes)
σορτς *sohrts n* shorts
σουβενίρ *soo•veh•neer* souvenir
σουπερμάρκετ *soo•pehr•mahr•keht* supermarket
σουτιέν *soo•tiehn* bra
σπα *spah* spa
σπάγγος *spah•gohs n* string (cord)
σπάνιος *spah•nee•ohs* rare (unusual)
σπασμένος *spahz•meh•nohs* broken
σπάω *spah•oh v* break
σπήλαιο *spee•leh•oh n* cave
σπίρτο *speer•toh n* match (to start fire)
σπονδυλική στήλη *spohn•THee•lee•kee stee•lee* spine
σπουδάζω *spoo•THah•zoh v* study
σταματώ *stah•mah•toh v* stop
στάδιο *stah•THee•oh* stadium
σταθμός μετρό *stahth•mohs meh•troh* subway [underground BE] station
σταθμός λεωφορείων *stahTH•mohs leh•oh•foh•ree•ohn* bus station
στάση *stah•see* exposure (photos), stop (bus)
στάση λεωφορείου *stah•see leh•oh•foh•ree•oo* bus stop
στέγη *steh•yee n* roof
στέλνω *stehl•noh* send
στενός *steh•nohs adj* narrow, tight
στήθος *stee•THohs* breast
στόμα *stoh•mah n* mouth
στομάχι *stoh•mah•khee n* stomach
στομαχόπονος *stoh•mah•khoh•poh•nohs* stomach ache
στολή *stoh•lee n* uniform
στολή δύτη *stoh•lee THee•tee* wetsuit
στρογγυλός *strohn•gkee•lohs adj* round
στυλ *steel n* style
στυλό *stee•loh n* pen
συμπεριλαμβάνεται *seem•beh•ree•lahm•vah•neh•teh* included
σύζυγος *see•zee•ghohs* husband, wife
συκώτι *see•koh•tee* liver
σύμπτωμα *seem•ptoh•mah* symptom
συναγερμός πυρκαγιάς *see•nah•yehr•mohs peer•kah•yahs* fire alarm
συναντώ *see•nahn•doh* meet
συνέδριο *see•neh•THree•oh* conference
συνταγή γιατρού *seen•dah•yee yaht•roo* prescription
συνταγογραφώ *seen•dah•ghoh•ghrah•foh* prescribe
συνταξιούχος *seen•dah•ksee•oo•khohs* retired
σύντομα *seen•doh•mah* soon
συντριβάνι *seen•dree•vah•nee* fountain
συστάσεις *see•stah•sees* introductions
συστήνω *see•stee•noh* introduce, recommend
συχνός *seekh•nohs adj* frequent
σφηνωμένος *sfee•noh•meh•nohs* jammed
σφράγισμα *sfrah•yeez•mah* filling (dental)
σφυρί *sfee•ree* hammer
σχέδιο *skheh•THee•oh n* plan
σχήμα *skhee•mah n* shape
σχισμένος *skheez•meh•nohs* torn
σχοινί *skhee•nee n* rope
σχολή σκι *skhoh•lee skee* ski school
σωσίβιο *soh•see•vee•oh* lifejacket
σωστός *sohs•stohs adj* right (correct)

Τ

ταμπόν *tahm•bohn* tampon
τάβλι *tah•vlee* backgammon
ταγιέρ *tah•yehr* women's suit
ταΐζω *tah•ee•zoh v* feed
ταινία *teh•nee•ah* movie
ταξί *tah•ksee* taxi
ταξίδι *tah•ksee•THee* journey
ταξίδι με πλοίο *tah•ksee•THee meh plee•oh* boat trip
ταξιδιωτική επιταγή *tah•ksee•THee•oh•tee•kee eh•pee•tah•yee* traveler's check [traveller's cheque BE]
ταξιδιωτικό γραφείο *tah•ksee•THyoh•tee•koh ghrah•fee•oh* travel agency
ταξιτζής *tah•ksee•jees* taxi driver
ταυτότητα *tahf•toh•tee•tah* identification
ταχυδρομείο *tah•kheeTH•roh•mee•oh* post office
ταχυδρομική επιταγή *tah•kheeTH•roh•mee•kee eh•pee•tah•yee* money order

ταχυδρομικό κουτί *tah•kheeTH•roh•mee•koh koo•tee* mailbox [postbox BE]
τεμάχιο *teh•mah•khee•oh* piece
τελειώνω *teh•lee•oh•noh v* end
τελευταί ος *teh•lehf•teh•ohs* last
τελεφερίκ *teh•leh•feh•reek* cablecar
τέλος *teh•lohs n* end
τελωνειακή δήλωση *teh•loh•nee•ah•kee THee•loh•see* customs declaration (tolls)
τελωνείο *teh•loh•nee•oh* customs (tolls)
τέννις *teh•nees* tennis
τετράγωνος *teht•rah•ghoh•nohs* square
τζετ-σκι *jeht skee* jet-ski
τζόγκιγκ *joh•geeng* jogging
τζόγος *joh•ghohs* gambling
τηλεκάρτα *tee•leh•kahr•tah* phone card
τηλεόραση *tee•leh•oh•rah•see* TV
τηλεφώνημα *tee•leh•foh•nee•mah* phone call
τηλεφωνικός θάλαμος *tee•leh•foh•nee•kohs thah•lah•mohs* telephone booth
τηλεφωνικός κατάλογος *tee•leh•foh•nee•kohs kah•tah•loh•ghohs* telephone directory
τηλέφωνο *tee•leh•foh•noh n* phone
την *teen* per
τιμή συναλλάγματος *tee•mee see•nah•lahgh•mah•tohs* exchange rate
τιμή εισόδου *tee•mee ee•soh•THoo* entrance fee
τιρμπουσόν *teer•boo•sohn* corkscrew
τοίχος *tee•khohs* wall
τοπικός *toh•pee•kohs* local
τοστιέρα *toh•stieh•rah* toaster
τουαλέτα *too•ah•leh•tah* restroom [toilet BE]
τούνελ *too•nehl* tunnel
τουρίστας *too•rees•tahs* tourist
τουριστική θέση *too•ree•stee•kee theh•see* economy class
τουριστικός οδηγός *too•ree•stee•kohs oh•THee•ghohs* guide book
τραβώ το καζανάκι *trah•voh toh kah•zah•nah•kee* flush
τραμ *trahm* tram
τράπεζα *trah•peh•zah* bank
τραπέζι *trah•peh•zee* table
τραπεζομάντηλο *trah•peh•zoh•mahn•dee•loh* tablecloth
τραυματισμένος *trahv•mah•teez•meh•nohs* injured
τρένο *treh•noh* train
τρέχω *treh•khoh v* run, speed
τρόμπα *troh•mbah n* pump
τρόλλεϋ *troh•leh•ee* trolley-bus
τρύπα *tree•pah* hole (in clothes)
τρώω *troh•oh* eat
τσάντα *tsahn•dah* handbag
τσίμπημα *tsee•bee•mah n* bite, sting (insect)
τσίμπημα κουνουπιού *tseem•bee•mah koo•noo•piooh* mosquito bite
τυπικός *tee•pee•kohs* typical
τύχη *tee•khee* luck

Υ

υγρό πιάτων *eegh•roh piah•tohn* dishwashing detergent
υπεραστικό λεωφορείο *ee•peh•rahs•tee•koh leh•oh•foh•ree•oh* long-distance bus
υπεραστικό τηλεφώνημα *ee•pehr•ahs•tee•koh tee•leh•foh•nee•mah* long-distance call
υπέρβαρο *ee•pehr•vah•roh* excess baggage [BE]
υπηκοότητα *ee•pee•koh•oh•tee•tah* nationality
υπηρεσία *ee•pee•reh•see•ah n* service (administration, business)
υπηρεσία δωματίου *ee•pee•reh•see•ah THoh•mah•tee•oo* room service
υπηρεσία πλυντηρίου *ee•pee•reh•see•ah pleen•dee•ree•oo* laundry service
υπνόσακκος *ee•pnoh•sah•kohs* sleeping bag
υπνωτικό χάπι *eep•noh•tee•koh khah•pee* sleeping pill
υπόγειος *ee•poh•ghee•ohs* underground [BE]
υπολογιστής *ee•poh•loh•yee•stees* computer
υπόνομος *ee•poh•noh•mohs* sewer
ύφασμα *ee•fahs•mah* fabric (cloth)
ύψος *ee•psohs* height

Φ

φακός *fah•kohs* flashlight, lens
φακός επαφής *fah•kohs eh•pah•fees* contact lens
υπηρεσία φαξ *ee•pee•reh•see•ah fahks* fax facility
φάρμα *fahr•mah n* farm
φάρμακα *fahr•mah•kah* medication
φαρδύς *fahr•THees* loose (fitting), wide
φάρος *fah•rohs* lighthouse
φέρνω *fehr•noh* bring
φέρυ-μπωτ *feh•ree boht* ferry

φεστιβάλ *fehs•tee•vahl* festival
φεύγω *fehv•ghoh v* leave (depart)
φιλμ *feelm n* film (camera)
φίλη *fee•lee* girlfriend
φιλί *fee•lee n* kiss
φιλοδώρημα *fee•loh•THoh•ree•mah* gratuity
φίλος *fee•lohs* friend, boyfriend
φίλτρο *feel•troh n* filter
φιλώ *fee•loh v* kiss
φλέβα *fleh•vah* vein
φλεγμονή *flegh•moh•nee* inflammation
φλυτζάνι *flee•jah•nee* cup
φοβερός *foh•veh•rohs* terrible
φοβισμένος *foh•veez•meh•nohs* frightened
φοιτητής *fee•tee•tees* student
φόρεμα *foh•reh•mah n* dress
φόρος *foh•rohs* duty (customs), tax
φορώ *foh•roh v* wear
φούρνος *foor•nohs* oven
φούρνος μικροκυμάτων *foor•nohs mee•kroh•kee•mah•tohn* microwave (oven)
φούστα *foo•stah* skirt
φούτερ *foo•tehr* sweatshirt
ΦΠΑ *fee•pee•ah* sales tax
φράγμα *frahgh•mah n* lock (river, canal)
φράση *frah•see n* phrase
φράχτης *frahkh•tees n* fence
φρέσκος *frehs•kohs adj* fresh
φτάνω *ftah•noh arrive*
φτηνός *ftee•nohs* cheap, inexpensive
φτιάχνω τις βαλίτσες *ftee•ahkh•noh tees vah•lee•tsehs v* pack (baggage)
φυλακή *fee•lah•kee n* prison
φύση *fee•see* nature
φυτό *fee•toh n* plant
φως *fohs n* light (electric)
φώτα *foh•tah* lights (car)
φωτογραφία *foh•tohgh•rah•fee•ah v* photo
φωτογραφική μηχανή *foh•tohgh•rah•fee•kee mee•khah•nee* camera
φωτοτυπικό *foh•toh•tee•pee•koh* photocopier

Χ

χαμηλώνω *khah•mee•loh•noh v* turn down (volume, heat)
χαλί *khah•lee* rug
χαλκός *khahl•kohs* copper
χάπι *khah•pee* tablet
χάρτης *khahr•tees n* map
χαρτί *khar•tee* paper
χαρτί κουζίνας *khah•rtee koo•zee•nahs* kitchen
χαρτί υγείας *khahr•tee ee•yee•ahs* toilet paper
χαρτομάντηλο *khahr•toh•mahn•dee•loh* tissue
χαρτομάντηλο *khah•rtoh•mahn•dee•loh* handkerchief
χείλη *khee•lee* lips
χειροκίνητος *khee•roh•kee•nee•tohs* manual (car)
χειρότερος *khee•roh•teh•rohs* worse
χιλιόμετρα *khee•lioh•meh•trah* mileage
χιονίζει *khioh•nee•zee v* snow
χλιαρός *khlee•ah•rohs* lukewarm
χόμπυ *khoh•bee* hobby (pastime)
χοντρός *khohn•drohs* thick
χορεύω *khoh•reh•voh v* dance
χορτοφάγος *khohr•toh•fah•ghohs* vegetarian
χρειάζομαι *khree•ah•zoh•meh v* need
χρέωση υπηρεσίας *khreh•oh•see ee•pee•reh•see•ahs* service charge
χρήματα *khree•mah•tah* money
χρησιμοποιώ *khree•see•moh•pee•oh v* use
χρήσιμος *khree•see•mohs* useful
χρονική περίοδος *khroh•nee•kee peh•ree•oh•THohs* period (time)
χρυσός *khree•sohs n* gold
χρώμα *khroh•mah n* color
χρωστώ *khroh•stoh* owe
χτένα *khteh•nah n* comb
χτενίζω *khteh•nee•zoh v* comb
χτες *khtehs* yesterday
χώρα *khoh•rah* country (nation)
χωριό *khohr•yoh* village
χωρίς *khoh•rees* without
χώρος *khoh•rohs n* space (area)
χώρος κάμπινγκ *kah•mpeeng khoh•rohs* campsite
χώρος στάθμευσης *khoh•rohs stahth•mehf•sees* car park [BE]
χώρος στάθμευσης *khoh•rohs stahth•mehf•sees* parking lot

Ψ

ψαλίδι *psah•lee•THee* scissors
ψάρεμα *psah•reh•mah* fishing
ψάχνω *psahkh•noh* look for
ψηλός *psee•lohs* tall
ψύλλος *psee•lohs* flea

Ω

ώμος *oh•mohs n* shoulder (anatomy)
ώρα αιχμής *oh•rah ehkh•mees* rush hour
ώρες λειτουργίας *oh•rehs lee•toor•yee•ahs* opening hours

INDEX

Accommodation 115, 136
Agía Kiourá 77
Agia Marína 76
Ágios Ioánnis 46
Ágios Ioánnis Thymianós monastery 53
Ágios Stéfanos 50
Ágios Theológos 53
airports 116
Álinda 76
Alykí salt pan 45
Andimáhia 46
Andimáhia castle 47
Arkí 82
Asklepion 39
Astypalaia 52

Bicycle and scooter hire 116
Bodrum 82
Bros Thermá 42
budgeting for your trip 117

Camel 50
Cape Ágios Fokás 42
car rental 118
climate 118
crime and safety 119

Driving 120

Electricity 122
embassies and consulates 123
Emboriós 71
entertainment 94
Evangelístria 57

Getting there 123
guides and tours 124

Health and medical care 125
Hippokrates 17
history 15
Hóra 81
Hristós peak 58

Kálymnos 66
Kamári 51
Kandoúni 70
Kardámena 48
Kávo Paradíso 54
Kéfalos 52
Kos Town 29
agora 32
Albergo Gelsomino 36
Amnós tou Theoú 37
Apothíki Alatíou Hamam 32
Archaeological Museum 34
Casa del Fascio 37
Casa Romana 34
covered market 37
Evangelismós Church 37
Fascist Youth building 37
Haluvaziá 35
Loggia Mosque 32
Neratziá Castle 30
odeion 34
Pórta tou Fórou 32
primary school 37
synagogue 37
western excavations 33

Lagoúdi 57
Lakkí 74
Lakkí volcanic zone 63
Lámbi 41, 82
Langádes (Markos) 50
language 126
Léros 74
LGBTQ travellers 128
Limniónas 54
Lipsí 82
Livádi Geranoú 82

Magic 50
Mandráki 62
maps 128
Maráthi 82
Marmári 44
Mastihári 45
media 128
Melitsáhas 71
money 128
Myrtiés 71

Nightlife 95
Nikiá 64
Nísyros 61

Opening times 129

Pahiá Ámmos 66
Paleó Pylí 55
Pátmos 78
Píso Thermá 43
Pláka 49
Platáni 38
police 130
post offices 130
Póthia 67
Psalídi 41
Psérimos 72
Psilí Ammos 82
public holidays 131
Pylí 55

Religion 131

Shopping 89
Skála 79
sports 85
hiking 86
horse-riding 89
mountain-biking 87
rock-climbing 87
watersports 85

Télendos 71
telephones 131
time zones 132
Tingáki 44
tipping 132
toilets 133
tourist information 133
transport 133

Vathýs 69
visas and entry requirements 134
Vromólithos 75

Websites and internet access 135
winery tourism 94

Berlitz pocket guide

KOS

Second Edition 2020

Editor: Tatiana Wilde
Author: Marc Dubin
Head of DTP and Pre-Press: Rebeka Davies
Managing Editor: Carine Tracanelli
Picture Editor: Tom Smyth
Layout: Aga Bylica
Cartography Update: Carte
Photography Credits: Alamy 4TL, 41, 43, 58, 68, 77, 99; Britta Jaschinski/Apa Publications 6L, 7, 7R, 11, 13, 30, 33, 35, 39, 61, 62, 64, 92, 102; Corbis 5M, 22, 87; Getty Images 4MC, 24, 28, 48, 80, 84, 89, 91, 95, 105; iStock 4TC, 5M, 5MC, 37, 47, 54, 56, 71, 79, 83; Public domain 18; Shutterstock 1, 4ML, 5T, 5TC, 5MC, 6R, 14, 21, 45, 51, 53, 67, 72, 75, 100
Cover Picture: Shutterstock

Distribution
UK, Ireland and Europe: Apa Publications (UK) Ltd; sales@insightguides.com
United States and Canada: Ingram Publisher Services; ips@ingramcontent.com
Australia and New Zealand: Woodslane; info@woodslane.com.au
Southeast Asia: Apa Publications (SN) Pte; singaporeoffice@insightguides.com
Worldwide: Apa Publications (UK) Ltd; sales@insightguides.com

Special Sales, Content Licensing and CoPublishing
Insight Guides can be purchased in bulk quantities at discounted prices. We can create special editions, personalised jackets and corporate imprints tailored to your needs. sales@insightguides.com; www.insightguides.biz

Printed in Poland by Interak

Contact us
Every effort has been made to provide accurate information in this publication, but changes are inevitable. The publisher cannot be responsible for any resulting loss, inconvenience or injury. We would appreciate it if readers would call our attention to any errors or outdated information. We also welcome your suggestions; please contact us at: berlitz@apaguide.co.uk
www.insightguides.com/berlitz